THE EVERYTHING

Women of the Bible Book

Dear Reader,

I first started reading the Bible when I was a kid in elementary school. I suppose in some ways I was mimicking what I saw in the women around me. I grew up in a rural area of the Midwest where, on Sunday afternoons, farmwomen who had toiled from dawn to dusk on all of the other days rested, visited, and caught up on their reading of the Good Book. They'd sit on the front porch in their rockers and read the Bible, all the while keeping one eye on the kids who were often playing in the yard or a nearby field.

One of my earliest and fondest childhood memories was walking through the woods with my mom and brother to the house of an elderly farmer and his wife. My little brother and I would stretch out on the guest featherbed or, if it was a blazing hot day, on a quilt spread upon the floor, and listen to my mom or the farmer's wife read from the Scriptures until we fell asleep.

I believe that the ages-old ritual I experienced as a child was similar to that of the nomadic Hebrew women of Abraham's time. They likely gathered on the Sabbath in one of the tents to talk, perhaps have a honeyed sweet or fruit and a beverage, and share fellowship in their own cultural tradition. As a child, I'd listened to their stories being read to me, and I thought those women were pretty interesting people, even though some of them were not too nice. It is my honor to offer their stories to you, my readers, with the hope that you will find them to be as fascinating as I have.

Meera Lester

The EVERYTHING® Series

Editorial

Innovation Director	Paula Munier
Editorial Director	Laura M. Daly
Executive Editor, Series Books	Brielle K. Matson
Associate Copy Chief	Sheila Zwiebel
Acquisitions Editor	Lisa Laing
Development Editor	Katie McDonough
Production Editor	Casey Ebert

Production

Director of Manufacturing	Susan Beale
Production Project Manager	Michelle Roy Kelly
Prepress	Erick DaCosta
	Matt LeBlanc
Interior Layout	Heather Barrett
	Brewster Brownville
	Colleen Cunningham
	Jennifer Oliveira
Cover Design	Erin Alexander
	Stephanie Chrusz
	Frank Rivera
Interior Illustrator	Michelle Dorenkamp

THE
EVERYTHING®
WOMEN OF
THE BIBLE
BOOK

From Eve to Mary Magdalene—
a history of saints, queens, and matriarchs

Meera Lester

◢
Adams Media
Avon, Massachusetts

*This book is dedicated to women everywhere whose hearts and
minds seek to understand the ebb and flow of life, of birth and
death, of bounty and the reversal of fortune, of weakness and forti-
tude, and the blessed stream of Light that shines through it all.*

An Everything® Series Book.
Everything® and everything.com® are registered trademarks of F+W Publications, Inc.

Published by Adams Media, an F+W Publications Company
57 Littlefield Street, Avon, MA 02322 U.S.A.
www.adamsmedia.com

ISBN-10: 1-59869-385-9
ISBN-13: 978-1-59869-385-0

Printed in the United States of America.

J   I   H   G   F   E   D   C   B   A

Library of Congress Cataloging-in-Publication Data
The everything women of the Bible book / Meera Lester.
p. cm. — (An everything series book)
Includes bibliographical references.
ISBN-13: 978-1-59869-385-0 (pbk.)
ISBN-10: 1-59869-385-9 (pbk.)
1. Bible—Biography. 2. Women in the Bible. I. Title.

Unless otherwise noted, the Bibles used as sources are listed on p. 267.

*This book is available at quantity discounts for bulk purchases.
For information, please call 1-800-289-0963.*

Contents

Top Ten Interesting Facts about the Women of the Bible / x

Introduction / xi

1 Women Who Were First / 1
Eve: First Woman, Wife, and Mother **2** • Rebelling Against God **4** • Hassophereth **6** • Rebekah **7** • Rachel **9** • Zipporah **11**

2 Adulteresses, Harlots, and Deceivers / 13
The Adulterous Woman Brought Before Jesus **14** • Bathsheba **15** • Delilah **18** • Drusilla **21** • Lot's Daughters **22** • Potiphar's Wife **24** • Prostitutes Who Forced Solomon to Split the Baby **26**

3 Women Who Caused Murder / 27
Athaliah **28** • Herodius **29** • Jael **31** • Laodice **32** • Salome **32** • Two Starving Mothers **34**

4 Women of Virtue and Goodness / 35
Anna **36** • Miriam, Sister of Moses and Aaron **37** • Ruth and Naomi **40** • Ruth **42** • The Book of Ruth **44**

5 Slaves, Handmaidens, Nursemaids, and Midwives / 45
Deborah, Rebekah's Nurse **46** • Bilhah **47** • Hagar **48** • Puah and Shiphrah **50** • Rachel's Midwife **52** • Rhoda **52** • Zilpah **53**

6

Women Who Prophesied / 55

Deborah **56** • Huldah **59** • Isaiah's Wife **60** • Necromancer of Endor **61** • Jezebel **63** • Slave-Girl Soothsayer of Philippi **65**

7

Women Favored by God / 69

Elisheba **70** • Hannah **72** • Sarah **74** • Shunammite Mother **77**

8

Temptresses, Harlots, and Sinful Women / 81

Babylonian Sacred Sex Workers **82** • Cozbi, Daughter of Zur **83** • Gomer **85** • Jephthah's Mother **87** • Prostitutes Washing Themselves in Ahab's Blood **89** • Rahab **90** • The Sinful Woman Who Wiped Jesus' Feet **92**

9

Women Who Tasted Bitterness / 95

Asenath **96** • Berenice **97** • Dinah **98** • Naomi **100** • Rizpah **101** • Thamar **103** • The Daughters of Amaziah **105** • The Women of Joppa **106**

10

Beautiful Women of the Bible / 107

Abigail **108** • Ahinoam **110** • Jemima **112** • Sarah **114** • Susanna **117**

11

Women Who Were Queens / 119

Azubah **120** • Esther **121** • Hephzibah **124** • Nehushta **125** • Queen of Sheba **125**

12

Women Healed by Jesus and the Apostles / 131

Jairus's Daughter **132** • Joanna, Wife of Chuza **133** • Peter's Mother-in-Law **134** • Susanna **135** • Slave Girl Freed from a Divining Spirit **136** • Tabitha **137** • Woman with the Issue of Blood **138**

13   **Women Disciples and Followers of Christ / 141**
Martha **142** • Mary Magdalene **143** • Mary of Bethany **147** • Mary, Wife of Cleophas **148** • Salome, Wife of Zebedee **150**

14   **Women Workers in Christ / 151**
Apphia **152** • Chloe **153** • Euodia and Syntyche **154** • Junia **155** • Lydia **156** • Nympha **157** • Priscilla, Wife of Aquila **158**

15   **Women Who Opposed Certain Men / 161**
Job's Wife **162** • Judith **163** • Lot's Wife **165** • Michal **167** • Sapphira **170**

16   **Women Who Were Concubines / 171**
Abishag **172** • Antiochis **174** • Keturah **177** • Reumah **178** • Rizpah **179**

17   **Women Who Advised, Taunted, or Lied / 183**
Arsinoe, Sister and Advisor of Ptolemy IV Philopator **184** • Peninnah **185** • Samarian Women at the Well **187** • The Woman at the Well **189** • Wife of Naaman **191** • Wives of Midian's Warriors **193**

18   **Women Who Sacrificed and Suffered / 195**
Jochebed, Mother of Moses **196** • Mother of Seven Tortured and Murdered Sons **199** • Prayerful Maccabees Women **200** • Pregnant Women Destined to Be Torn Apart **202** • The Virgin Daughter of the Elderly Man of Gibeah **203** • Expendable Women **204**

19   **Women Who Showed Courage and Commitment / 207**
Mary, Mother of John Mark **208** • Mothers Put to Death for Having Their Sons Circumcised **210** • Women Who Aided in Sanctuary Construction **212** • Zibiah **214**

20   **Remarkable Mothers / 217**

Ann **218** • Elisabeth **220** • Manoah's Wife, Samson's Mother **221** • The Blessed Virgin Mary **224**

21   **Ancient Hebrew Women in Their World / 231**

Marriage **232** • Divorce **235** • Consequences of Rape **236** • Taboos and Abominations **237** • Children and Heirs **238** • Widowhood **239** • A Woman's Place in Hebrew Society **240** • Religious Responsibilities **241**

22   **Women of the Bible in Popular Culture / 243**

Images of Biblical Women in Earliest Christian Culture **244** • Early Christians Grapple with Virginity and Divinity **245** • The Esoteric Gnostic Fascination with Eve **247** • Medieval Portrayal of the Sacred Feminine and the Witch **248** • The Renaissance **253** • Images of the Virgin Mary and Eve in the 1700s and 1800s **254** • PreRaphaelite Portrayals of Mary **255** • Paintings of Biblical Women in the Modern Era **256** • Stories of Biblical Women in Movies and Television **257** • Tales of Biblical Heroines and Martyrs in Books **258** • Heroines of the Bible in Music **260**

Appendix A: Glossary / 263
Appendix B: Additional Resources / 267
Index / 270

Acknowledgments

I offer my deepest appreciation to Lisa Laing, Paula Munier, and everyone at Adams Media involved in offering me such a wonderful project. I'm especially grateful to Lisa for her incredible skill at pulling together all of the elements that make this work exceptional in its scope, organization, and clarity.

Special thanks goes to Katerina Lorenzatos Makris, who walked with me to the house of Mary on Ephesus and prayed with me in the Cave of the Apocalypse on the island of Patmos. Our days in Greece and Turkey and our many discussions of biblical women and men inspired me to work on this book even as village roads invited me to explore the landscape and the Ionian and Aegean drew me into the sea.

I wish to thank Carlos Carvajal for his love, support, opposing points of view, and the many late-night conversations about spirituality, religion, and the mysteries of life. Understanding, I've come to believe, often emerges from an obscure place when the light of vigorous discussion and heated debate is turned upon it.

Top Ten Interesting Facts about the Women of the Bible

1. Antiochis, the concubine of Antiochus IV Epiphanes, was given the towns of Tarsus and Mallus by her lover, leading to a revolt by those communities.

2. Susanna, daughter of Hilkiah, was trapped by two local judges who lusted after her. Daniel rescued her from the men's false charges.

3. The Slave Girl of Philippi made a lot of money for her masters divining the future until the Apostle Paul cast a demon out of her.

4. Rahab was known as the "Harlot of Jericho."

5. Ruth, the Moabitess daughter-in-law of Naomi, married Boaz when he was eighty and she was forty, and subsequently had a child.

6. Sarah, the wife of Abraham, did not have a child until she was ninety.

7. The wife of the great Old Testament prophet Isaiah was also a prophet.

8. The Women of Joppa were placed on pleasure boats to drown with their children.

9. Junia was called "notable among the apostles" by the Apostle Paul, suggesting to some modern scholars that she (and perhaps other women) may have actually served as apostles.

10. Rachel was deeply loved by Jacob, who worked for seven years to pay her bride price. He believed he was marrying her, but discovered too late that through the trickery of her father, he had just married her sister, Leah.

Introduction

▶ FOR MANY WOMEN, the Bible offers a lens through which to view ancient womanhood. There are stories of women with many different qualities and gifts, life experiences, and spiritual challenges. There are dark tales filled with despicable deeds of depravity and despair. But there are also inspiring stories of hope, healing, and dreams of a better tomorrow.

While the women of the Hebrew Scriptures (the Old Testament) led lives severely restricted by a patriarchal culture, many of their situations (like that of Sarah and Rachel, who were barren for a long time) resonate with modern women who are experiencing infertility. Others (like the mother in the Second Book of Maccabees who lost her seven sons in one day because her beliefs differed from that of a "mad king") deeply mourned the reversals in their lives; in a post-9/11 world, such senseless loss and the mourning that follows is something modern people can relate to. Ancient women who were marginalized because they became widows (like the women in the Book of Ruth), or suffered illness (such as the New Testament woman with the issue of blood, whose only hope was to touch the hem of Jesus' garment), or were overcome by demons of mental illness (such as the Slave Girl of Philippi or Mary Magdalene) have modern counterparts who are also suffering and desperate for understanding and help.

Much has been written about the fact that the Bible was written by men, and that the portrayals of women are therefore colored by a male point of view. Some have said that in biblical narrative, women pretty much fall into certain types of roles and paradigms that male scribes assigned them, so much so that the women lose their uniqueness because they and their roles border on cliché. I disagree.

It is true that the majority of women in the Bible lived lives limited to the domestic sphere, regulated by a patriarchal society. Yet, what I took away from my study of the Bible was that each woman was an individual. Although some women shared many things in common, each woman was unique, and many could not be labeled simply as a Jewish woman caring for home and family. There were women living a hard life in a nomadic tent culture, others raising families in small villages, and still others who thrived or suffered in cities. There were queens and prostitutes, warriors and judges, martyrs and deceivers, and devoted wives and mothers who sacrificed their own lives for others. Some were prophetesses. Where did the idea of female personification of wisdom come from, if not from the wise women of the Bible?

You will draw something unique from each of these women's stories, depending upon how you view the Bible. Some people believe the Bible to be literally the Word of God, while others believe it to be inspired, and still others hold a more critical view. But there is something universal in the experience of womanhood. I have attempted to reveal the information about each woman's story without editorializing or inserting my own interpretations and feelings. It is my hope that if there is something specific you are seeking, a secret or a key to unlock meaning in your own life, you will find it here.

May the richly diverse stories of these ancient women echo through time to bless and enrich your life in myriad ways.

Chapter 1

Women Who
Were First

The biblical narrative spans thousands of years, focusing on the all-important, and often turbulent, relationship between God and His children. While the text of the Bible features stories of notable men, equally compelling are the tales of women. Some were deeply spiritual; others served as military leaders, prophetesses, and queens. A small number committed crimes, including murder. There were even a few who were first to perform a particular feat or to experience life-altering events. But among them all, Eve stands out as the woman who could claim the most significant "firsts."

Eve: First Woman, Wife, and Mother

Eve was the first earthly woman. She was not born of the flesh, but created by God. She had no mother to teach her the things that mothers impart to their daughters. There was no one to model for Eve how to be a wife and mother. No one told her about pregnancy, coached her on how to stay healthy while pregnant, or nourished her emotionally and spiritually through the pregnancy process. She endured the pain of childbirth without an understanding of what was happening within her own body. She reared her children without any knowledge of how to do such things and without another woman on earth to guide or support her. She suffered the murder of one of her children by her other child. Eve, who was placed in paradise, had a life filled with beauty and pleasure and wonderment, but also one weighted by sadness and suffering.

FACT

The version of the Adam and Eve story in midrashi writings (an ancient interpretive system in Jewish literature to reconcile contradictions in biblical text) states that before creating Eve, God made Lilith, an evil and licentious woman who rebelled against Adam (refusing to take a submissive position to him in sex). Lilith abandoned Adam. Eve, according to midrashic writings, was Lilith's replacement.

In the Judeo-Christian tradition, the image of God is portrayed as masculine. Adam could have looked to God for cues about all things male, but Eve must have had difficulty relating to her femaleness, with no image of a divine feminine counterpart to Adam's God. Eve shoulders the blame associated with the first sinful act. Rightly or wrongly, humankind's fall from grace has long been blamed on the "Original Sin" committed by Eve, when she was tempted by the serpent to defy God's rule not to eat the fruit of the tree of knowledge.

Adam and Eve recognized God through the Divine presence and voice, but no description is given in Genesis of God as seen through their eyes. However, perhaps what is meant by "our likeness" is that a divine spark entered Adam and Eve at their creation, and the spark mirrored, in some way, an image (or images) of God.

After the story of the creation of male and female in Genesis 1:27, a second version of the creation of the first couple appears in Genesis 2:7–25. According to that version, God created Adam first and then Eve, and he used a different process for each. Adam was created from the dust of the ground. God breathed the breath of life into Adam's nostrils, making Adam a living soul. God placed Adam in the Garden of Eden. After warning him not to eat from the tree of knowledge of good and evil (with death as the threatened punishment), God caused Adam to fall into a deep sleep. While Adam slept, God created Eve (Genesis 2:21–22). Instead of making Eve from dust as he had made Adam, God fashioned her from one of Adam's ribs.

Adam chose Eve's name. In Old Testament times, naming a thing equaled having authority over it. Her name derives from the Hebrew word *Hava*, and means "the Mother of All Living" (Genesis 3:20). In both the Judeo-Christian tradition and the Islamic faith, Eve is the mother of the human species and Adam is the father.

Inferior or Equal

Some who believe in a literal interpretation of the Bible might argue that because Eve was created after Adam and from his rib, her position as woman was inferior to that of man. This idea was one espoused in the New Testament by the Apostle Paul in Timothy 2:13–15. However, another interpretation suggests that from unity or wholeness, God created two halves, male and female. Without his female counterpart, Adam could never be complete; he could not generate offspring and continue the human species. God created Eve not just as a helper or companion for Adam, but as an equal to complete him.

Longing for Knowledge

The newly created Eve and her husband, though naked, had no sense of self-consciousness. All they knew and all they could see was the perfection of God's creation and themselves as part of it. They hid nothing from each other or from God. Darkness, negativity, deception, and imperfection had not yet entered into their consciousness. Eve had been created differently

Eve

from Adam, and yet was profoundly part of him. Perhaps separate from each other they both felt a deep inner longing to be united. Whatever the reason, Eve began to desire knowledge. Perhaps it was carnal knowledge. The Hebrew word for knowledge, *da'at,* means sexual knowledge.

Rebelling Against God

In a roundabout way, the serpent asked Eve if God had denied her the right to eat from the trees in the garden. Eve explained that there was only one tree she and Adam could not eat from, and it was in the middle of the garden. Eating from that tree meant suffering the penalty of death. This would have been based upon her understanding of Adam's instruction, since God had not told her about the tree (at least nothing is recorded in Genesis about a conversation between God and Eve in which God forbade Eve to eat from the tree). When God forbade Adam to partake of the fruit of that tree, he had not yet even created Eve. The serpent told Eve that God knew that on the day that she and Adam ate from that tree, they would be divine beings, their eyes would be opened, and they would not die, but would know good and evil.

Loss of Innocence

The possibility that she could possess divine knowledge must have roused a deep desire within Eve. But she did not act in haste; instead, she took time to consider that the tree of knowledge "was good for food, and that it was pleasant to the eyes, and a tree to be desired to make one wise" (Genesis 3:6). Then, not only did she eat from the tree, but she also shared the fruit with her husband. Neither of them died in the literal sense; however, the act brought the death of their innocence. Their eyes were opened, and their minds and hearts grasped the knowledge of good and evil. They must have also experienced a sickening, sinking feeling at having disobeyed God. Their feelings of bliss and perfection shifted to guilt, remorse, and shame. They now saw their own nakedness and covered their bodies with aprons fashioned out of fig leaves.

Sexual Allegory

The tasting of the forbidden fruit works well as an allegory for the sexual awakening of Adam and Eve. God gave them free will. Instead of using self-discipline to stay away from the tree, they chose to indulge themselves in arousal and pleasure. Their eyes became open as they came "to know" each other as sexual beings. They were evolving as humans. God's punishment enabled them to develop moral responsibility as they learned that there are consequences to every choice and course of action.

Some say that the serpent symbolized Eve's sexual yearning. Scholars are aware of a long tradition linking fertility symbolism with ancient snake motifs. In ancient societies in the Middle East, snakes played a role in the efforts of some fertility cults to acquire divine knowledge. The Adam and Eve story could have been a warning to ancient Hebrews against being seduced by certain rival cults with such practices.

God's Punishment

God punished the serpent first. Formerly able to move upright, the snake would ever after slither upon its belly and eat dust. As for Adam, God told him that he would have to labor upon the earth to produce food for survival. God punished Eve by making her, and all generations of women, suffer the pains of childbirth, desire their husbands, and have their husbands rule over them (Genesis 3:16). Adam and Eve were banished from the Garden of Eden. The Book of Genesis does not establish a timeline for their departure;

however, some sources assert that the couple remained in the garden less than a day. After leaving paradise, Eve conceived.

Eve's sons brought offerings to the Lord. Cain's was the first fruit born of the ground, and Abel's was a newborn from his flock of sheep. Abel's offering pleased the Lord more than Cain's, causing enmity between brothers that turned to violence—Cain murdered his brother. Genesis does not say how the murder of one of her sons by the other affected Eve, but it must have been devastating. To make matters worse for the first mother, her son Cain left to dwell in the land of Nod, east of Eden. Eve's story ends there, only to pick up much later when she gives birth to Seth. Adam was 130 years old when Seth was born. Eve must have been the same age, if we are to believe that she and Adam were created on the same day, as suggested in Genesis. Eve's later life and death are not mentioned in Genesis. But her story, intertwined as it is with Adam's, some say, points less to being about sin than it does to becoming the perfect human who, through wisdom and will, mirrors the Creator.

And Adam knew Eve his wife; and she conceived, and bare Cain, and said, I have gotten a man from the Lord. And she again bare his brother Abel. And Abel was a keeper of sheep, but Cain was a tiller of the ground. (Genesis 4:1–2)

Hassophereth

Hassophereth (also referred to as Sophereth) is the first woman writer whose name is mentioned in the Old Testament. The Hebrew meaning of the name Sophereth is "the female scribe," and she may have been either one of a family of scribes, or the head of a guild of scribes. The name first appears in Ezra, one of the last four books of the Hebrew canon (the canon includes Ezra, Nehemiah, and 1 and 2 Chronicles). The Persian king Cyrus desired to have the Hebrews build a temple in Jerusalem. His desire paved the way for their departure from Babylonian exile, along with their families and slaves. The following E-Quote shows how Ezra chronicled the names in an ancient list.

The children of Bazluth, the children of Mehida, the children of Harsha, the children of Barkos, the children of Sisera, the children of Thamah, the children of Neziah, the children of Hatipha. The children of Solomon's servants: the children of Sotai, the children of Sophereth, the children of Peruda. (Ezra 2:52–55)

A parallel passage that includes the name Sophereth appears in Nehemiah 7:57. Not much is known about the authorship of the Old Testament, but some scholars assert that women contributed to the final shaping of the writings of at least some of the Old Testament. This theory is based on the numerous instances of direct quotes by women and the fact that there were women writers in Babylon.

Rebekah

Rebekah married Isaac, son of the great patriarch Abraham. When Abraham's servant Eliezer saw Rebekah, he believed that God had guided him to her. He spoke to Rebekah gently and gave her gifts, and Rebekah's family agreed to the marriage. Rebekah accompanied Eliezer back to Isaac's village.

Rebekah remained childless for twenty years before becoming the first woman to give birth to twins. Hers was not an easy pregnancy. It seemed to Rebekah that a fierce battle was being waged inside her body. She asked the Lord why this was happening, to which He replied, "Two nations are in thy womb, and two manner of people shall be separated from thy bowels; and the one people shall be stronger than the other people; and the elder shall serve the younger" (Genesis 25:23). Rebekah named her twin boys Esau and Jacob. The Bible says that Esau appeared red and covered with hair, but does not describe Jacob except to say that he grabbed Esau's heel soon after birth.

As if guided by the hands of angels, the marriage between Rebekah and Isaac turned out to be a heavenly match. But Rebekah and Isaac did not love their sons in an equal manner. Rebekah favored Jacob because of his fine temperament, as opposed to his brother's wild and forceful nature. Isaac, however, loved Esau. No good could come of such preferential feelings toward one child.

Rebekah's sons grew to manhood. Jacob was a plain and gentle man who lived in tents, while Esau became a man of the fields, a skillful hunter who brought home the venison his father loved to eat. Esau, as first-born son, occupied an important position in the family that included the line of succession of patriarchal authority and inheritance, but Esau thought so little of his birthright that he sold it to Jacob for a meal of lentils and bread. He further disappointed Rebekah and Isaac by his choice of wives.

QUESTION?

Why was it significant that Jacob's fingers grabbed the heel of Esau at birth?

It might be seen as a prophetic sign that the second-born would struggle to usurp the position of the first-born. That is exactly what took place after the boys grew into manhood, fulfilling God's words that "the elder shall serve the younger."

One day Rebekah overheard Isaac, then old and nearly blind, tell Esau that death was near and that he wanted a meal of venison before pronouncing the blessing of the first-born. Rebekah knew that the blessing ensured Esau would inherit his father's property, something she wanted for Jacob. She devised a scheme to secure the blessing for her favorite son. Jacob feared that such deception would bring a curse instead, but followed his mother's wishes and put on Esau's clothes, covering his hands and neck with goatskins before taking the venison to his father.

Through Rebekah's clever scheme, Jacob acquired the blessing of his father, but the curse of his brother. Esau vowed to murder Jacob as soon as the days of mourning were over. Rebekah advised Jacob to flee to her brother Laban's place in Haran. Rebekah then spoke to her husband Isaac and said she was weary and worried that Jacob might take a wife from among the daughters of Heth. Her concerns must have had resonance in

Isaac's heart as well, for he called Jacob and charged him "not to take a wife of the daughters of Canaan" (Genesis 28:1).

Twenty years passed before Jacob returned to mend the relationship with his brother and see his father. Though she must have longed through the years to see her beloved son again, Rebekah would not live to see him return.

And Esau was forty years old when he took to wife Judith the daughter of Beeri the Hittite, and Bashemath the daughter of Elon the Hittite: Which were a grief of mind unto Isaac and to Rebekah. (Genesis 26:34–35)

Rachel

Rachel was the first woman in the Bible to die while giving birth to a child. Her story reveals how deception can spawn tragedy. In Rachel's family, the deception was between father and daughter, but in the family of Jacob (Rachel's husband), the deception occurred between mother and son.

Rachel's name, which means "ewe," was given to her by her father Laban, who owned sheep. She fell in love with Jacob, the youngest son of Isaac and Rebekah, when she saw him approaching the well where she often drew water for the sheep.

Jacob had fled his parents' home after he and his mother had deceived the aging and nearly blind Isaac, when he approached the well. Isaac had told Jacob not to take a wife from the Canaanite women, but rather to choose from among Laban's daughters (Laban was Rebekah's brother, and Rachel and Leah were Jacob's cousins). The chance meeting at the well between Jacob and Rachel seemed to be divinely ordained. The two experienced an instant attraction and soon Jacob sought Laban's permission to marry Rachel. Laban saw how the love between his daughter and Jacob could work out well for him. He forced Jacob to labor for him for seven years in exchange for agreeing to the marriage.

As her wedding day approached, Rachel did not know the devious scheme that her father and older sister Leah had worked out. Leah disguised herself in Rachel's wedding garments, married Jacob, and spent the wedding night

Rachel at the well

with the new groom. Only when the sun rose the next day did Jacob discover he had been tricked; it was too late to undo the marriage. After about a week, Laban offered Rachel to Jacob if Jacob would agree to work for Laban for an additional seven years. It was a harsh pact, but Jacob's desire for Rachel was so great, he agreed to it.

Rachel stood by as her sister Leah conceived and bore six sons and a daughter by Jacob. Eventually, Rachel also married Jacob, but unlike her sister, she could not conceive. She cried out in anguish, "Give me children, or else I die" (Genesis 30:1). In desperation, she gave her maid Bilhah to Jacob to bear children for her. Bilhah bore two sons—Dan and Napthali. Rachel eventually conceived and bore a son that she named Joseph, and another son named Benjamin.

The family was the keystone of ancient Hebrew society, and the tribe was simply an extension of the family on a larger scale. Family size quickly increased in many cases due to polygamy, the practice of men taking multiple wives, as Jacob did when he married Leah and Rachel and had children by their handmaidens.

After serving out the allotted time to Laban as a laborer, Jacob, who had increased his and Laban's wealth, asked for release. Having received inspiration from God, Jacob wished to return to the land of his family, and to rebuild his relationship with his brother Esau. Rachel desired that they would continue to prosper in their new life. Without telling Jacob, she stole some small religious idols from her father's house. Outraged at finding the idols gone, Laban believed Jacob was the thief. He set out to find him.

Rachel, upon seeing her father approaching their camp along the road, hid the idols in a saddle bag on a horse, and then climbed onto the saddle. On the pretext of having her monthly period, Rachel refused to dismount.

And Laban said, It is better that I give her to thee, than I should give her to another man: abide with me. And Jacob served seven years for Rachel; and they seemed unto him but a few days, for the love he had for her. (Genesis 29:19–20)

Jacob, unaware that Rachel had taken the idols, asked Laban what he had done to cause Laban to pursue him. Jacob went on to remind Laban of all that he had done during two decades, "Thus have I been twenty years in thy house; I served thee fourteen years for thy two daughters, and six years for thy cattle: and thou hast changed my wages ten times" (Genesis 31:41). Jacob's quiet reasoning cooled Laban's rage. Jacob offered a sacrifice and invited Laban and those with him to eat. The next day, Laban and his companions left.

Eventually, Rachel became pregnant again. The labor was extremely difficult. She gave birth to a son, calling him Ben-oni (Son of My Sorrow), just before dying. Rachel, the woman who had cried out "give me children or else I die" perished in childbirth. Her husband changed the newborn's name to Benjamin (Son of Happy Omen), and buried Rachel on the way to Ephrath in Bethlehem. He built a monument on the road at the place where he buried her, with eleven stones put there by Rachel's sons. The largest stone was set into place by Jacob.

Zipporah

Zipporah had the distinction of being the Bible's first woman to circumcise her child. She was given in marriage to Moses by her father Jethro, a Midian priest, after Moses rescued her and six of her sisters from shepherds harassing them while they attempted to water their sheep at a desert well. Moses came upon the women after fleeing from Egypt, where he had taken a man's life for maltreatment of a Hebrew slave. Although their religious beliefs were different, Zipporah and Moses had a good marriage and produced two boys, Gershom and Eliezer.

And it came to pass by the way in the inn, that the Lord met him, and sought to kill him. Then Zipporah took a sharp stone, and cut off the foreskin of her son, and cast it at his feet and said, "Surely a bloody husband art thou to me" … she said, "a bloody husband thou art, because of the circumcision." (Exodus 4:24–26)

Zipporah proved herself to be decisive and determined when faced with God's seeming displeasure toward her and Moses. God spoke through a burning bush to Moses, telling him to return to Egypt to free his brethren from the pharaoh's bondage. He told Moses to take the rod that the Lord had given him (which Moses would use to "make signs" or miracles), and that the men who wanted to kill him were themselves all dead. While on the return journey, Zipporah, Moses, and the boys stopped at an inn. There God met Moses and "sought to kill him" (Exodus 4:24). Zipporah, perhaps fearing that God was angry because their son was not circumcised, took matters into her own hands…literally.

The Hebrews used circumcision as the symbol of their covenant with God as his chosen people. Exodus does not reveal which son Zipporah circumcised. It does reveal that she threw the piece of bloody foreskin at his feet, but that raises another question: To whom does "his" refer? Did she throw the skin at God, Moses, or the child? Still, her swift action saved the life of her husband and restored Moses' favor in the sight of God.

The narrative about Zipporah may have been instrumental in warning ancient Hebrews about the importance of circumcision, and that neglecting it could have dire consequences, even death. The story may also support the idea that marriages of Hebrews to nonHebrews can be good matches and work out well. Finally, Zipporah perhaps served as a powerful example for women's faith and abilities to conduct religious ritual.

Chapter 2
Adulteresses, Harlots, and Deceivers

The Bible is full of stories of virtuous women, but within the ancient narrative are also tales showing the darker side of womanhood. Unrestrained desire ultimately led to entrapment of one kind or another; lust was often at the heart of marital deception, infidelity, and betrayal. Women featured in the Old Testament stories had little power to thwart men intent on being with them. However, in some instances, the women themselves were the agents of deceit, manipulating a situation for personal gain, sometimes with dire consequences.

The Adulterous Woman Brought Before Jesus

To be caught in an adulterous act in ancient times was to know that your time on earth would soon end in a terrible death by stoning. That was the punishment faced by the woman brought to Jesus by the scribes and Pharisees. Biblical scholars say that the woman was a convenient ploy in the plan of those men to trap Jesus into somehow breaking the Law of Moses. The scribes and Pharisees reminded Jesus that Mosaic Law required that she be stoned, but they asked Jesus, "what sayest thou?" (John 8:5). Even Jesus recognized that it was a question with enormous implications for both himself and the woman.

The adulterous woman brought before Jesus

The poor woman stood there, her fate being decided by a group of men, yet there is no mention of the whereabouts of her lover. Jesus can't very well tell the men to release her, because he would essentially be saying to disobey the Mosaic Law. But Jesus knew that the group of men was no less guilty of sin than the woman. He doesn't judge her, but instead stoops down and writes on the ground with his finger. Some have suggested that he wrote the names of the men in the group who were themselves adulterers. The Gospel of John, in which this story is found, does not reveal exactly what Jesus wrote. But pressured by the men to give his opinion, Jesus takes his time to give a measured response.

One by one the men began to leave. The woman apparently stands before Jesus in silence, waiting for her fate to be decided by a group of men rapidly shrinking in size. Finally, only she and Jesus remain. The woman must have felt relief and bewilderment. In her world, men held great power over the means of life and death of a woman. She might have just as easily fled after the men had left, but she didn't. Jesus stood up to face her and asked, "…where are those, thine accusers? Hath no man condemned thee?" (John 8:10). The woman replied no man [remained]. Jesus told her that neither did he condemn her. He counseled her to go and sin no more.

So when they continued asking him, he lifted up himself, and said unto them, He that is without sin among you, let him first cast a stone at her. And again he stooped down, and wrote on the ground. (John 8:7–8)

The Gospel of John says no more about the woman. She may have decided to follow Jesus' advice to live more virtuously after coming so close to death in her quest for sensual pleasure. The story is both a morality lesson and also an example of how Jesus viewed women differently than the way other men saw them in first-century Palestine. He showed a more egalitarian, loving, and respectful way of treating them than they were generally treated with in their society. Not surprisingly, all types of women chose to follow him, among them the outcasts of society, widows, the lame and sick, and others who were displaced or disenfranchised.

Bathsheba

From among the many ancient women who exploited the flaws in the character of rich and powerful men, no one stands out quite like Bathsheba. She was a wife, an illicit lover, a mother, and a queen. Her intriguing story starts with a serene bath she took on a rooftop before sunset. It is not known whether she was an exhibitionist and knew she was being watched, or if she was simply cleansing herself as part of a purity ritual, in which case the bathing would have been somewhat explicit. Whichever the case, she was bathing in view of the palace of King David, and he was watching.

Bathsheba may have come across as a self-assured, confident, and articulate young woman. But biblical scholars assert that such characterization of her involves pure speculation. She certainly must have appeared beguiling to have captured the interest of David, who already had many wives and concubines. Whether or not she sought the interest of the king, Bathsheba was married to Uriah the Hittite, a professional soldier in the king's army. Uriah served on the battlefield, leaving Bathsheba alone for long periods of time. He was away on the afternoon of her infamous bath, engaged in the war the Israelites were fighting against the Ammonites.

King David was not on the battlefield with his soldiers. Instead, he "tarried still at Jerusalem" (II Samuel 11:1). As he observed the beautiful woman bathing on the distant rooftop, David was overcome with feelings of lust. Instead of averting his eyes or resisting the temptation to give into his sexual desire, David sent for her.

God gave many laws to Moses and Aaron for the children of Israel concerning uncleanness (especially Leviticus 15:1–33). One such rule was that a woman who had her monthly period was required after seven days to take a ritual bath known as a mikveh. Perhaps this was the bath that Bathsheba was engaged in when she was spied by David.

If Bathsheba had intended to seduce the king, then she would likely have been elated to go meet him. But if that were not her purpose, she would have felt fear and dread upon discovering his carnal desire for her, because death by stoning was the punishment for committing adultery.

When Bathsheba told David that she was with child, the ruler had to figure out how to hide what he had done to the wife of one of his soldiers. He sent word to Uriah to come from the battlefield, hoping that Uriah would spend the night with Bathsheba and thus create the appearance that Uriah was the father of the unborn child. Uriah returned at the behest of the king, but he did not sleep with his wife. He slept with the servants of the king at the door of the palace. When David learned that Uriah had not gone home to Bathsheba, he asked him why. Uriah replied that since the soldiers were staying in tents and the king's servants camped in an open field, Uriah didn't feel right about going to his house to enjoy a good meal, having something to drink, and lying with his wife.

Murder as a Cover Up

Out of options, David ordered Uriah to the battle's front line. There was little question that Uriah would be killed. And indeed he was. David received word that his faithful soldier had fallen in battle. The ruler replied matter-of-factly that, "the sword devoureth one as well as another."

FACT

Bathsheba's story inspired many images of her through the ages. Artists, including among others Rembrandt and Jan Metsys, have depicted her as a partially clad or nude woman, often with a full figure, reaching for water, sitting quietly absorbed in thought, boldly speaking to David, or simply washing her feet.

Their Act Offends God

Bathsheba mourned the loss of her husband for the required period before marrying David. Perhaps she felt remorse over the death of Uriah, but there was little question that her station in life suddenly shifted upward. The steamy, sexual bond between her and David may not have been love, but it was a strong bond nevertheless. The Scriptures do not mention love between the king and the soldier's wife, nor do they suggest that Uriah was necessarily an attentive and devoted husband. The adultery between Bathsheba and David, and the subsequent murder of Uriah to cover it up, displeased the Lord, who sent the prophet Nathan to David with a message: "...the sword shall never depart from thine house..." (II Samuel 12:10).

Wages of Sin

Nathan told David that he and Bathsheba would not lose their lives in punishment for the sin, but that the child Bathsheba carried in her womb would die. Soon Bathsheba gave birth to a sickly infant. On the seventh day, the infant died; the wages for the sin of the father and mother fell upon the innocent infant. The sexual attraction between Bathsheba and David, however, must have remained strong, for he comforted Bathsheba and lay with her again to conceive another child. In time, she gave birth to Solomon, a baby that the Lord loved. In all, Bathsheba would have three children by David.

Bathsheba's Power Grows as Queen Mother

As the years went by, Bathsheba's power increased, even as David's waned. The Lord forgave the couple for their adulterous act, and Bathsheba proved to be an insightful wife and an intelligent and powerful queen. She raised Solomon to honor God and adhere to his laws with diligence. When it appeared that David's son Adonijah would claim the throne while David lay upon his deathbed, Bathsheba convinced her husband to proclaim Solomon his successor. According to some sources, Bathsheba wrote Proverbs 31 in honor of Solomon's marriage to the pharaoh's daughter. In her recitation of that text on Solomon's wedding day, she issued warnings against giving his strength to women or doing things that destroy kings.

As a bathing beauty, she may have been a masterful manipulator, or simply a beautiful young woman performing a mikveh. In any case, Bathsheba would be remembered as a politically perceptive queen, beautiful wife to David, diligent mother of Solomon, and a woman who would be included in the genealogy of Jesus (Matthew 1:6).

Delilah

Delilah was another biblical beauty who showed how a pretty woman could bring down a man, even if he was a powerhouse of strength. She lived in the valley of Sorek, and may have been a widow, for she had means to live without a husband. The Bible does not reveal her lineage, whether Israelite, Philistine, or something else, and does not say Delilah loved Samson, hero of the Israelites. It does say that she became the object of Samson's desire after he had been betrayed by his Philistine wife. His enemies must have thought that they could exploit Samson's weakness for her. The lords of the Philistines approached Delilah with an extraordinary offer of 1,100 pieces of silver per man if she would discover for them the source of Samson's strength, and how he could be bound so as not to break free. Was Delilah coerced into betraying Samson? Was she loyal to the Philistines? Did she desire the money? The Scripture does not reveal Delilah's motivation, but does recount the steps in her betrayal. Three times she asked Samson about what could bind him that he could not break, and three times he told her a lie. Delilah pressed him daily for the answer to that question, but Samson resisted.

Before Samson was born, an angel appeared to his mother and foretold his birth. The angel warned her not to drink wine or strong drink, and not to eat anything unclean, "for the child shall be a Nazarite to God from the womb to the day of his death" (Judges 13:7). In other words, the child would be consecrated to God. Samson grew up blessed with extraordinary powers, including strength, but only if his hair was never cut. Before he met Delilah, he had a fondness for Philistine women, one in particular. She was a woman from Timnath, and Samson demanded his parents get her for him.

Then his father and his mother said unto him, Is there never a woman among the daughters of thy brethren, or among all my people, that thou goest to take a wife of the uncircumcised Philistines? And Samson said unto his father, Get her for me; for she pleaseth me well. (Judges 14:3)

Samson's father made the arrangements for Samson to marry the woman (unnamed in the Bible). During the engagement feast, Samson made a wager with some young Philistine men, telling them a riddle that they would have to solve within seven days in order to get thirty sheets and thirty changes of garments. Upset that they could not solve the riddle, the men went to the young bride-to-be and asked her to get Samson to reveal the riddle. They threatened to burn her and her father's house if she didn't get it for them. She wept and asked Samson to reveal it. He held off for most of the week, but on the seventh day gave in, broke his Nazarite vow, and shared it with her. She, in turn, gave it to the Philistines. Enraged, Samson murdered thirty Philistine men and his wife was given to his companion.

Tradition paints Delilah as a fallen woman and a deceiver, but some scholars say that the image is not supported by the Scriptures. She didn't lie to Samson or trick him with her words. On the contrary, she asked quite directly: "Tell me, I pray thee, wherein thy great strength lieth, and wherewith thou mightest be bound to afflict thee" (Judges 16:6). It was Samson who repeatedly lied.

Samson then met Deliliah and loved her. He told Delilah that if he were tied with seven green withes or new ropes or seven locks of his hair woven with the web, that he would not be able to break free. Delilah put him to the test, and each time Samson broke the restraints. She protested and asked him how he could possibly love her when he continued to mock her with lies. Samson finally poured out his heart to Delilah. He confessed that a razor had never touched his head. If his hair were cut, he would lose his strength. Delilah wasted no time summoning the Philistines.

Delilah placed Samson's head in her lap and lulled him to sleep. She then summoned a man to cut Samson's hair. With his locks shorn, Samson's vow to God was broken. The Philistines bound him and gouged out his eyes. In the ultimate humiliation, Samson was put to work in prison pounding grain, the task of a woman.

After betraying Samson, Delilah disappeared from the story, although some scholars suggest that she may have been present during the Philistine agricultural festival at the Temple of Dagon where Samson was brought out so all could see the vanquished hero of the Israelites. In that version of the story, what no one seemed to have noticed was that Samson's hair had started growing again. After calling upon the Lord to

Delilah holding Samson's hair

strengthen him, Samson put his hands upon the pillars of the temple and pulled the structure down, killing himself and 3,000 Philistines, and Delilah, too, if she were present that day to see the culmination of her deed. To see Flemish painter Peter Paul Ruben's masterwork of Samson and Delilah, visit: *www.vincent.nl/?/gallery/oilreproduction.asp?vagnr=a1046&ref*

Drusilla

Drusilla, a gorgeous Jewess who belonged to a powerful family of officials working for the Roman Empire, became known as an immoral woman and an adulterer who was unrepentant to the end of her life. Her father was Herod Agrippa I, and her uncle was Herod Antipas, the man who ordered the beheading of John the Baptist. Drusilla was the loveliest and the youngest of her three sisters. At the age of fifteen, she married King Aziz after his conversion to Judaism. She soon became an unfaithful wife, turning her attention to the Roman governor Felix, who abducted her. She married him; however, the marriage was not legal, since Drusilla was neither divorced nor widowed. Drusilla took Felix as a husband, although he was a heathen and not inclined to convert to Judaism. In fact, he was a former slave whose savagery and brutality helped him move up the ladder of power to provincial ruler. The marriage cemented Drusilla's reputation as an immoral woman.

FACT

Numbers 5:11–31 explains the test for adultery. A woman suspected of infidelity was forced to drink a concoction made of sweeping debris from the temple floor mixed with holy water over which the priest pronounced ritual words. She was deemed innocent if she felt nothing, and guilty if she suffered a painful discharge from her womb, dropping of her uterus, abdominal swelling, or shrinking thighs.

Drusilla was present when Felix called the Apostle Paul before him to answer charges by Jews of being a "pestilent fellow, and a mover of sedition among all the Jews throughout the world, and a ringleader of the sect of the Nazarenes: Who also hath gone about to profane the temple" (Acts 24:5–

6). The couple listened as Paul reasoned out righteousness, temperance, and the judgment to come. He spoke of his faith in the Christ. Felix, the Bible says, began to tremble, suggesting that his heart may have received the Apostle's holy words, and that Paul's teaching had a powerful effect. Perhaps Felix felt remorse for all of the bad things he'd done. Maybe he regretted abducting and marrying Drusilla. He might have converted, some say, if Drusilla hadn't been present. Felix abruptly told Paul to go, and that he would call him later in a "convenient season" (Acts 24:25).

Some biblical writers suggest that Drusilla may have wanted the meeting to end. Perhaps the Apostle's words had made her uncomfortable and forced her to recall her sins. Whatever happened that day, the meeting ended and the Apostle Paul was returned to prison. Felix sent for Paul often and communed with him, but it is unclear what happened to Drusilla after that meeting; references to her in the Bible stop at that point. After two years, Felix transferred Paul's case to Procius Festus for trial against the charges the Jews had levied against the apostle. According to one source, Drusilla died some twenty years later with her child Agrippa, trying to flee the eruption of Mount Vesuvius.

Lot's Daughters

The Bible says that Lot's daughters made their father drink wine and then each had a sexual relationship with him in order to perpetuate his line of male descendents. The really surprising part of the story is that they accomplished their mission without the father knowing what had transpired. The older of the two bore a child and named him Moab. He became the father of the Moabites. The younger sister also gave birth to a boy, who she named Ben-ammi, and he became the leader of the Ammonites. The Bible never reveals the names of the sisters.

The story actually began much earlier, when two angels appeared to Lot where he dwelled in the city of Sodom. He pressed the angels to stay with him for the night and he made them a feast, including unleavened bread. The wicked men of Sodom came to Lot, even before the household had gone to sleep for the night, and said that they wanted to have sex with Lot's two guests. Lot stepped outside of his door and closed it, begging the men not to act so wickedly. He offered his two daughters instead.

Behold now, I have two daughters which have not known man; let me, I pray you, bring them out unto you, and do ye to them as is good in your eyes: only unto these men do nothing; for therefore came they under the shadow of my roof. (Genesis: 19:8)

Lot's offer of his daughters did not appease the men, and they became more determined than ever to get into Lot's house. They nearly knocked the door down before the angels pulled Lot inside and shut the door. The angels brought a blindness upon the men and told Lot to gather his family together and leave the town, for it was about to be destroyed. Lot, according to rabbinical literature, may have had four daughters—two married and two unmarried, for the Bible says that he ran to his sons-in-law, told them what had happened, and urged them to go with him, but they mocked him. The next morning, the angels told Lot again to get his wife and daughters out of the city, but Lot tarried. The angels laid hold of him and his wife and daughters and set them outside the city, telling the family not to look back and not to stay on the plain, but to go to the mountain.

Perhaps the community of Sodom held many memories for Lot's wife. Maybe she knew how much she would miss it and the friends she'd made. Perhaps she wondered if her married daughters were following. Whatever the reason, Lot's wife looked back just once to see the destruction taking place behind them, and instantly became a pillar of salt. Lot and his daughters, however, continued on to the town of Zoar, where they lived in a cave. Husbandless and motherless, the girls worried that their aging father would also die, and no man would want them. Most likely out of a concern for self-preservation, the older sister concocted the plan to give their father wine and then have sex with him. It is interesting that the father "perceived not when she lay down, nor when she arose" (Genesis 19:33), absolving him of any responsibility for the incestuous act.

Potiphar's Wife

Like some of the other vixens of the Old Testament, Potiphar's wife, whom the Bible never names, lusted after a particular man. The object of her affection was Joseph, son of Jacob. The boy had been sold to Ishmaelite traders after his brothers had stripped him of his coat of many colors and pushed him into a pit. Midianite merchants came upon Joseph, pulled him out of the pit, and sold him for twenty pieces of silver to the Ishmaelites, who took him in their camel caravan to Egypt. There Joseph was again sold, this time to Potiphar, an Egyptian officer of the pharaoh and captain of the guard. Potiphar respected and trusted Joseph and made him the overseer of his palatial home. He placed all of his possessions under Joseph's control; all, that is, except his wife.

Potiphar's wife held a prominent position as the wife of an official of the pharaoh. She was spoiled and a slave to sensual pleasure. She might have secretly deceived her husband with any man in Egypt, but she lusted after Joseph, demanding he give her what she desired. Living as she did in the licentious culture of Roman society in Egypt, she apparently was used to getting whatever she wanted. But Joseph was as equally intent on not betraying his master's trust. Joseph kept close to the Lord in his heart and mind, and dared not engage in "this great wickedness, and sin against God" (Genesis 39:9).

QUOTE

…and she said, Lie with me. But he refused, and said unto his master's wife, Behold my master wotteth not what is with me in the house, and he hath committed all he hath to my hand; there is none greater in this house than I; neither hath he kept back any thing from me but thee, because thou art his wife… (Genesis 39:7–8)

Perhaps Potiphar's wife did not mind the sting of rejection, because she kept pursuing Joseph; but he kept refusing her advances. Joseph harbored no desire to betray the master who had trusted him, but his spurning of Potiphar's wife only further inflamed her. One day she demanded that he lie with her, and when he refused, she grabbed his tunic. Joseph fled the house in such haste that his garment was ripped from him. The scorned woman's desire turned to hate, and she quickly decided Joseph's ripped tunic was just the thing she needed to get even. She told all of the men of the house that Joseph, "the Hebrew servant," had raped her (Genesis 39:17). She kept the tunic by her side and waited until her husband returned, then told him the same lie.

QUESTION?

Did Potiphar believe his wife or his trustworthy servant?
While Potiphar may have suspected that his wife was faithless, his anger at the thought of her lying with Joseph consumed him. The Bible says that Potiphar took Joseph into the prison where the king's other prisoners were bound.

The jailer was sympathetic and let Joseph have a great deal of freedom within the prison. He could have contact with the other prisoners. There is no biblical record that Joseph ever complained about Potiphar's wife or slandered her in any way. The Bible does reveal that in prison Joseph became the interpreter of dreams. Word of his great spiritual power got around, and eventually Joseph interpreted the pharaoh's dreams. Because Joseph was wise and discreet with the pharaoh, he was put in charge of the pharaoh's palace. The pharaoh so believed in the visionary gifts that God had given Joseph that he said, "Thou shalt be over my house, and according unto thy word shall all my people be ruled: only in the throne will I be greater than thou...I have set thee over all the land of Egypt" (Genesis 41:40–41).

As for Potiphar's wife, nothing more is revealed about her life after the incident with Joseph. Perhaps she sought to satisfy her carnal cravings with others, or maybe she always longed for Joseph, the one man she couldn't have.

Prostitutes Who Forced Solomon to Split the Baby

During the reign of King Solomon, son of David and Bathsheba, two women known as harlots came before him in a dispute over which one of them was the rightful mother of a child. The two women lived alone in the same house and had given birth within three days of each other. One of the women told the king that the other woman's child died during the night, because the mother had rolled over on it. The mother of the dead infant then switched the babies, so that in the morning she had a living son.

The harlot's complaint proved to be a most difficult test of Solomon's abilities. Solomon had previously dreamed of God coming to him and asking him what he desired, to which Solomon answered "an understanding heart to judge thy people" (1 Kings 3:9). Before him were two mothers—one of them was the mother of the living child, the other was a liar. Solomon asked for a sword.

> And the king said, Divide the living child in two, and give half to the one, and half to the other. Then spake the woman whose living child was unto the king...O my lord, give her the living child, and in no wise slay it. But the other said, Let it be neither mine nor thine, but divide it. (1 Kings 3:25–26)

It was clear to Solomon that the true mother of the child couldn't bear to see harm come to her infant, so was willing to let the other woman have it. To her, Solomon gave the child. The Scriptures do not mention what, if anything, was done to the woman who lied. King Solomon must have known that she had suffered the loss of her child, and perhaps considered that her pain drove her to such a heartless act.

Chapter 3

Women Who Caused Murder

In biblical times, bad blood was often blamed for bloodthirsty acts of brutality and murder. The ancients passed stories through oral tradition of instances when a bad seed was sown in a previous generation, only to reappear later. The Old Testament, replete with stories of murders, is no different. Life to the ancients was a precious thing, but death could come from any corridor, and not just at the hands of soldiers, despotic rulers, warring tribes, power-grabbing brothers, or vengeful fathers. The most intriguing evildoers of ancient times were often the women who gave life, but also took it!

Athaliah

Athaliah, the daughter of Ahab and Jezebel and the granddaughter of King Omri, one of Israel's most evil rulers, had the blood of idolaters and murderers coursing through her veins from birth. Half Phoenician, half Israelite, Athaliah chose to worship Baal rather than Jehovah, making her an idolater in the eyes of the Hebrews. And like her mother, she, too, lusted for power. So much so that she destroyed all of her grandsons, the "seed of royal stock," so that she could seize the throne as Queen of Judah.

Athaliah married King Jehoram of Judah, who had murdered all of his brothers with a sword because they were loyal to Jehovah. From the union of Athaliah and Jehoram came a son, named Ahaziah. He would be forty-two before following his father to the throne. Jehoram was stricken with an incurable disease and died after two years when "his bowels fell out by reason of his sickness" (2 Chronicles 21:19).

Athaliah had prepared Ahaziah to become king by teaching him the many wicked ways of her father, Ahab. Thus, Ahaziah ruled with Athaliah's guidance. However, his reign lasted for only one year before he perished at the hands of Jehu, the anointed king of Israel.

And Jehoiada made a covenant between him, and between all the people, and between the king, that they should be the Lord's people. Then all the people went to the house of Baal, and brake it down, and brake his altars and his images in pieces, and slew Mattan the priest of Baal before the altars. (2 Chronicles 23:16–17)

Athaliah knew that Ahaziah's sons now stood in line to become king. But the more she thought about the throne, the more she desired it for herself. So in one of the most wicked acts recounted in the Old Testament, Athaliah slaughtered her grandsons, the royal princes, to become queen.

Ahaziah's sister, the wife of Jehoiada the high priest, took Joash, the only grandson to escape the slaughter, and hid him in a bedchamber. The boy remained in hiding for six years in the house of God. Not surprisingly,

Athaliah showed herself to be a ruthless despot. She did many things during her seven-year reign that offended her subjects, including destroying their Temple of Jehovah and using the materials to erect a temple honoring Baal. What she didn't know was that the high priest was quietly working to raise a rebellion against her. He provided the people with swords, bucklers, and shields that had belonged to King David. He orchestrated the overthrow of Athaliah and installed Ahaziah's surviving son on the throne.

Athaliah heard the commotion and cheers of the coronation of Joash. All she could do was tear her clothes and cry, "Treason, treason." Jehoiada put men at all corners and alleys and gates. He commanded that Athaliah not be killed inside the temple, for that would defile it. When Athaliah came through a horse gate by the king's house, the guards posted there stabbed her with their swords—thus the murderess was murdered herself.

Herodius

Herodius, the female version of the name Herod, was the woman responsible for the savage beheading of John the Baptist. Herod is one of the most recognizable names in the Bible. It identifies a family of political rulers that persecuted Jesus and his followers, among others. Aristobulus (son of Herod the Great and Mariamne) and his wife had a child and named her Herodius. Herodius grew into womanhood, married her uncle Herod Philip, and soon gave birth to a daughter she named Salome.

QUESTION?

Who was the famous male in Herodius's lineage?
Herod the Great, her grandfather, was King of Judea from 37 B.C. to 4 B.C. Herod the Great was told by wise men of a star foretelling the birth of the King of the Jews. Pretending to want to worship Jesus, but really desiring to destroy him, the ruler told them to find the child.

Herodius helped her husband entertain Herod Antipas, Philip's half-brother, when he came to Rome to visit them in their home. Herod Antipas took a great liking to Herodius, so much so that he abducted her with the intent of making her his wife, and Salome his stepdaughter. However, there was a complication: Herod Antipas was married to an Arabian princess he had to divorce in order to marry Herodius. It seems that Herod Philip had little to say about the whole affair, or if he did, his words were not recorded.

For Herodius's sake, Herod Antipas imprisoned John the Baptist after John told him that it was not lawful for him to have his brother's wife. It wasn't the first time John had criticized the incestuous union. Herodius wanted John put to death, but Herod Antipas understood that the masses saw John as a prophet, and that the religious movement he started was growing ever more popular. Herod Antipas didn't want to make a martyr of John and then face an uprising, rebellion, or reprisal by the masses. Besides, he had met John and found some of his ideas interesting. So Herod Antipas imprisoned John in a fortress near the Dead Sea and turned his attention back to the banquet to be held in honor of his birthday.

Salome presenting John the Baptist's head to Herodius

Herodius had taught her daughter to perform a sensual dance for the pleasure of Herod on his birthday. She must have known that when Herod was aroused, he would grant her daughter's fondest wish. When Salome's dance ended, Herod Antipas asked her what she wanted. She turned to her mother for suggestions. It was a triumphant moment for Herodius: she told Salome to ask for the head of John the Baptist, and Salome did. His blood-soaked head was put on a platter and presented to her. Salome gave it to her mother, who was finally satisfied that John's tongue would no longer criticize her. Herod Antipas felt a twinge of sorrow, but he had made a promise that others had heard; and an oath by a ruler, even one whose weakness was to love a manipulative, strong-willed woman intent on murder, had to be kept.

Jael

One day Jael was the wife of Heber the Kenite, a Bedouin, and the next she became a heroine of the Israelites because of her murderous deed. Her name means "wild goat," "gazelle," or "mountain goat." She lived at a time when Israel suffered under the foreign rule of Jaban, king of Canaan. Jaban's fiercest Canaanite warrior was Sisera. Jael certainly knew of Sisera, army commander and oppressor of the children of Israel. She must also have heard of Deborah, the Hebrew prophetess and patriot. But Jael may not have known she would play a role in the battle between Sisera and Deborah.

FACT

In biblical times, the land of Canaan was divided among twelve tribes: Naphtali, Asher, Manasseh, Zebulon, Land of Tob, Sachar, Ephraim, Dan, Reuben, Judah, Simeon, and Benjamin.

Deborah had a plan to throw off the Canaanite's yoke of oppression on the Israelites. Summoning Barak, a Jewish military leader from the north, Deborah told him to assemble his troops, go to Mt. Tabor, and take Sisera and his men by force. Barak feared Sisera's well-equipped army with its iron chariots. He told Deborah he would go, but only if she would join him; he needed her presence and faith to sustain him in a battle against Sisera. Deborah agreed, but replied that because of his lack of faith, God would deliver Sisera into the hands of a woman.

The battle ensued, and Barak's men overcame Sisera's; however, Sisera escaped and came upon the tent of Heber the Kenite. Jael greeted him in a friendly, hospitable manner, as was the custom among the desert people. She invited him into the tent, encouraged him to sleep, and covered him with a blanket.

Jael seemed to be an ally: Sisera had no reason to suspect that she harbored murder in her heart toward him, a man she saw as the cruel enemy of God's children. When she said she would watch the door of the tent for enemies or strangers, Sisera believed her and drifted off to sleep. Jael moved toward him ever so quietly, her fingers clutching a hammer and tent peg. As the weary Sisera lay sleeping, Jael hammered the tent peg into his brain, fastening it into the ground.

The killing of Sisera finished the freeing of Israel from the Canaanites, inspiring Deborah and Barak to sing a triumphal ode in which Deborah praised Jael. "Blessed above women shall Jael the wife of Heber the Kenite be, blessed shall she be above women in the tent" (Judges 5:24).

Women of Jael's time did all of the work associated with tent life in the desert. They learned how to make tents, pitch them, and pull them down. Jael would have known how to handle a hammer and tent nail, her weapons in the murder of Sisera.

Laodice

Laodice was the wife and half sister of Antiochus II Theos. Antiochus set aside Laodice as a wife in order to marry Berenice (also, Bernice). Berenice's father was the Egyptian king Ptolemy II Philadelphus. Her father sought an alliance with Antiochus, who ruled over the northern Seleucid Empire. When the men had reached an agreement, Berenice's father sealed his part of the bargain by giving Berenice to Antiochus II Theos in marriage. Laodice must have obsessed about how to get Berenice out of her half brother's life. Her rage toward the woman was fueled when Berenice gave birth to a son by Antiochus named Ptolemy. Unable to put up with the wife of her former husband any longer, Laodice devised a plan to do away with Berenice: She poisoned Berenice, her son Ptolemy, and all of Berenice's attendants.

Laodice's son, Seleucus II Callinicus, eventually took control of the northern Seleucid Empire, but was deposed by Ptolemy III Euergentes.

Salome

On the occasion of the birthday celebration for Herod Antipas, the lascivious gyrations of Salome culminated in an offering from her shocked and aroused uncle for anything her heart desired, including half of his kingdom. Salome said to her mother, "What shall I ask?" The gospels of Matthew, Mark, and Luke all mention the dance of young Salome before her uncle that brought about the murder of John the Baptist.

And she went forth, and said unto her mother, What shall I ask? And she said, The head of John the Baptist. And she came in straightway with haste unto the king, and asked, saying, I will that thou give me by and by in a charger the head of John the Baptist. And the king was exceeding sorry; yet for his oath's sake, and for their sakes which sat with him, he would not reject her. (Mark 6:24–26)

Herodius hated John the Baptist for often criticizing her incestuous marriage to Herod Antipas (see Herodius). Though tradition blames Salome for John's death, her mother and stepfather were directly responsible—Herodius for telling Salome what to request as her gift, and Herod Antipas for ordering the execution.

Had Herod Antipas not made such a generous offer to his niece/stepdaughter within earshot of so many, perhaps he might have reconsidered. John, then, might have been spared a vicious and humiliating death. But though Herod Antipas was surely shocked, and possibly knew he had been manipulated, he was the highest authority in the room, and he had to save face. Some scholars say it illustrates the weakness of Herod Antipas and the corruption of the Herodian court.

Some Bible scholars assert that the entire story of Salome's seductive dance was a fabrication, citing questions over differing dates in the canonical Gospels and in the accounts of the historian Josephus, a contemporary of John the Baptist. Also, a young girl of the royal household would never have been asked to be the entertainment for guests of the king, since that would have been considered improper in the ancient world. Others say Josephus would not have made up Salome's existence and marriage to the king of Chalcis, and that the account of her is supported by the Gospels.

The story of Salome ends badly for the young woman whose page in history will forever be stained with the blood of John the Baptist. Legend says that she was decapitated when she fell through a partially frozen lake and the ice shards cut through her neck. The historian Josephus recorded a different account. He said the scandalous behavior began and ended with the infamous dance. Salome married a cousin and bore three children—her life apparently had one extraordinary moment, and the rest of it was uneventful and normal.

Two Starving Mothers

The Old Testament account of two mothers starving during the siege of King Ben-hadad in Samaria at the time of great famine tugs at the heart, but does not justify the act of murder. The siege and famine drove prices for food out of reach for poor people. One day the king of Israel passed a wall, where a woman cried out, "Help, my lord, O king" (2 Kings 6:26). Approaching, he asked her what was wrong. She replied that she had a son, and that the woman with her had told her to boil the son so they could eat him, which they did. The next day, the woman who no longer had a child asked the other woman to hand over her son for them to eat, but the woman hid her son. The king felt a great heaviness upon his heart. In mournful horror at what they had done and sadness for the dead child, he tore his clothes.

And it came to pass, when the king heard the words of the woman, that he rent his clothes; and he passed by upon the wall, and the people looked, and, behold, he had sackcloth within upon his flesh. (2 Kings 6:30)

He did not punish the women for the murder of the boy, but sent a messenger to Elisha swearing his vengeance upon him as God's representative. As the King saw it, God had cursed the land with misery and suffering.

The narrative of the two starving mothers was most likely used to illustrate the desperate situation in Samaria; for what could be worse than the plight of women who would devour their own young in order to survive? Then, as now, the idea was reprehensible.

Chapter 4

Women of Virtue and Goodness

The Scriptures preserve the stories of women in ancient times whose weaknesses and darker tendencies got the better of them, but they also include narratives about women whose lives were filled with goodness, grace, and love. A virtuous woman's love, it has been said, approaches the love of the Divine. Many women of ancient times hoped for good alliances that could develop into loving relationships. Some got their wish, while others made the best of their circumstances. Still others focused their hearts and minds on the will of God and took comfort in the presence of the Holy One in their lives.

Anna

Anna, daughter of Phanuel of the Asher tribe (referred to by biblical historians as one of the "lost tribes"), was a widow serving at Temple in Jerusalem when Mary and Joseph took the infant Jesus for presentation to the Lord forty days after his birth. Anna had been married as a virgin and lived with her husband for seven years. The Bible does not reveal his name or mention how old he was when he died. It does say that Anna was forty-four. After becoming a widow, she no longer left the temple but spent untold hours over many years on that holy ground continually serving God, fasting, and praying.

FACT

The book of Deuteronomy explains the fate of widows: A widow was required to marry her late husband's brother (Deuteronomy 25:5–10). Such a marriage was called a "levirate marriage." The brother-in-law could refuse, but the woman could not. If she became pregnant and had a son, the boy would take the name of the woman's dead husband.

A widow's life during ancient times was precarious, as she was often entirely alone, and vulnerable without male family members to provide for her. Anna would have placed herself under God's care with the hope that no one would hurt or exploit her. Admonishments to treat widows well are to be found in Exodus, Deuteronomy, Samuel, Kings, Isaiah, and Jeremiah.

Through her penances, Anna had purified herself, and the Lord favored her with the gift of prophecy. When Jesus was brought into the temple, Anna's heart must have quickened, for she believed that the Lord was allowing her to gaze upon the Holy One whose coming had been foretold by the Hebrew prophets of the past. Anna had just heard the old man Simeon, a regular visitor to the temple, blessing the family of Jesus, saying to Mary, "Behold, this child is set for the fall and rising again of many in Israel; and for a sign which shall be spoken against; (Yea, a sword shall pierce through thy own soul also) that the thoughts of many hearts may be revealed" (Luke 2:34–35).

The Bible says nothing more about Anna. Her name means "grace," and it seems she was aptly named, for her story suggests that she was a woman who required little in life except the grace of God.

Miriam, Sister of Moses and Aaron

Miriam was the sister of two powerful biblical figures, Moses and Aaron. Her name derives from the root Mary, Mariamne, or Maria, meaning "bitterness." She served the Lord all of her life, remained steadfast in her determination to free the Hebrew people from the pharaoh's oppression, and demonstrated repeatedly that the love of her country and people exceeded her personal desires as a woman. But Miriam was human, and not perfect. For her pride and insubordination to the power of God working through Moses, she became afflicted with a disfiguring skin disease. It was of short duration, but long enough for her to reflect on the error she made in criticizing the instrument of the Lord.

FACT

Miriam accompanied her brothers and the Children of Israel out of Egypt. Four books of the Old Testament—Exodus, Leviticus, Numbers, and Deuteronomy—tell their story and provide details of their arduous journey, as well as their trials and triumphs.

Hiding Her Brother Moses

Miriam's mother, Jocheved, hid her newborn baby boy for three months. The pharaoh had ordered that "every son that is born [of Hebrew slaves] ye shall cast into the river…" (Exodus 1:22). Her mother must have been terrified that her deception would be discovered and her baby drowned. Most likely, she pondered myriad ways to keep her son alive, and finally enlisted the help of her dutiful daughter, Miriam.

Guarding Moses

When Jocheved could no longer conceal the fact that she had a three-month-old infant, Miriam became the infant's guardian. Miriam watched over Moses after their mother placed him in a boat among the reeds near the edge of a stream where the pharaoh's daughter regularly came to wash herself. When the baby was spotted, plucked from the boat, and shown to the princess, she named him Moses, because she "drew him out of the water" (Exodus 2:10).

Nurturing the Baby Brother

Moses cried with the pain of hunger in his tiny belly. That was Miriam's opportunity. The quick-witted girl stepped from behind the reeds and bushes where she hid and faced the princess. While Moses wailed for his feeding, Miriam addressed the princess. "...Shall I go and call to thee a nurse of the Hebrew women that she may nurse the child for thee?" (Exodus 2:7). Miriam knew of the perfect wet nurse: the baby's own mother, Jocheved. The pharaoh's daughter told Miriam's mother to wet nurse the child until the child was weaned and, in return, she would pay her wages.

Miriam beholding her baby brother, Moses

Receiving the Gift of Prophecy

As Miriam grew older, she became known as a prophetess. She gave herself over to the will of God and doing his work. The longer she remained at the side of her brother Moses, however, the wearier she grew of standing in the giant shadow that he cast. She longed for her own recognition and power.

Standing Strong

The Bible doesn't say how Miriam reacted to the news that her brother Moses killed an Egyptian slave master who was abusing his Hebrew worker. Undoubtedly, feeling as strongly about the plight of the Hebrews as she did, Miriam most likely would have remained his staunchest ally. However, when the pharaoh learned about it and threatened to kill Moses, he fled to Midian, where he married Zipporah. Because she was not an Israelite, but a Midianite, Miriam did not particularly like her.

Chapter 4 in Exodus reveals that God told his chosen representative Moses, who was slow of speech, to use his brother Aaron as an eloquent spokesman for the Divine. Later, God tells Moses that Aaron and his sons are to become priests and are to wear robes. There are no mentions of any such special honor for Miriam.

Turning Against Foreign Influence

When Moses took a second wife, a beautiful Ethiopian Cushite woman, Miriam liked her even less. His wives represented foreign alliances, and Miriam was staunchly pro-Hebrew. She had concerns about nonHebrew influences upon her brother Moses, and through him, God's chosen people. She allowed her negative feelings toward her sisters-in-law, especially the Cushite woman, to overshadow her dedication and commitment to the work of Moses. Miriam began criticizing Moses, questioning openly whether or not God spoke through only Moses, or also through her and Aaron.

When God let his people leave Egypt, the land of plagues, Moses led them accompanied by Miriam and his brother, Aaron, a high priest. Miriam was a worker for God, a patriot for the Israelites, and a dutiful sister to Moses, but she also complained about Moses. Miriam and Aaron were jealous of their brother, believing that God favored him, but also spoke through the two of them. At first they kept their feelings to themselves, but later became critical of Moses. At a time when they should have inspired unity, they introduced divisiveness. The Lord called them into his presence for an accounting of their behavior. Miriam shouldered the blame as the instigator. When the meeting was over, she was afflicted with leprosy and banished from the camp for seven days. After her isolation, her health was restored. Although not entirely blameless, Aaron received no such punishment. He had tabernacle duties to perform and God must have seen that work as imminently important to keep his children on course.

The Bible suggests that Miriam never married; however, Josephus noted that she married Hur, a Hebrew leader and judge. She undertook the arduous forty-year trek with Moses, Aaron, and the Hebrew people, but her dream of seeing the Promised Land was never fulfilled—she died before reaching it and was buried by Moses and Aaron at Kadesh-Barnea in the Zin desert.

Miriam is credited with composing a jubilant hymn after the Hebrews crossed the Red Sea during their journey to the Promised Land. Exodus 15:20 states that she took a timbrel in her hand and began to sing and dance ecstatically and all of the other women followed her example. In that moment, the bitterness she had felt in the past must have been replaced with rapture, glorious and triumphant. Miriam demonstrated that even a virtuous woman, focused on doing the Lord's work, can have shortcomings like jealousy and desire for the power that belongs to another. But shortcomings can be forgiven, and a woman can become stronger for having had them. Miriam surely understood that God has a purpose for every life, and hers was to protect and watch over the baby Moses, the deliverer of the Children of the Lord.

Ruth and Naomi

During the famine in Judah, Elimelech of Bethlehem moved his wife Naomi and his two sons to Moab, where his sons married local women, Ruth and her sister Orpah. Generally, the Hebrews did not like the Moabites. They believed Moabites were descendants of Lot and his daughters, and considered Moabite women loose. Elimelech died, and ten years later Elimelech's sons died. Naomi, Ruth, and Orpah mourned the loss of their husbands and struggled to survive. Starving, the three decided to go to Judah; they had heard that the land there no longer suffered from famine. Along the way, Naomi kissed the young women and told them to return to their own people in Moab where they might marry again. Orpah obeyed, but Ruth refused to abandon Naomi. Ruth voluntarily gave up the option of returning to Moab to stay with her mother-in-law. Her attachment and deep feelings touched Naomi, and they continued on together to Judah.

And Ruth said, Entreat me not to leave thee, or to return from following after thee: for whither thou goest, I will go; and where thou lodgest, I will lodge; thy people shall be my people, and thy God my God: Where thou diest, will I die, and there will I be buried: the Lord do so to me, and more also if aught but death part thee and me. (Ruth 1:16–17)

Ruth begging Naomi

The two women returned to the town of Bethlehem at the beginning of the barley harvest. When the groups of old friends and acquaintances gathered around Naomi to welcome her back, she told them not to call her Naomi, but rather Mara ("bitterness"), "…for the Almighty hath dealt very bitterly with me. I went out full, and the Lord hath brought me home again empty…" (Ruth 1:20–21).

Naomi's late husband had a wealthy relative, a learned judge known for his piety and fairness, whose name was Boaz. He had some fields of barley that were being gleaned. Ruth begged Naomi to let her go to one of the fields and gather up some grains.

Ruth

While picking up grain in the fields, Ruth was spotted by Boaz. He noticed how graceful she seemed. He asked the foreman of the reapers who she was. The foreman replied that she was the "...damsel that came back with Naomi out of the country of Moab" (Ruth 2:6). Some sources assert that Boaz knew that she was to be the ancestress of the royal house of David, and also of the Messiah (Matthew 1:5).

Ruth in the wheat field

Boaz worried that Ruth, scavenging in a field of men, might be molested by one of them. He instructed her not to pick from any fields but his, and he instructed his men not to touch her. Ruth asked him why he was so kind to her, a total stranger. Boaz explained that, "It hath fully been showed me all that thou hast done unto thy mother-in-law since the death of thine husband: and how thou hast left thy father and thy mother and the land of thy nativity, and art come unto a people which thou knewest not heretofore" (Ruth 2:11). He told her to go to one of his fields where women worked. Ruth, overcome with gratitude, fell at his feet, thanking him. Boaz invited her to stay for lunch with him. When she did leave, he gave her six measures of grain to take back to Naomi.

Ruth Does as Naomi Tells Her

When Ruth told her story to Naomi, her mother-in-law remembered Boaz as a rich relative. The two women discussed a plan for Ruth to marry Boaz. Following Naomi's instructions, Ruth washed and perfumed herself. Then she slipped unseen to where Boaz slept in the darkness after his evening meal and cup of wine. Uncovering his feet, she lay down next to him.

Boaz Responds

Boaz agreed to Ruth's request to be her keeper and provider. He surely felt honored to have such a wonderful woman ask him to be her kinsman. He told her, "Blessed be thou of the Lord, my daughter, for thou hast showed more kindness in the latter end than at the beginning, inasmuch as thou followedst not young men, whether poor or rich…. I will do to thee all that thou requirest: for all the city of my people doth know that thou art a virtuous woman" (Ruth 3:10–11).

And it came to pass at midnight, that the man was afraid, and turned himself: and behold, a woman lay at his feet. And he said, Who art thou? And she answered, I am Ruth thine handmaid: spread therefore thy skirt over thine handmaid; for thou art a near kinsman. (Ruth 3:8–9)

Ruth Waits Patiently

But the path for Ruth to marry Boaz still had an obstacle: there was a kinsman closer than Boaz who could claim her. Boaz allowed her to lie upon his floor until early morning, when she could slip out unnoticed. When Boaz asked for her veil she gave it to him, and he filled it with barley to take back to Naomi. So Ruth returned to her mother-in-law and waited to see if Boaz would settle the matter with the other kinsman.

Ruth Gets Her Wish

Boaz found that particular kinsman on the road and invited him to sit a while. Ten others joined the men. Boaz told the kinsman that Naomi wished to sell some of her late husband's land and the first right of refusal belonged to the kinsman. The man wanted to buy the property, until Boaz told him he had to take the widow Ruth as well. At that, the man balked. Boaz then said he would buy the property and take the widow as his wife.

Boaz, at eighty, was forty years older than Ruth when they married. Although Boaz, some sources say, died the day after their wedding, he fathered a son whom Ruth named Obed. The birth of the baby boy reinvigorated Naomi, who nurtured and cared for him as she had her own sons. Through her daughter-in-law Ruth, Naomi found a way to feel hope again, along with a measure of peace. She had a renewed purpose—to help raise Obed, who, the Bible states, became the father of Jesse, who became the father of King David. The Scriptures do not mention Ruth beyond that point.

The Book of Ruth

The Book of Ruth, some feminist scholars of biblical studies assert, shows female ingenuity, strength, commitment, and love. Some sources even suggest that a woman may have written the Book of Ruth. The point of the story is a little ambiguous. Was it the story of the linkage or lineage to King David, or a story celebrating ethnic diversity and accepting it into ancient Hebrew culture, or a means to justify the levirate marriage practice? The Book of Ruth certainly invites reflection on all of the above, but more importantly, the story shows how two women, under extremely adverse conditions, served as extraordinary examples of pious and virtuous womanhood.

Chapter 5

Slaves, Handmaidens, Nursemaids, and Midwives

Some of the most extraordinary tales of the Old Testament are about women who possessed a strong maternal instinct to nurture and serve others. Sometimes, their life circumstances dictated that they serve other women as midwives or nurses. In other cases, they were simply slaves or handmaidens required to serve a mistress or master, sometimes even expected to bear children by their mistress' husband. For such women, life could be extraordinarily difficult. Some remained committed to the families they served, while others, like Hagar, fled in peril of their lives.

5

Deborah, Rebekah's Nurse

Deborah was both nurse and confidante to Rebekah, wife of Isaac and mother of Jacob. She spent her life with Rebekah and Jacob and their children; she was probably part of Rebekah's household before the young woman married. Old Testament references to Deborah are scant, but the Bible says that Deborah accompanied Rebekah when she agreed to go with the servant of Abraham to meet Isaac (Genesis 24:59). Deborah helped Rebekah give birth to Esau and Jacob, and would have been an integral part of Rebekah's and Isaac's family, helping to care for the boys as they grew into men. She may have witnessed the deception of Isaac and Esau by Jacob and Rebekah. Years later, when Jacob fled, perhaps Rebekah turned to her faithful nurse for loving support and words of wisdom. Deborah, ever patient and an eyewitness to all that went on in the tent of Jacob, may have reassured her mistress that the day would surely come when she would be able to send for Jacob and welcome him home.

While on the run from Esau, Jacob had slept on the road and dreamed of the angel's ladder. In Jacob's dream, the Lord God told him "the land whereon thou liest, to thee will I give it, and to thy seed" (Genesis 28:13). Jacob had awakened from the dream and marked the site, and called it El Beth-el. He placed a stone pillar there and poured oil on it to consecrate it as a holy place of God. When he returned home, he went there and constructed an altar. One fateful day, Deborah died on the road to Beth-el. There, Jacob buried her under a tree, referred to as Allon-bachuth, or "oak of tears" (Genesis 35:8).

Some sources say that the ancient women who carried on the oral tradition about Rebekah's nurse called the tree where she was buried a Deborah palm. It represented Deborah, the loyal nurse, as well as another Deborah, a judge who lived about 600 years later. That Deborah presided over an open-air court in the shade of the Deborah palm, located between Beth-El and Ramah (Judges 4:5).

Bilhah

Bilhah was a handmaid to Rachel's father, Laban. He gave Bilhah to Rachel upon her marriage to Jacob. Leah, Rachel's sister (first married to Jacob through a ruse planned by Laban to get Jacob to labor for him for seven years), had six sons and a daughter with him. But Jacob loved Rachel very much. When the two were finally married, Rachel looked forward to bearing his children, but had difficulty conceiving. Heartsick that she might never bear a child with her husband, Rachel brought Bilhah to him. Bilhah had two sons by Jacob, Dan and Naphtali. The boys were considered Rachel's sons, and therefore Jacob's rightful heirs. Rachel eventually had two sons of her own, but she died in childbirth with the second. After her death, Reuben, firstborn son of Jacob and Leah, committed incest with Billhah, an act that Jacob overheard.

And Jacob set a pillar upon her grave: that is the pillar of Rachel's grave unto this day. And Israel [Jacob's name after Rachel died] journeyed, and spread his tent beyond the tower of Edar. And it came to pass, when Israel dwelt in that land, that Reuben went and lay with Bilhah, his father's concubine: and Israel heard it. (Genesis 35:20–22)

The act of defiling Bilhah meant Reuben forfeited his birthright. It was given instead to Joseph, firstborn son of Jacob and Rachel.

Some sources assert Bilhah was, in fact, a daughter of Laban, and that after Rachel died, Jacob turned to Bilhah for affection. Reuben found the relationship between his father and Bilhah worrisome, because Bilhah was in competition with his mother Leah for Jacob's time and attention. To sleep with his father's concubine or wife was an egregious thing to do. The Bible doesn't say Reuben had any affection for Bilhah, so he may have forced himself upon her. It was also a betrayal of trust between Reuben and his father.

Hagar

Hagar was the Egyptian maidservant of Sarah, wife of Abraham. Sarah and her husband had lived in Canaan for ten years and still had no children. Sarah must have believed that God, who had the power to open or close wombs, had closed hers. She compelled Hagar to sleep with Abraham so he could have an heir. Hagar was to be Abraham's wife, but not have the same status as Sarah. It is unlikely that Hagar was consulted: Sarah, the free-woman, had the authority to order Hagar, the bondwoman, to do whatever she wished, and Hagar was expected to submit.

Once Hagar had conceived a child by Abraham, Sarah became jealous. Tensions between the women began to rise, escalating throughout Hagar's pregnancy. Sarah came to despise Hagar, and believed the maidservant no longer respected her. Sarah treated Hagar so harshly that the woman, pregnant and alone, fled into the desert, weeping along the way to Shur.

An angel found Hagar by a fountain and asked her where she was going. Hagar told the angel that she was fleeing from her mistress. Hagar's fear of Sarah must have been great to risk having to give birth alone in the desert without food or water or anyone to help. So many times she had cried out to God about her plight, but was he listening? The angel told her that God had heard her and that she should call her son Ishmael (meaning "God hears"), but also that she must return and submit to her mistress.

FACT

Because the societies of the ancient world were patrilineal, it was imperative to produce a son to carry forward the genes of the father. Inheritance went only to males. When a woman married, she went to live with her husband's family. If a married woman could not conceive, the husband could legally impregnate his wife's slaves, and the child was his legal heir.

Hagar lived in an uneasy accord with her mistress, Abraham, and the son she bore him. One day, God told Abraham that Sarah would give birth

Hagar and her son in the desert

to a son. Knowing that she was long past the childbearing years, the aged Sarah and Abraham (who was nearly 100 years old) laughed, but she soon conceived and gave birth to Isaac. As Isaac grew and was finally weaned, Sarah could no longer bear the company of Hagar and Ishmael. She told Abraham to banish them, "...for the son of this bondwoman shall not be heir with my son..." (Genesis 21:10). Abraham struggled with guilt and worry; how could Sarah have asked him to do such a thing? He didn't want to turn out Hagar and his son, but God told Abraham to let them go. God also told him that he would make a nation from Ishmael because he was the "seed" of Abraham (Genesis 21:13).

Abraham, concerned about the heat of the desert, gave Hagar some bread (symbol of sustenance) and a bottle of water (symbol of life) for their journey. The banishment was effectively Abraham's divorce of Hagar, but the items of food and water signaled to all the tribal members that the two were still under his protection. With great sadness in his heart, he watched the young mother take his son and walk into the wilderness of Beer-sheba.

With the water gone, Hagar knew that death was near. Unable to watch her child die, she placed him under some shrubs and walked some distance away, where she collapsed. She could hear Ishmael's weak cries. In deep despair, Hagar called out to God and wept. The angel of God responded, "What aileth thee, Hagar? Fear not; for God hath heard the voice of the lad where he is. Arise, lift up the lad, and hold him in thine hand; for I will make him a great nation" (Genesis 21:17–18). God opened Hagar's eyes, and she saw a well. She filled her bottle with water and gave her son a drink.

Ishmael grew and became an archer. Hagar is last mentioned in the Bible seeking a wife for Ishmael. The place where she sought a bride for her son was not in or around the places where the Hebrews dwelled, but rather in Egypt, her homeland.

The Koran states that Mecca is the place where God showed Hagar the well and saved her and Ishmael from death. Muslims see Abraham, Hagar, and Ishmael as ancestors of the prophet Mohammed. Today, devout Muslims do pilgrimage by retracing Hagar's steps to find water.

The story of Hagar and Ishmael shows the importance to the ancients of male supremacy. God, whom the ancients considered male, had the greatest power and could make it possible for a woman to be barren or fertile. Men had power over a woman's body to create heirs to carry his seed forward to future generations. Inheritance went to the firstborn male. The narrative also addresses the issue of Abraham's rightful heir. Ishmael was his firstborn, but by an Egyptian maidservant and, in Sarah's eyes, not worthy or legitimate to receive Abraham's property. Hagar shows the challenges faced by a single pregnant woman, who is both a victim and a survivor.

Puah and Shiphrah

Puah and Shiphrah were midwives in ancient Egypt who refused to comply with the pharaoh's order to kill all male babies born to Hebrew women (Exodus 1:15–17). While the Jews chafed under enslavement and were forced to do backbreaking labor for untold hours each day, their numbers continued to increase through live births. The pharaoh told the midwives if they saw a Hebrew woman on a birthing stool and she gave birth to girl, let her live; but if the baby was a boy, they should kill him. Puah and Shiphrah, who were God-fearing Hebrew women, dared not tell the pharaoh no, for that would ensure their own quick deaths. They kept quiet and continued to help women deliver their babies—girls and boys. In time, however, the pharaoh discovered what they were doing and called them before him.

The women explained to the pharaoh that by the time they got to the Jewish women, their babies were already born, and to kill them after the birth would reveal that they were agents of the pharaoh. The pregnant Jewish women would then give the midwives a later due date and conceal the birth. They told the pharaoh that if the women did that, they would never know when a birth had taken place. Thus, they couldn't get a true accounting of the numbers of new Jewish babies. The pharaoh followed their reasoning and released them. The pharaoh still trusted them, and the first chapter of Exodus says that because the women feared God, the pharaoh made them houses.

And the king of Egypt called for the midwives, and said unto them, Why have ye done this thing, and have saved the men children alive? And the midwives said unto Pharaoh, Because the Hebrew women are not as the Egyptian women; for they are lively, and are delivered ere the midwives come in unto them. (Exodus 1:18–19)

The ancient Hebrews desired many children. Couples understood even before they were married that the woman was expected to bear children and expand the family. In fact, it was a great honor for women to bear children. Puah and Shiphrah did not have to explain to the Hebrew women, although they may have, that pregnancy involved a growth process of not only the child inside of them, but also their own bodies. Most believed that the process was overseen by God. When labor pains started and it was time to give birth, pregnant women, assisted by midwives, crouched to push out their babies. The Bible mentions a birthstool (Exodus 1:16) that was also used, but doesn't elaborate, and information about it is scant. Because a woman's labor could last for hours, it seems reasonable to think it was some type of low stool that the woman could sit on during her labor. Puah and Shiphrah became heroines in Jewish history as instruments of God to ensure the survival of the Lord's children. The population of the Hebrews increased and the people prospered.

Rachel's Midwife

Although she remains unnamed, Rachel's midwife helped her with her labor during the birth of Benjamin. The Bible says that her labor was hard and protracted. After grueling hours of painful labor, perhaps Rachel feared that the angel of death was hovering nearby. The midwife comforted Rachel and told her not to be afraid, that she would bear the child. But despite the midwife's heroic efforts to save her life, Rachel died, whispering the name of her son, Ben-oni (Genesis 35:16–18).

QUESTION?

What were the risks of giving birth during the time in which Rachel lived?
Excessive bleeding and infection were two common hazards mothers faced in ancient times. Conditions such as breech births (coming down the birth canal feet-first) or an umbilical cord wrapped around the infant's neck could threaten the normal delivery of otherwise healthy babies.

Rhoda

Rhoda's name in Greek means "rose." She was the foreign-born maidservant first mentioned in Acts 12:13 as the woman who is in the house of Mary, a wealthy Jerusalem widow and mother of John Mark. Mary, John Mark, and Rhoda were followers of Christ. After Herod had killed James, brother of John, he imprisoned Peter. Those in the Jerusalem Christian community began to pray unceasingly for him. The angel of God intervened and delivered Peter from the dungeon. Peter went straight to the house of Mary, where the faithful had gathered together for prayer. Peter knocked at the door of the bolted gate and called out.

Rhoda went to see who was calling at such a late hour (they may have been saying midnight prayers on Peter's behalf). Recognizing Peter's voice, she ran to tell the others, leaving Peter standing on the other side of the unopened gate, a dangerous place to be if the guards woke up and found him gone. When Rhoda told those inside the house who was at the gate, they told her she was mad. After repeatedly insisting that it was indeed Peter, he was finally welcomed by his astonished friends.

There is little else in the Bible about Rhoda. She appears to have been a loyal servant to Mary, and must have had a good heart, for she was happy to hear Peter's voice; so happy that she lost her head for a moment and left him standing outside the locked gate while she ran to tell the others. She must have felt jubilant that their prayers for his safe release had been answered. However, those gathered inside the house repeatedly called her mad. So firm was her faith that God had heard and answered their prayers, that Rhoda never wavered in her belief, unlike those inside Mary's house who were astonished. It was as if they couldn't believe that their prayers could actually be answered.

Zilpah

Zilpah

When Leah married Jacob, Laban gave his daughter a handmaid named Zilpah. Leah produced six sons and a daughter, and when she could no longer conceive, she gave Zilpah to Jacob to increase the size of her family. Zilpah bore two children by Jacob, Gad and Asher (Genesis 29:24, 46:18). Both grew into manhood and became founders and leaders of two tribes. Leah named both of Zilpah's sons and helped care for them. Some biblical scholars assert that Zilpah and Bilhah (handmaiden to Leah's sister Rachel) were actually Laban's younger daughters. She is buried in Tiberias at the Tomb of the Matriarchs. The Bible doesn't provide any further details about Zilpah.

Chapter 6

Women Who Prophesied

The "angel of God spoke to me" was the ancient Hebrews' way of saying that they had received divine inspiration or certitude that God was speaking to them. The expression appears throughout the Old Testament, especially in the sayings of the prophets. From among them, several women exhibited an extraordinary gift of prophecy, including Deborah, Huldah, Isaiah's wife, the Necromancer of Endor, Jezebel, and the slave-girl soothsayer of Philippi.

Deborah

Deborah, whose name means "bee," was the wife of Lappidoth. An online Jewish encyclopedia states that she was one of seven Hebrew women in ancient times known as prophetesses. They included Sarah, Hannah, Abigail, Miriam, Esther, Huldah, and Deborah.

All of the above-mentioned women are found in this book; however, only Huldah's story is included in this chapter. The remaining women are grouped into categories other than prophecy. Deborah alone stands out in biblical history as an adept female military commander, and unique among the five leaders or "Judges" of Israel that God inspired and empowered to lead Israelites in throwing off the yoke of their oppressors. In the Old Testament narratives, women often led sheltered lives. However, a few had contact with military men, luring enemies to their deaths through sexual prowess. Deborah, however, served her people as a holy prophetess, woman warrior, and a just and righteous judge.

Deborah

Deborah's people, the Hebrews, had been oppressed for some twenty years by a group of Canaanite rulers whose military strength was unsurpassed. Their ruler was King Jabon, who resided in the city of Hazor, and whose general, Sisera, was a formidable warrior. Sisera believed that his military power was invincible, and that the Hebrews would not challenge him because a woman, Deborah, was leading them. But, inspired by God, Deborah threw down the gauntlet, summoned her own general, named Barak, and told him to gather together 10,000 soldiers and take them to Mount Tabor; she would lure Sisera to the river Kishon and "...deliver him into thine hand" (Judges 4:7).

Sisera heard of the plan and went to the Kishon Wadi (a dry riverbed). He must have felt quite confident, since his army substantially outnumbered the Israelites and his iron chariots represented the best in the world. But Deborah had God on her side. The Bible says that "the stars in their courses fought against Sisera," and "the river of Kishon swept them away." Many sources say that the Kishon River flooded in a torrential downpour that rendered the iron chariots useless, and Sisera's men died by the sword. Sisera fled to Jael's tent (see the section on Jael in Chapter 3), where he perished when she plunged a tent peg through his brain.

And Deborah said unto Barak, Up; for this is the day in which the Lord hath delivered Sisera into thine hand: is not the Lord gone out before thee? So Barak went down from mount Tabor, and ten thousand men after him. (Judges 4:14)

Prophetess

Deborah had a powerful and abiding faith in God, and she was blessed with the gift of prophecy. Receiving divine inspiration in a message from God, she ordered Barak from his home at Kedesh in Naphtali to lead the Israelites against the Canaanites. Barak said he would go only if she would accompany him; he wanted his ruler and prophetess by his side. Deborah said she would go with him, but prophesized that "...the journey that thou takest shall not be for thine honor; for the Lord shall sell Sisera into the hand of a woman" (Judges 4:9). Jael murdered Sisera, and Deborah's prophecy proved accurate.

Woman Warrior

Deborah summoned General Barak, a male military leader who was the son of Abinoam, and ordered him in the name of God to lead the armies of Israel to Mount Tabor in an all-out assault on the Canaanites. The Canaanites, led by Sisera, had 100,000 men and 900 iron chariots, the best in the land. Deborah and Barak defeated Sisera and the Canaanites with only 10,000 men. For the next forty years, the people lived in peace.

Just and Righteous Judge

For a woman in ancient times, Deborah occupied an almost unheard of position of power as a leader or Judge of Israel. It would have been unseemly for her to hear petitions and complaints in private quarters, so she held court "…under the palm tree of Deborah between Ramah and Bethel in mount Ephraim…" and there dispensed wisdom and justice to the children of Israel (Judges 4:5).

Mother of Israel

Deborah called herself "…a mother in Israel" (Judges 5:7). The Old Testament says she was a wife, but doesn't say whether or not she ever had children. As a "mother in Israel" she shouldered the responsibility for the entire Hebrew nation—the children of God. Barak, in biblical mentions, clearly occupied a subordinate position to Deborah. In Rabbinical literature, Barak's name means "lightning," and some say that he was Lapidoth, Deborah's husband, whose expression after the victory flashed brightly.

Singer/Songwriter

After inciting the rebellion and successfully winning the battle against Sisera and the Canaanites, Deborah and Barak sing a triumphant song. Some sources suggest that Deborah composed that song. The complete song is found in Chapter 5 of The Book of Judges. It is a lovely example of the poetry of the ancient Hebrews. Her ode of triumph exalts the Lord, who led Israel against the Canaanites and empowered them to conquer their foes.

Then sang Deborah and Barak the son of Ahinoam on that day, saying, Praise ye the Lord for the avenging of Israel, when the people willingly offered themselves. Hear, O ye kings; give ear, O ye princes; I, even I, will sing unto the Lord; I will sing praise to the Lord God of Israel. (Judges 5:1–3)

Deborah emerges as an icon among the women of Scripture, as a woman of strong faith, vision, and resolve. She saw how her people had become weak from years of oppression by idolaters, and when called by God to be a deliverer, she did not question Him, but took action to free the weak from the iron grip of the oppressors.

Huldah

Huldah, a professed prophetess in the time of King Josiah, was married to Shallum, son of Tokhath and grandson of Harhas, keeper of the king's wardrobe. She lived in Jerusalem, and was accustomed to speaking to representatives of the king, as well as the high priest, in a direct and stern manner. She had the authority to interpret whether or not something was genuine Law or a corruption of it. She was thought of as a prophetess, a powerful spokeswoman for the word of God. What is known about her personally is through her husband's connections. She may have been related to Jeremiah, the prophet. She also served as a teacher in the school.

Huldah, whose name means "weasel," was a messenger of God blessed with the power of prophecy. King Josiah summoned her instead of the prophet Jeremiah when the high priest Hilkiah discovered the Book of the Law in the Temple.

...Tell the man that sent you to me, Thus saith the Lord...Because they have forsaken me, and have burned incense unto other gods, that they might provoke me to anger with all the works of their hands; therefore my wrath shall be kindled against this place, and shall not be quenched. (2 Kings 22:15–17)

Hilkiah, Ahikam, Asahiah, Achbor, and Shaphan consulted Huldah for her understanding of the Lord's opinion when they found the lost book. The text of the missing book addressed the coming wrath of the Lord against his children. The king wanted to know if the book (possibly later known as Deuteronomy) was authentic, and if the prophecy in the book would be fulfilled. Huldah unrolled the scroll, verified its authenticity, and read the narrative. She told King Josiah that because the people and their fathers had disobeyed God, the Lord would do what was stated; that is, bring upon them and their land disaster and ruin.

Huldah's understanding of the prophecy proclaimed many frightening events to come. One small flicker of hope remained that children of God would not be completely wiped out. A few years before Huldah was given the scroll to decipher, the prophet Isaiah had predicted a future time when the people would rise up, rebuild, and restore that which would be destroyed.

QUESTION?

What is significant about Huldah's expression, "Tell the man that sent you ..."?
It shows that Huldah was not impressed by positions of power and stature. A king or any other powerful man could consult her, but would exert no influence upon her prophetic pronouncements, because she revealed the words of the highest power—God.

Huldah told the men to tell King Josiah that because of his piety and love of the Lord, he would be spared witnessing the destruction of his kingdom, for God had spoken: "...I will gather thee unto thy fathers, and thou shalt be gathered into thy grave in peace; and thine eyes shall not see all the evil which I will bring upon this place" (2 Kings 22:20). Huldah's words were accepted as Divine revelation, and the king took her words to heart. He instituted reforms, and the people returned to the faith of their fathers and became deeply spiritual.

Isaiah's Wife

She is not named in the Bible, but Isaiah's wife is referred to as a prophetess. Some sources say the reason for her designation as a prophetess is that she possessed the gift of prophecy like Deborah, Huldah, and others, and others say it is because she was a prophet's wife.

Her husband, Isaiah, lived circa 765 B.C., and served as a prophet during the reigns of Jotham, Ahaz, and Hezekiah, the successors of Uzziah, king of

Judah. Isaiah foretold the birth of Jesus (Isaiah 7:14), one of the most important prophecies from the Old Testament to be fulfilled and written about in the New Testament. Shortly after that reference in Chapter 7, Isaiah refers to his wife as "the prophetess."

And I went unto the prophetess; and she conceived, and bare a son. Then said the Lord to me, Call his name Mahershalalhashbaz. For before the child shall have knowledge to cry, My father and my mother, the riches of Damascus and the spoil of Samaria shall be taken away before the king of Assyria. (Isaiah 8:3–4)

A rough translation of the Lord's name for the child of the prophetess and Isaiah means "quick defeat and access to the spoils of war." The child's name foretold a time when Judah would overpower and defeat her enemies. Damascus at that time was the capital of Aramaea, and Samaria was the capital of Israel. There are no other mentions of the prophetess wife of Isaiah following that reference.

Necromancer of Endor

The prophetess who foretold future events in the reign of King Saul was simply called the Necromancer of Endor (also the "witch" of Endor). When Saul saw the Philistines had gathered together and pitched camp in Shunem, he feared the buildup of hostile forces and the coming war. He decided to assemble all of Israel and pitch his own camp in Gilboa. He prayed to God for insight and inspiration. God didn't answer his prayers, send messages to him in his dreams, or speak to Saul through the prophets.

Because she knew that Saul had recently rid the country of all wizards and soothsayers, the woman was afraid to meet the king. She thought he was attempting to expose her prophetic gift by asking her to invoke a ghost. When she did what he requested, she would be trapped. Saul put on a disguise and, with two other men, went to see her at night.

As already noted, the woman feared reprisals, and refused to give Saul predictions of his future. Not realizing who he was, she said to him, "Behold, thou knowest what Saul hath done, how he hath cut off those that have familiar spirits, and the wizards, out of the land: wherefore then layest thou a snare for my life, to cause me to die?" (1 Samuel 28:9).

Then said Saul unto his servants, Seek me a woman that hath a familiar spirit, that I may go to her, and inquire of her. And his servants said to him, Behold, there is a woman that hath a familiar spirit at Endor. (1 Samuel 28:7)

The Necromancer Conjures Samuel

Saul swore an oath that no harm would come to her. She finally agreed to his wishes and asked whom she should conjure. He replied, "Samuel." The woman had a vision of an old man with a shawl draped over his shoulders. Saul believed it was Samuel, and asked him to predict the future outcome of the war with the Philistines. Samuel confirmed Saul's worst fears: The king not only would not prevail against his enemies, but because he had disobeyed God, he was going to die, along with his sons.

Necromancer is an old-fashioned word with a root form in Greek, Latin, and Old English. It also means "sorcery." A necromancer, in Old Testament usage, was one who used black magic to predict the future by means of communicating with the dead, rather than hearing the voice of God. The Necromancer of Endor conjured a deceased prophet of Saul's choosing.

The Necromancer Offers Bread to the King

King Saul's worst fears had been confirmed, and he collapsed to the ground. The necromancer told him that she was going to give him a morsel of bread for strength. Saul had not eaten in days, but he refused, saying he didn't want food. But the woman and Saul's servants convinced the king that he ought to eat before going back to his men, so she made some unleavened bread and prepared a fatted calf, and the king and his men ate before leaving to meet up with his army (1 Samuel 28:20–25).

Just as shamans summoned spirits or ancestral ghosts, necromancers or witches called forth such beings using specific intonations and incantations. Necromancy was widespread among the Chaldeans and Babylonians. The book of Deuteronomy warns against the use of necromancers for consulting the dead (Deuteronomy 18:9–12).

The Prophecy Proves True

The battle between the Philistines and the Israelites ensued, resulting in defeat of Saul's forces. His sons, Jonathan, Abinadab, and Melchishua died in battle. Saul asked his armor bearer to thrust a sword through him, but the man was afraid and refused. King Saul then took his sword and fell upon it. (1 Samuel 31:4). Thus, the prophecy of Samuel through the Necromancer proved true.

Jezebel

Jezebel, daughter of Ethbaal, the King of Sidon, was a self-proclaimed prophetess and wife of Ahab, king of Israel. The Bible says that Jezebel "stirred up" Ahab to wickedness (1 Kings 21:25). To the Hebrews, she was an idolatress, because she worshipped Baal, a pagan god. Many Hebrew prophets were persecuted while Jezebel enjoyed the affection of her husband. The Hebrew prophet Elijah the Tishbite was particularly troublesome for the royal couple. Elijah warned the king that the country would suffer from drought if the cult of Baal were not removed. After the country had suffered three long years of drought, Elijah issued a challenge to Ahab and his priests to offer their prayers to Baal to render a miracle on Mount Carmel. The priests' prayers failed to produce any miracle, so the people turned away from Baal and embraced God.

Jezebel

Elijah ordered all of the idolatrous prophets of Baal killed. Jezebel, infuriated that her prophets had perished, wanted Elijah murdered, so he was forced into hiding.

The palace of King Ahab was situated very near a vineyard, and a man named Naboth owned the land. Ahab wanted the vineyard for growing herbs for his kitchen. He offered Naboth money or another vineyard in exchange. Naboth, however, would not sell the vineyard, telling the king that he had inherited the vineyard from his forefathers. Ahab became quite unhappy and stopped eating. Jezebel decided to secure the vineyard for the king by getting two men to testify that Naboth had blasphemed God and the king—the punishment was death by stoning. The plan worked, and with Naboth dead, the king went to Jezreel to take possession of his vineyard.

God told Elijah to go to the vineyard of Naboth to tell Ahab that he and Jezebel would perish for the killing of Naboth. Jezebel would die by the wall of Jezreel, where the dogs there would devour her (1 Kings 21:23).

QUESTION?

What was the name of Jezebel and Ahab's daughter?
Their child was named Athaliah. She must have inherited some of the evil genes of her mother, because Athaliah grew up to become a powerful schemer. She became Queen of Judah by having all of the royal princes murdered.

Elijah told Ahab, "Thus saith the Lord, in the place where dogs licked the blood of Naboth shall dogs lick thy blood, even thine" (1 Kings 21:19). Ahab started a war in which he allied himself with the king of Judah against Ben-hadad. During battle, a stray arrow ended the life of Ahab. Some sources say that dogs licked up the blood washed from his chariot, fulfilling Elijah's prophecy.

After Jehu ascended the throne as king of Israel, he set out to avenge those killed by Jezebel. One day he saw her in the window of the palace and told the people inside to throw her down. Jezebel, the self-proclaimed prophetess who exerted incredible influence over Ahab, must not have seen her own fate unfolding, for just as Elijah had prophesied, she was pushed out the window by those loyal to Jehu and was devoured by dogs.

Slave-Girl Soothsayer of Philippi

In A.D. 49 or 50, Paul and some companions, including Silas, Luke, and Timothy, entered the Macedonian city of Philippi. Paul encountered a slave girl who made money for her owner by telling people's fortunes and predicting the future. The Bible does not name the girl, but refers to her as "...a certain damsel possessed with a spirit of divination..." (Acts 16:16).

After having a vision in which a man appeared praying to him to go to Macedonia to help the people, Paul set out for Philippi. There, he and his companions planned to share the gospel with others. Philippi in those days had become a thriving Roman colony, vibrant with Greco-Roman traditions. Paul and his companions remained in Philippi for some time.

Just west of town, near a river where people gathered to pray on the Sabbath (mostly women, possibly Jewish and without a synagogue), Paul met Lydia, a wealthy businesswoman and seller of purple cloth, from Thyatira. The Bible says the Lord had opened her heart, which may have meant that she was already predisposed to receiving the gospel message from Paul. When she offered to open her home to Paul and his friends, they accepted her hospitality and stayed with her.

One day, the men encountered the young slave-girl soothsayer who, through possession by a spirit, made a lot of money for her owners using her occult powers. One source suggested that the girl might have been under the influence of a spirit of the cult of Apollo, whose devotees often had the powers of clairvoyance. She was a fortuneteller, according to the Acts of the Apostles. Many of the words for fortunetelling end in "mancy," which derives from *manteia*, Greek for "divination." In order to get her messages, she may have fallen into a trance, allowing the demon to take over and convey messages through her.

From the moment the girl first saw Paul, she followed him and his companions around, shouting, "These men are the servants of the most high God, which shew unto us the way of salvation" (Acts 16:17). Day after day, she continued to follow Paul and shout her chant. Paul found it annoying and finally, could bear it no longer. Believing that the girl's psychic abilities stemmed from possession by a spirit, he ordered the demon to depart.

And this did she many days. But Paul, being grieved, turned and said to the spirit, I command thee in the name of Jesus Christ to come out of her. And he came out the same hour. (Acts 16:18)

The slave girl's owners soon realized that her powers were gone and, consequently, their economic future altered. Seething with anger, they went looking for Paul and his companion Silas. The girl's owners took Paul and Silas to the city's rulers and complained that the two were Jews who were making trouble in the city. Anti-Semitism had been intensifying in Philippi, and the slave masters must have thought that by calling Paul and Silas Jewish troublemakers they could bring the wrath of city officials upon them. The slave masters' supposition proved right, and the magistrates ordered Paul and Silas beaten. Savagely flogged and bearing many stripes upon their bodies, the men were then thrown into a dungeon. The jailer, a Roman civil servant, was charged with safeguarding them.

At midnight, while Paul and Silas prayed and sang hymns of praise to God, a violent earthquake shook the land, causing the jail doors to fly open and the inmates' chains to come loose. The jailer, believing all of the prisoners had fled into the darkness, prepared to kill himself with a sword, "But Paul cried with a loud voice, saying, Do thyself no harm: for we are all here" (Acts 16:28). The jailer called for a light and went to the dungeon where Paul and Silas were chained. He brought the men out of the dungeon and asked how he could be saved: He was told to believe in Jesus Christ. The jailer thanked them and took them to his home, where he washed their wounds and was baptized. The next day, Paul and Silas were released.

The text of Acts doesn't mention the slave girl again. Her story is important in the context of the ancients' belief in demonic possession as a way to explain the girl's extraordinary powers. But the power of God working through his holy emissary, Paul, showed a greater power—one that restored the girl to wholeness. Thanks to Paul, she was free of her demonic imprisonment. Although the Bible doesn't say that the exploited slave girl then became a Christian, it seems likely.

FACT

Philip II established Philippi in 356 B.C. Today, the Hellenic Ministry of Culture claims that in terms of important archaeological sites, Philippi ranks at the top of sites in eastern Macedonia. Christians consider the city holy, and make pilgrimages there because Paul did missionary work in Philippi, and later sent a letter to the Philippians (now part of the canon). See *www.sacred-destinations.com/greece/philippi.htm*.

Modern Christian ministers use the story of the slave girl of Philippi to illustrate how people of different socioeconomic backgrounds all became united through the gospel. Lydia was Turkish and wealthy, the slave girl may have been Greek, and certainly owned nothing, and the jailer was a Roman civil servant whose economic status was between that of the two women.

Chapter 7

Women Favored by God

The main purpose of a woman's life during biblical times was to marry and bear children. Children were the hope of the future and the promise of a strong Hebrew nation that could fight off its enemies. Barren women sought God's grace, believing that only the Lord had the power to open or close a woman's womb. Psalm 127 addressed the importance of children as "…an heritage of the Lord…," noting that, "…the fruit of the womb is his reward." God made many barren women fertile, and gave special children to others, according to the Old Testament.

Elisheba

Elisheba (also Elisheva) means "God is my oath" or "God's oath." She became the sister-in-law of Moses when she married his brother, Aaron, member and high priest of the Levite tribe. Her brother, Naashon, served in the army of Judah. Naashon was referred to as "prince of the children of Judah" in 1 Chronicles 2:10. The Bible notes little else about Elisheba and her family, but does say that she gave birth to four sons who became the patriarchs of the Levitical priesthood, a priesthood that God had instituted. You may recall that God told Aaron that he and his sons would be priests: Elisheba is mentioned briefly in the book of Exodus as the mother of those would-be priests.

And Aaron took him Elisheba, daughter of Amminadab, sister of Naashon, to wife; and she bare him Nadab, and Abihu, Eleazar, and Ithamar (Exodus 6:23). And Eleazar Aaron's son took him one of the daughters of Putiel to wife; and she bare him Phinehas: these are the heads of the fathers of the Levites according to their families (6:25).

Elisheba's father, Amminadab, belonged to the tribe of Judah. Elisheba's marriage to Aaron fused the royal line of Judah with the priestly Levites. Her husband Aaron (of the Levite tribe) was born when the people of Israel were in exile in Egypt, some eighty-three years before God's "Chosen Ones" would reach the Promised Land. Elisheba most likely would have been with Aaron as he traveled with his brother Moses and sister Miriam toward the Promised Land.

What did Elisheba think about her husband yielding to the demands of the people and making the golden calf for them to worship while Moses was high up on the mountain receiving the Ten Commandments from God? It was a low point in Aaron's life, a life that had many highs and lows. Did she think he was just placating the desire of the people and buying time until Moses could return? Did Elisheba fear God might strike her husband down for making an idol? Did she simply acquiesce and remain silent? The Bible doesn't say.

When the Hebrew people believed that Moses would not return (after he'd gone to the mountain where God gave him the Ten Commandments), they went to Aaron, their priest, and demanded to worship an idol. Aaron appeased them using gold rings from the ears of the Hebrew wives, sons, and daughters to make a molten golden calf.

The incident with the golden calf was only one of what must have been many challenging moments in Elisheba's life. Lack of further mention of her in the Bible suggests that she did not attract attention to herself or incur the wrath of God. She may have quietly served the Lord without offending him or others. Perhaps she was alive to see her sons, Nadab and Abihu, die in a fire after having offered incense to the Lord that was not in compliance with the law he had given (Leviticus 10:1–20, Exodus 30:9). She may have witnessed her husband's transference of his priestly power and authority (when he was 123 years old) to his third son, Eleazar, presenting him with the sacred garments to be worn by the high priest. Maybe Elisheba even witnessed the death of her husband at Mount Hor, and participated in the people's mourning of him for thirty days.

She may have lived long enough to enter the Promised Land with her son, Eleazar, but Aaron, Moses, and Miriam died before they could complete that journey—a punishment by God for their sins. Moses' shortcoming was lack of faith and anger. God had told him to get water from a rock by speaking to it. Instead, Moses hit the rock with a rod (Deuteronomy 32:48–52, Numbers 20:7–13). Aaron and Miriam, similarly, were punished for their defiance against God and lapses in faith. The Bible does not reveal how or when Elishaba died. The most important detail of her life was that she had found favor in the sight of the Lord, such that he blessed her with sons to carry on the work of the priesthood.

Hannah

Although Hannah's story belongs with those of other ancient biblical tales about women, it has modern resonance. She was a woman who deeply wanted a child, but could not conceive. The Old Testament expression for a barren woman is that God had "shut up her womb" (1 Samuel 1:5). Hebrew women during Hannah's lifetime had a sacred duty to bear children; it was considered an honor and blessing from God to have sons and daughters. The identity of many women was tied to being a wife and mother; to remain barren equated with being cursed. For many such women, life had no purpose. In Hannah's case, her barrenness was made worse by the fact that she was one of two wives of Elkanah, a Levite from Ramahthaim-zophim near Mount Ephraim. Elkanah's other wife, Peninnah, produced many children and cruelly ridiculed Hannah (1 Samuel 1:2, 6).

Hannah's name derives from the Hebrew words for "grace" and "favor." She was faithful and diligent in her love for God, praying to the Lord often to bless her with children. Hannah was so desperate to have a baby that she promised God that if she could conceive and bear a child, she would give the child to the service of the Lord as a Nazarite. The child would remain the rest of his life in the tabernacle. Hannah vowed that "…there shall no razor come upon his head" (1 Samuel 1:11), a symbol of a life of dedication.

The Law of Separation and Consecration, found in Chapter 6 in the Old Testament's Book of Numbers, presents guidelines for the children of Israel who took vows to become Nazarites. For example, when they separated themselves from the general populace to become servants of the Lord, they could not cut their hair, drink vinegar, wine, or strong beverages, or eat grapes, whether moist or dried.

Hannah felt deep misery and sadness over her barrenness, and went to pray at the tabernacle. The Hebrews believed that the tabernacle was the holy dwelling place of God on earth, and that it was originally established by Moses following precise geometric criteria. At the tabernacle Hannah poured out her heart to God. On a seat near one of the posts of the temple, the priest Eli saw her and noted that her lips were not moving in prayer. As she continued to pray, Hannah spoke words to God in her heart, but not through her mouth. Eli thought that she had been drinking and asked her, "How long wilt thou be drunken? Put away thy wine from thee" (1 Samuel 1:14). But Hannah explained to the priest that she was of a sorrowful spirit, and had not been drinking. Eli, believing her, took pity and prayed on her behalf.

Hannah and Elkanah rose the next day, went out before the Lord to say their prayers, and then returned home and were intimate. God had heard the prayers of Hannah and Eli, the priest; soon she was pregnant with a baby boy, which she named Samuel. True to her word, Hannah returned Samuel to God upon weaning him. She took him to the tabernacle and left him there to be raised as a Nazarite. He grew up to become an important Old Testament leader and prophet.

QUESTION?

How did Eli, the priest, treat Samuel?
Eli treated Samuel as a loving foster father. Eli's own sons were priests, but they were wicked and corrupt and lay with women who congregated near the tabernacle. Eli was permissive and unable to discipline his own sons, but Samuel "grew before the Lord" (1 Samuel 2:21).

Every year after that, Hannah went to the tabernacle at Shiloh with her husband to offer the yearly sacrifice and leave Samuel the little coat she had made for him. The Lord was pleased with Hannah and blessed her with three sons and two daughters (1 Samuel 2:21). These children were to bring her joy in place of Samuel, who lived with Eli at the tabernacle at Shiloh.

Hannah's story, in some ways, parallels the stories of other biblical women who were barren, including Sarah (Abraham's wife), Rebekah (wife of Isaac), Rachel (wife of Jacob), Samson's mother, Michal (first wife of David), and Elizabeth (wife of Zacharias). Some believe that God may have had a special purpose for each of these women, making them fertile in order that they might conceive and bear sons who, in turn, rendered important service to individual tribes of the Hebrews and their nation.

Sarah

Sarah, childless until the age of ninety, is considered the first matriarch of the Hebrew people. At the beginning of her biblical story, Sarah is known as Sarai, married to Abram (later changed to Abraham). Some sources characterized her as a loving, loyal, and capable partner in every way to her husband. Others praised her beauty and called her idealistic and resourceful.

Sarah and Abraham started their lives together in Ur, Babylonia (modern-day Iraq). God promised to make a great nation of Abraham. Sarah may initially have been an obedient, even submissive wife; however, as the years began to pass and Sarah saw other women bearing their husbands' children while she remained childless, she may have decided to take action. If God had not intervened after all of that time, Sarah would have had a child one way or another. The Lord had promised a child, and yet Sarah was growing old. She was ten years younger than Abraham, and must have been in her mid-eighties when she decided upon her course of action. Perhaps her faith momentarily weakened. Perhaps she thought that the Lord had changed his mind or was taking too long. Maybe she had given up on believing that through God all things are possible. The biblical texts do not reveal whether or not Sarah sought her husband's counsel; nor do the texts say she undertook fasting, penance, and prayer to prepare the way for seeking God's counsel. Whatever went through Sarah's mind and heart, her patience with the Lord had run out. She made a decision and took Hagar, her young Egyptian handmaiden, to Abraham.

Sarah

Sarah's Initial Intent

Some sources say that Sarah's act was one of selflessness. Hagar was given to Sarah by the pharaoh after she had spent a brief period in the pharaoh's court (Genesis 12:11–20). One story states that Hagar was the daughter of the pharaoh, and thus royalty. Sarah might have looked upon Hagar, with her royal lineage, as an appropriate choice as a mother for Abraham's heir. After all, the beautiful Hagar and Abraham would create a wonderful child, perhaps one having the best traits of both father and mother. Such a child would begin the nation of Abraham.

And Sarai, Abram's wife, took Hagar her maid the Egyptian, after Abram had dwelt ten years in the land of Canaan, and gave her to her husband Abram to be his wife. And he went in unto Hagar, and she conceived: and when she saw that she had conceived, her mistress was despised in her eyes. (Genesis 16:3–4)

Conflict Between the Women Erupts

Hagar may not have wanted to be intimate with the husband of her mistress, but it's unlikely that Sarah would have asked the girl's permission. Once Hagar gave birth to Abraham's firstborn son, Ishmael, she may have believed that her status was on equal par with, or even exceeded, Sarah's. The household became filled with tension and rivalry, shattering the peace that once existed in Abraham's tent.

Dissent and Rivalry Erupt

As daughter of the pharaoh, Hagar was born into nobility and could have become a queen. Possibly, she believed that she would assume the primary position in Abraham's life, producing the children that Sarah could not. What Hagar didn't understand was that Sarah and Abraham were partners in love and in life. Both were spiritual giants, working together to serve the Lord. God would make of Abraham's seed a nation of people, but Sarah, not Hagar, was to become the matriarch of that nation.

Sarah Becomes Pregnant

The Bible says that when God told Abraham and Sarah that she would conceive, the two of them laughed. Sarah was already ninety and had given up on the idea that she would ever bear children by her husband, who was also quite old. Abraham called his son Isaac, and complying with God's command, he circumcised Isaac when the baby was eight days old.

FACT

Kirjatharba was the same as Hebron in the Old Testament. Today, Hebron is a divided city occupied by both Israelis and Palestinians. Abraham and his followers settled in Hebron. Some believe that not only Sarah, but also Abraham, Isaac, Rebekah, Jacob, and Leah are buried in Hebron's Tomb of the Patriarchs, a site considered sacred by both Jews and Muslims.

Hagar Is Cast Out

After weaning Isaac, Sarah made a great feast, and she and her husband celebrated. Soon, however, Sarah told Abraham that the time had come for Hagar and her son to go. She saw Ishmael as mocking, and didn't want her own son to share his inheritance with Abraham's firstborn. Abraham felt saddened and resisted, but God told him that "...in all that Sarah hath said unto thee, hearken unto her voice; for in Isaac shall thy seed be called. And also of the son of the bondwoman will I make a nation, because he is thy seed" (Genesis 21:12–13).

Abraham's Faith Is Tested

Did Sarah know about God's testing of her husband's faith? The Bible doesn't say, but what a tribulation that would have been for her if she had known that Abraham, following God's instruction, had taken their son Isaac to the land of Moriah to sacrifice him as a burnt offering. Abraham had built the altar, placed wood upon it, bound Isaac, and raised his knife to slay his son, when the angel of the Lord stopped him. Abraham had passed the test. The Lord was pleased and sent a ram for Abraham to use as the offering in

Isaac's place. The writer of Genesis does not reveal how Sarah reacted, or even if Abraham ever told her.

Sarah passed away in Kirjatharba, in the land of Canaan, when she reached the age of 127. Her husband greatly mourned her passing. He purchased the cave at Machpelah at the end of a field belonging to Ephron, the son of Zohar, a Hittite man. There, Abraham buried his beloved Sarah.

Shunammite Mother

The prophet Elisha often passed by the house of a wealthy and respectable woman in Shunem. The woman believed him to be a holy man and offered him bread each time he passed through the area. She convinced her husband that they should create a small chamber for the prophet, putting in a bed, table, stool, and candlestick, so that whenever he came to their home he had room of his own in which to rest.

The prophet began to use the chamber. One day he asked Gehazi, his servant, to summon the Shunammite woman in order that he might ask her what he could do for her in return. The woman stood before him, but didn't ask for anything. She had a kind heart, and only desired to use her wealth to care for the holy man. Gehazi told Elisha that the woman's husband was quite old and that the woman had no child. So Elisha asked her if she could embrace a child at that point in her life.

And he said, About this season, according to the time of life, thou shalt embrace a son. And she said, Nay, my lord, thou man of God, do not lie unto thine handmaid. And the woman conceived, and bare a son at that season that Elisha had said unto her, according to the time of life. (2 Kings 4:16–17)

The Child Dies

Her child grew healthy and strong. One morning, the boy accompanied his father to a field to work with the reapers. However, when he fell on his head and screamed in pain, his father carried him to his mother and placed him on her lap. The child remained in her embrace until noon, when he died.

The Shunammite mother carried the boy to the little room she had made for the prophet Elisha. She gently laid the lifeless body upon the bed. Then she called for a donkey and rode as fast as she could to Mount Carmel.

FACT

Mount Carmel in ancient times was associated with Elijah and Elisha, two notable Old Testament prophets. The mountain juts up 1,792 feet and is part of a mountain ridge in northwest Israel that stretches from the Plain of Esdraelon down to a part of the Mediterranean Sea known as the Bay of Haifa. The port city of Haifa is located at the base of Mount Carmel.

Elisha saw her coming and called out to Gehazi, his servant, to go to the woman and find out what was troubling her. The Shunammite mother did not want to waste precious time explaining things to Gehazi, but instead threw herself at the feet of Elisha. Her gesture demonstrated great humility and respect, and in an anguished voice she pleaded with Elisha to help her child. The old prophet understood her pain and told his servant to take his staff and go heal the boy. The Shunnamite mother insisted that she would not leave Elisha's side, so the two followed after Gehazi.

Gehazi was unsuccessful in reviving the boy, and some sources assert that he may not have tried very hard; but Elisha took over when he arrived. He entered the room and closed it, keeping everyone out. He prayed to God, "And he went up, and lay upon the child, and put his mouth upon his mouth, and his eyes upon his eyes, and his hands upon his hands: and stretched himself upon the child; and the flesh of the child waxed warm" (2 Kings 4:34).

Elisha, the Bible says, then got up and paced before once again stretching himself upon the boy. This time the child sneezed seven times and opened his eyes.

Elisha called in Gehazi and told him to get the Shunammite woman. When the woman entered the room, Elisha told her, "Take up thy son" (2

Kings 4:36). The woman, who had much faith in God and had freely given of her wealth to make life more comfortable for the Lord's prophet, was surely rewarded with Divine favor; nothing short of a miracle was performed through the aging prophet. Overcome with gratitude, she fell at Elisha's feet.

QUESTION?

What is the significance of seven sneezes?
To the ancients, seven symbolized a protracted state of something (a severe illness or demonic possession), but also completion. Some sources assert that the boy's sneezes are to be understood as breaths Elisha exhaled into him. The ancients believed that the soul temporarily flew out of the body during a sneeze.

The Shunammite woman was to again receive God's grace through his prophet Elisha. The holy man told her that she must take her son and travel as far as she could, because a famine would soon ravage the land for seven years. The Shunammite took her son and went to territory occupied by the Philistines. At the end of seven years, she returned.

Gehazi was speaking to the king about how Elisha had restored the woman's son to life at precisely the moment the woman reappeared. She asked the king to return her house and land. Not only did the king honor her request, but he also ordered that all of the fruit of her land (all that it had produced in her seven-year absence) be given to her.

These are only a few of the stories to be found in the Bible about how God favored women in ancient times. Their lives were fraught with many of the same problems that plague modern women, but their faith, resourcefulness, and perseverance was often rewarded through divine intervention.

Chapter 8

Temptresses, Harlots, and Sinful Women

The ancient Hebrews spent a period of exile in Babylonian captivity from 586 B.C. to 538 B.C. During that time, they would have been exposed to Babylonian religious customs and the roles of women. The Babylonians were pagans and, like the Sumerians, worshipped Ishtar, the goddess of life, love, and fertility. The Bible called her the Whore of Babylon, a euphemism for evil. The harlots made up an organized hierarchy of temple workers who engaged in sacred sex. In the act, a man became a god, worshipped in the arms of the harlot as a representative of the goddess.

Babylonian Sacred Sex Workers

Babylonian women, obliged to serve as cult prostitutes once in their lifetimes, would sit along different roads and byways and burn chaff. The chaff was used for ancient erotic rites and considered a type of aphrodisiac, according to scholarly interpretations of Baruch 6:42 in the Old Testament of The New American Bible. Baruch served as the prophet Jeremiah's scribe, and his book contains prayers and praises of God, as well as poetry and admonitions against idolatry. (The Book of Baruch is not included in the Old Testament of the King James Version of the Bible.)

And the woman was arrayed in purple and scarlet colour, and decked with gold and precious stones and pearls, having a golden cup in her hand full of abominations and filthiness of her fornication: And upon her forehead was a name written, MYSTERY, BABYLON THE GREAT, THE MOTHER OF HARLOTS AND ABOMINATIONS OF THE EARTH. (Revelation 17:4–5)

The Babylonian women serving as sacred sex workers in the temple of Ishtar accepted money for their lovemaking, but the amount did not matter and the men offering money were never refused. The act was considered sacred, and the money therefore consecrated. The women were made holy through the conjugal act. They wore an unbroken cord to signify that they had not yet fulfilled their obligation. The more beautiful the woman, the faster she could be "made holy." The less attractive among them might spend a few years in an effort to fulfill their obligation. Once they had performed their duty, the women were free to leave the temple, marry, and have children. The Babylonians granted women the same status as men. As wives, however, later Sumerian texts noted that temple women could be indifferent and unsympathetic wives, having been treated as goddesses while in the temple.

The Whore of Babylon came to symbolize evil doings in the world. Jesus' Apostle John the Divine, at the end of his lifetime in the last few years of the Common Era, used the Great Whore in his book of Revelation to depict evil.

Scholars assert that the Whore of Babylon's identity in Revelation cannot be known with certainty, but most likely represented the evil-doing, debauchery, and pagan worship associated with Rome, seat of the Roman empire, during John's lifetime. The fledgling Christian communities believed that idolatry and pagan worship was wrong, and preached against it. And although Jesus demonstrated through his actions egalitarian treatment of women, the Hebrews continued a patriarchal system that accorded men the superior position above women and children in the social strata of their communities.

Cozbi, Daughter of Zur

Cozbi was a Midianitish princess who was slain for idolatry and immorality after being brought by Zimri, an Israelite chief of the tribe of Simeon, into his tent. The Hebrews were encamped near Mount Peor. A plague had ravaged their numbers. The mountain of Peor was the last the Israelites had to ascend before they could cross the Jordan River into the land of Canaan. But with Hebrew immorality running rampant, and the plague decimating the population, the Lord instructed Moses to kill his own leaders and to display them in daylight. In that way, the wrath of God could be appeased.

QUESTION?

Who were the Moabites and Midianites?
The Moabites were a peaceful people dwelling east of the Dead Sea in modern-day Jordan. The Midianites were mainly nomadic shepherding families living in the desert of what is now northwest Arabia. They descended from Abraham and Keturah, who dwelled in the land of the East (Genesis 25:1–6). Moses took a Midianite wife, Zipporah (Exodus 2:21).

When Moses and the Hebrews heard God's pronouncement, they began to weep at the door of the tabernacle. Some of the men had sinned with Moabite and Midianite women; they had worshipped and made sacrifices to the god Baal at Peor. Many Hebrews felt their own people bore responsibility for bringing the plague upon the rest of them.

According to the Bible, Cozbi's father, Zur, was the leader of a people and head of an important house in Midian. Zimri was the son of Salu, and a Hebrew tribal leader with a bright future ahead of him when he became hopelessly infatuated with Cozbi. According to some sources, Zimri confronted Moses, asking why he couldn't cohabitate with Cozbi if Moses could take a gentile woman as a wife and have her accepted within the Jewish nation. Allegedly, Moses did not answer, but when Phinehas, his nephew, cited a principle that zealots could slay anyone who cohabitated with non-Jewish women, Moses may have nodded agreement.

Cozbi and Zimri possibly loved each other. Perhaps they had been lovers for a while. That day, their timing could not have been worse. When Zimri escorted Cozbi past the Israelites, those assembled became incensed. Phinehas, grandson of Aaron (the high priest and brother of Moses), watched them walk toward the tent, possibly thinking that they were about to commit an act of fornication. Phinehas rose, followed the couple into the tent, and thrust a spear through Zimri, killing him. He then turned his spear upon Cozbi, plunging it through her belly. The Hebrews considered it a righteous act, since God had told Moses to smite the Midianites.

And the Lord spake unto Moses, saying, Vex the Midianites, and smite them: For they vex you with their wiles, wherewith they have beguiled you in the matter of Peor, and in the matter of Cozbi, the daughter of a prince of Midian, their sister, which was slain in the day of the plague for Peor's sake. (Numbers 25:16–18)

If Phinehas had killed Cozbi and Zimri out of rage, he had simply murdered two people. However, as a zealot committing the act, Phinehas earned God's blessing of "...the covenant of an everlasting priesthood; because he was zealous for his God, and made an atonement for the children of Israel" (Numbers 25:13).

Gomer

Gomer was the unfaithful wife of Hosea, one of the so-called Minor Prophets. His name means "salvation." Details about his life and death are scant. He was the son of Beeri and lived in the Northern Kingdom during the rule of Jeroboam II, around 786 B.C.–746 B.C. This historical period saw the decline of the covenant between God and the Israelites. The Jews, having broken God's commandments and violated the terms of his covenant with them, are collectively depicted in the book of Hosea as a harlot.

"And the Lord said to Hosea, Go, take unto thee a wife of whoredoms and children of whoredoms: for the land hath committed great whoredom, departing from the Lord" (Hosea 1:2). Some scholars suggest that the command of God to Hosea was symbolic, and many Jews have a problem with the idea that God would order a devoted follower to take a prostitute for a wife. But Hosea used the travails of his relationship with his wife as a mirror and metaphor to prophesy about the relationship between God and the Jews at that juncture of history.

Their Marriage Produces Three Children

Gomer, daughter of Diblaim and, possibly, a prostitute, married Hosea. She bore three children in succession. The firstborn was a boy, and God commanded Hosea to name him Jezreel. The second child was a girl; Hosea called her Lo-ruhamah. The third child was another boy, named Lo-ammi. The children's names are significant because they symbolize the Lord's relationship with the children of Israel and, in another way, the travails of the marital life of Hosea and Gomer.

Gomer Leaves the Marriage

Some scholars have asserted that Gomer was not a harlot before her marriage to Hosea (although some sources assert that she may have been and that Hosea was her client). One possible explanation for the passage "...take unto thee a wife of whoredoms and children of whoredoms..." is the foretelling of what was to come; that is, that Gomer would become unfaithful after marriage. Just as Israel broke her covenant with God, Gomer broke hers with Hosea.

The Children's Names Have Meaning

The naming of Gomer's and Hosea's children is significant in a historical context. The first child was named Jezreel, a valley in which the kings of the Northern Kingdom had caused much bloodshed. The Northern Kingdom's retribution was coming, and God would not show pity. Lo-ruhamah's name means "no pity" or "she is not pitied." The name Lo-ammi means "not mine" or "not my people." It was a terrible name with which to saddle a child, yet taken symbolically, it could be said that God wanted the Northern Kingdom to bear the shame of no longer being claimed by the Divine.

Accusations of Infidelity Cause Divorce

Hosea sent Gomer away, saying, "And she shall follow after her lovers, but she shall not overtake them; and she shall seek them, but shall not find them: then shall she say, I will go and return to my first husband; for then was it better with me than now" (Hosea 2:7). While this mirrors Israel's departure from the covenant with God, it also suggests that Hosea had split from Gomer for good.

Hosea Pays to Get Gomer Back

Gomer may have been living with a lover who demanded money for her release, or perhaps she had become a slave to pay a debt. Whatever the reason, she was not free to return to Hosea. He had to purchase her to get her back. He abstained from sexual relations with her for some time.

So I bought her to me for fifteen pieces of silver, and for an homer of barley, and an half homer of barley: And I said unto her, Thou shalt abide for me many days; thou shalt not play the harlot, and thou shalt not be for another man: so will I also be for thee (Hosea 3:2).

Again, symbolically, the return of Hosea's wife mirrored God taking back the Israelites, but not until they had floundered without a ruler for some time (punishment, some might say, for a harlot's bad behavior, or divine retribution for Israel's worship of false gods). However, just as Gomer returned to Hosea, so, too, did Israel again receive God's favor.

Jephthah's Mother

Jephthah's father, Gilead, had a wife and numerous children when he met the mother of Jephthah, a woman that the Bible does not name, but calls a harlot (Judges 11:1). Gilead had a brief affair with her. She may have been a cult temple worker, or simply a prostitute. When Jephthah was born, his father Gilead took him to raise him. The name Jephthah means "he will open" in Hebrew. Perhaps in naming his son, Gilead believed that God would open passages for him through difficult situations and times ahead. The boy was raised in Gilead's home with the rest of his family, in the land east of the Jordan River.

FACT

Some sources assert that Jephthah's mother was a pagan temple prostitute. The Hebrew word for such a prostitute is *qedesha*. The Hebrew word for whore is *zona*, and that is the word some Bibles use to describe her. The King James version calls her a harlot (Judges 11:1).

When Gilead died, his legitimate sons went to Jephthah and told him to leave. They had never accepted him as their brother, and did not desire to share any of their inheritance with him. It seems reasonable to believe that Jephthah's mother may have been banished from Gilead's family home as well, though the Bible does not say Gilead had ever taken her in, or that she had any further contact with their son. Jephthah's path would lead to greatness, but also to great sadness.

Jephthah Becomes a Powerful Warrior

Jephthah sought refuge in the wilderness. There, he eventually developed friendships with others who were societal outcasts. Jephthah must have developed strong survival skills, because he became a fierce warrior in Tob. Eventually, the elders of Gilead went searching for Jephthah. They asked him to return to be their leader in a fight against the invading Ammonites. Jephthah asked them why they wanted him when they had previously cast him from his father's home. They more or less dismissed his question, and convinced him that if he would return they would make him their military leader and commander.

He Makes a Promise to God

Jephthah agreed and attempted to resolve the dispute with the Ammonites through a dialogue with their king. However, failing that, he prayed to God to grant him a victory over the aggressors. In return, he would give a burnt offering of the first thing he saw coming out of his door to meet him when he returned home. Of all of the people dwelling in that home, who did Jephthah think would come to meet him: His stepmother? His brothers who had banished him? His own mother? What Jephthah saw caused his heart to sink, and he tore his clothes in sadness.

Jephthah Keeps His Vow

His virginal daughter (born of a wife that the Bible doesn't name) came dancing out of the door with timbrels in her hands. "And it came to pass, when he saw her, that he rent his clothes, and said, Alas, my daughter! thou hast brought me very low, and thou art one of them that trouble me: for I have opened my mouth unto the Lord, and I cannot go back" (Judges 11:35). Jephthah's daughter, his only child, begged him to let her spend two weeks in the mountains with her female companions before he sacrificed her, a request that he honored.

The Bible doesn't say if Jephthah's own mother was involved in raising him, if she knew about his leadership abilities, his victory over the Ammonites, or his vow to God to sacrifice her granddaughter. Perhaps his mother had already passed away, or had long ago taken up with another man. She may not have been around to witness the unfolding of events in her son's life, but Jephthah, like her, made certain choices and became bound by them. He became a judge for Israel and a strong leader; some sources called him a deliverer of the Israelites.

Prostitutes Washing Themselves in Ahab's Blood

The biblical story of these prostitutes is intrinsically tied to the story of Ahab's death. Ahab served as king of Israel from 874 B.C. to 853 B.C. He received a life-threatening wound in battle against the Syrians as he and his army attempted to regain Ramoth-gilead. Ahab ordered his charioteer, "Turn thine hand, and carry me out of the host; for I am wounded" (1 Kings 22:34). The Bible states that Ahab stood up in his chariot and stayed in the battle until that evening, but died from a loss of blood due to his wound. He was taken to Samaria to be buried.

According to Canaanite mythology, Baal, god of fertility, was in a perpetual struggle with Mot, god of sterility. The outcome of their struggles was often a seven-year cycle of famine or prosperity. Baal was also seen as king among gods, and ruled over the rain, wind, and clouds. He was worshipped in high places in nature, usually with an altar for sacrifices along with a wooden image of the goddess Ashtoreth, his consort, and a stone pillar to represent him.

Ahab must have lost considerable blood, because his chariot and armor were covered with it. When the chariot was washed, the Pool of Samaria ran red, and dogs licked it up, fulfilling the prophecy of Elijah (1 Kings 21:19). Some biblical accounts add that not only dogs were at the pool, but also prostitutes. Scholars suggest that the harlots bathing in the bloody water was probably due to a superstitious belief that they might magically gain some of the fertility and power of Ahab from contact with his blood. They may also have been worshippers of Baal.

Rahab

Rahab was referred to in the Bible as "the harlot of Jericho." She and her family were the only people living in Jericho that survived the destruction of the community. One legend asserts that she married Joshua; another states she wed Salmon, one of the Hebrew spies sent by Joshua that she protected. If the latter legend were true, then she would have been among the line from whom Jesus was descended. Regardless, she came to be honored among women for her courage on behalf of the Hebrew people.

To set the stage for her story, it is first necessary to present a little background. Moses, the leader of the Hebrew people, was dead and Joshua, the son of Nun, had taken his place. While the Hebrews camped at Shittim before crossing the Jordan River into Canaan, the Promised Land, Joshua dispatched spies to provide information on the strength of the forces of the King of Jericho, since the Hebrew encampment stood just opposite Jericho.

Rahab

"And they went, and came into an harlot's house, named Rahab, and lodged there" (Joshua 2:1). Soon, the King of Jericho was told about the men at Rahab's house. The king promptly sent for the harlot.

Rahab told the king that she had seen the men come in, but they had left and she didn't know where they went. She told the king to send out his men in a hurry, and perhaps he would find the spies. In truth, however, she had taken the men up onto her roof and hidden them with stalks of flax. But before she hid them, Rahab voiced a request.

Rahab Strikes a Deal with Joshua's Spies

She told the men that she had heard how powerful the Hebrew god was, and that she understood that they had come to take over the land in which she lived. She asked them to show kindness to her as she had to them, and to spare her family. The men told her they would protect her family if she helped them.

The Spies Escape

Joshua's men climbed to safety down a scarlet cord hung from Rahab's window. She told them to hide for three days until the king's men gave up their search. When the spies returned to their camp, they told Joshua of their promise to spare Rahab and her family.

And the king of Jericho sent unto Rahab, saying, Bring forth the men that are come to thee, which are entered into thine house: for they be come to search out all the country. And the woman took the two men, and hid them… (Joshua 2:3–4)

Rahab's City Is Captured

The Hebrews readied themselves for the crossing of the Jordan, and the river dried up so that the children of the Lord could cross over. The people surrounded the city of Jericho. Trumpets blared and the people shouted, and the walls of Jericho came tumbling down. The Hebrews went to claim Jericho, destroying men, women, children, and animals "…with the edge of the sword" (Joshua 6:21).

Joshua Spares Rahab and Her Family

Joshua told his spies to go to Rahab's house and get her and everything she had with her, including her family. The men did as they were told, taking Rahab and her relatives to a place outside the camp of Israel. They then torched the city. "And Joshua saved Rahab, the harlot, alive, and her father's household, and all that she had; and she dwelleth in Israel even unto this day; because she hid the messengers, which Joshua sent to spy out Jericho" (Joshua 6:25).

The Sinful Woman Who Wiped Jesus' Feet

When Simon the Pharisee invited Jesus to come and dine at his house, he didn't expect a woman to show up with an alabaster box of ointment. In particular, Simon must have been surprised to see *that particular* woman appear. Luke's narrative says that this woman stood behind Jesus weeping, "...and began to wash his feet with tears, and did wipe them with the hairs of her head, and kissed his feet, and anointed them with the ointment" (Luke 7:38). The woman's identity may have been well known in the community, or at least known to Simon, for the narrative says that Simon thought to himself, "This man, if he were a prophet, would have known who and what manner of woman this is that toucheth him: for she is a sinner" (Luke 7:39).

Jesus, well aware of what Simon was thinking, told him he had something to tell him. Jesus told Simon a story about a creditor with two debtors: one owed 500 pence, and the other owed 50 pence. When they had nothing to pay, the creditor forgave them both. Jesus asked Simon which of the debtors would love the creditor more. Simon said the one whom he forgave the most, which Jesus said was the right answer. Then Jesus turned to the woman, and still talking with Simon, underscored his point.

...Seest thou this woman? I entered into thine house, thou gavest me no water for my feet: but she hath washed my feet with tears, and wiped them with the hairs of her head. Thou gavest me no kiss: but this woman since the time I came in hath not ceased to kiss my feet. My head with oil thou didst not anoint: but this woman hath anointed my feet with ointment. (Luke 7:44–46)

Jesus told Simon that her sins were many, but that he forgave them because she "...loved much. "...But," he continued, "to whom little is forgiven, the same loveth little" (Luke 7:47). Simon couldn't have missed the point, and the woman was saved by her faith.

Just four verses after the narrative of the Sinful Woman, Mary Magdalene is mentioned as the woman out of whom Jesus cast seven devils. Many confuse the Sinful Woman in Chapter 7 of Luke with Mary Magdalene, whose story begins in Chapter 8. The fact that the Sinful Woman carries an alabaster jar further adds to the confusion, since artists throughout the century have depicted Mary Magdalene with an alabaster jar.

Pope Gregory the Great, in his Homily XXXIII, even combined the stories of those two women with Mary of Bethany (sister of Martha and Lazarus) to create a compelling composite image to show the forgiving nature of the church. His effort turned out to be quite effective, and 2,000 years afterward, many Christians have believed that the woman named Mary Magdalene was a prostitute. However, the truth is that there was never any biblical or historical evidence to prove that Mary Magdalene was ever a prostitute, or that she was the Sinful Woman of Luke or Mary of Bethany. The stories of those women are nonetheless inspiring, and their tales will likely be retold for another 2,000 years.

Chapter 9

Women Who Tasted Bitterness

Life for a female in ancient times could be quite precarious. Like their modern counterparts, they longed for good marriages, healthy children, plentiful food, and a stable life. They put faith in God to provide their families food and shelter, knowing that malady and misfortune shadowed them wherever they went. Famine, war, plagues, and difficult childbirth could decimate their numbers; praising the Lord would not have been easy in such circumstances. While some women exhibited unshakable faith, others had great difficulty bearing their many and varied tribulations.

Asenath

The Egyptian-born Asenath was the daughter of Potipherah, priest of On. Some sources dispute that she was the flesh-and-blood daughter of Potipherah, asserting that he was unable to impregnate his wife. What isn't disputed is that Asenath's destiny was to be with Joseph, son of Jacob.

After Joseph was imprisoned by the pharaoh, and then correctly interpreted the ruler's dreams about seven years of abundance in Egypt to be followed by seven years of famine, the pharaoh gave Joseph control over all of Egypt. He called Joseph by the name of Zaphnathpaaneah, or "revealer of things hidden" (Genesis 41:45). The pharaoh gave Asenath to Joseph for his wife; Genesis doesn't reveal how old Asenath was when she married Joseph, but he was thirty.

Egyptian land at that time was fertile, harvests were good, and food was plentiful. Asenath, whose name means "gift of the sun god," bore Joseph two sons. He named the firstborn Manasseh, "For God, said he, hath made me forget all my toil, and all my father's house" (Genesis 41:51). He named his second son Ephraim, "For God hath caused me to be fruitful in the land of my affliction" (Genesis 41:52). Both Manasseh and Ephraim grow up to lead their own Hebrew tribes.

When the famine hit Egypt and all of the lands around it, the storehouses were full of grain, because God had given Joseph the insight to fill the storehouses in preparation for the coming lean years. People from other lands, including Joseph's father and brothers, came to Egypt seeking food. Joseph introduced them to the pharaoh, and the ruler gave Jacob the Patriarch the best land for his family, and good pastures for their sheep. Joseph lived to be 110, long enough to see his sons become leaders of their own tribes, and to enjoy his son's grandchildren.

The Bible says nothing more about Asenath, but there is a story in Jewish midrashic literature that states that Asenath was actually Joseph's niece, the daughter of his sister Dinah following Dinah's rape by Sechem.

There is another story about Asenath found in an apocryphal account of the couple. In that story, Asenath is a virgin pagan. Joseph, repelled by the idea of a pagan wife, rejects Asenath. Reeling from the bitterness of his rejection, she enters a tower to fast and pray, and undergoes a conversion. A visit by an angel, and a ritual that involves honeycomb, result in Joseph changing his mind. He marries her, and she bears their two sons. However, the pharaoh's own son harbors a smoldering desire for Asenath. He hatches a plan to kill Joseph. Benjamin, one of Joseph's brothers, foils the plan, and the pharaoh's son perishes instead. Asenath and Joseph govern Egypt for forty-eight more years before the pharaoh's grandson takes power.

QUESTION?

Who was Sechem?

Sechem, the son of King Hamor, saw Dinah attending a nature festival. He raped her, but then fell in love with her and wanted to marry her. He begged his father to help. The king asked Jacob for the girl; negotiations resulted in the nonHebrew men of the village undergoing circumcision. But when they were too sore to move, Dinah's brothers, Levi and Simeon, took their revenge, killing all of the men, including Sechem and his father.

Still other sources assert that the priest Potipherah fell sick, and his illness resulted in his inability to father any children. Potipherah, those sources assert, likely adopted Asenath and gave her to Joseph after Joseph interpreted his dreams.

Another version of the story has Dinah giving birth to a baby girl whose presence in the home of Jacob and his sons was intolerable, because it served as a constant reminder of the disgraced Dinah. Jacob decided to send the girl to Egypt, where she might be adopted. He made the child a gift of a necklace and an amulet. Words in the amulet stated that the baby's name was Asenath, and she was the product of a violent tragedy. By some divine hand, baby Asenath was adopted by the priest Potipherah in Egypt. Later, she became Joseph's wife.

Berenice

Berenice, whose name means "victorious," was the half-Jewish daughter of the Roman ruler Herod Agrippa I. Her lineage of power and wealth extended back to her great-grandfather, Herod the Great of Judea. Berenice had the good things that life could offer, but her world also had a dark side. She married three times—first Marcus, then her uncle Herod (king of Chalcis, who died), and finally Ptolemy (king of Cilicia). Her marriage to Ptolemy made her a queen, but she left him to supposedly cohabitate incestuously with M. Julius Agrippa II, her brother with whom she may have been having an illicit relationship while she was married to her uncle Herod. She served with Agrippa II as joint ruler over Galilee and the eastern side of the Jordan River.

Some sources say she had captured the heart of the aging Roman Emperor Vespasian through her beguiling good looks and her gifts, but it was the old man's son, Titus, who had actually taken her as a lover. At the time, Berenice was forty, and Titus thirty.

Josephus, the Jewish historian, and Tacitus, the historian of Roman antiquity, both wrote about Berenice's dalliances with men, the bizarre relationship with Agrippa II, and her affair with Titus. After Titus divorced his wife, Berenice lived openly with him as his concubine.

FACT

A concubine was a woman involved in a relationship of a quasi-matrimonial type. The man usually already had a wife in the legal and religious sense, and the wife had more rights than the concubine. A man's concubine, and children of his concubine, were of a lower status and had fewer rights of support than a wife and her offspring.

Some sources note that Berenice and Titus were in love, and that when she was forty-five (in A.D. 74), he wanted to marry her. However, the tide of popular Roman opinion swelled against the idea. When Titus became emperor in A.D. 79, he sent Berenice away. It was a sad and bitter end to the great love affair of her life.

Dinah

Her father, Jacob, had twelve sons through his marriages to Leah and Rachel and their respective handmaidens, but Dinah was his only daughter.

Jacob's girl was naturally inquisitive, so when her friends set off to attend a festival of nature, she went with them. Prince Shechem, the son of Hamor the Hevite (a local king), spotted her and lusted after her. Genesis 34:2–4 states that "…he took her, and lay with her, and defiled her. And his soul clave unto Dinah the daughter of Jacob, and he loved the damsel, and spake kindly unto the damsel. And Shechem spake unto his father Hamor, saying, Get me this damsel to wife." As you can see, the word "rape" is not used, but the writer of Genesis does not include the testimony of Dinah as to whether or not it was consensual. The key word may be "defiled."

Shechem went to his father and asked his help in securing the girl for his wife. But before Hamor could make an overture to Jacob on his son's behalf, Jacob heard about what had happened to his daughter. He stayed silent and waited for his sons to return from the fields where they had been taking care of the cattle.

King Hamor then appeared at Jacob's house to ask Jacob's permission for Shechem to marry Dinah, making an earnest plea.

…The soul of my son Shechem longeth for your daughter: I pray you give her him to wife. And make ye marriages with us, and give your daughters unto us, and take our daughters unto you. And ye shall dwell with us: and the land shall be before you; dwell and trade ye therein, and get you possessions therein. (Genesis 34:8–10)

Shechem, so desperate to have Dinah as a wife, also made a monetary offer to Jacob and his sons of a dowry fee, in whatever amount they wanted. According to custom, even if Jacob were to refuse, he could still keep the money. Jacob may have deliberated a moment too long, because his sons answered deceitfully for him. They told Shechem and his father that they would gladly take the money, but they had a custom that their sister could only be given to a circumcised male. Further, the Hebrew women could not intermarry with the men of Hamor's kingdom unless all his men were circumcised. To this, Shechem and Hamor agreed.

Dinah must have gone with Shechem to stay in his house as his guest (Genesis 34:17, 26). Three days after the mass circumcision, while Hamor's men were still in some pain, Dinah's brothers, Simeon and Levi, armed with swords, massacred all the newly circumcised men, including the king and Shechem. They took Dinah out of Shechem's house and returned to Jacob. But Jacob was not happy, and the boys found they now had to defend their actions to their father.

And Jacob said to Simeon and Levi, Ye have troubled me to make me to stink among the inhabitants of the land, among the Canaanites and the Perizzites: and I being few in number, they shall gather themselves together against me, and slay me; and I shall be destroyed, I and my house. And they said, Should he deal with our sister as with a harlot? (Genesis 34:30–31)

Some biblical scholars assert that the revenge of the brothers of Dinah upon the men of Shechem's community was the inciting incident used by the Hebrews to lay claim to the territory. The midrashic literature elaborates on the story by suggesting that the boys, Simeon and Levi, were just teenagers with a highly developed sense of morality, and zealous in their demonstration of it. The aging patriarch Jacob ensures that they will not be able to do such a thing again by reducing their portions of inherited tribal lands.

Naomi

Naomi changed her name to Mara, meaning "bitter," after a series of setbacks in her life left her a widow, without sons, destitute, and alone. In the end, her sole ally was her loyal and loving daughter-in-law Ruth, who stuck by Naomi when things couldn't get any worse.

Naomi, with her two sons, Mahlon and Chilion, had followed her husband Elimelech to Moab when the famine came and threatened their survival. Elimelech died first, followed by Naomi's sons. Following the deaths of their men, Naomi and her daughters-in-law, Ruth and Orpah, charted a new course toward the land of Judah, specifically Bethlehem, Naomi's homeland. But before they left Moab, Naomi turned to her daughters-in-law and counseled them to turn back and stay with their own kind, perhaps thinking that the young women might marry again. Orpah followed Naomi's suggestion, but Ruth could not be convinced. She chose to remain with Naomi, so the two women continued toward Bethlehem.

It must have been very touching to Naomi that Ruth would abandon her own people and religion to become part of Naomi's world, in the land of the Israelites where Moabites were despised. Naomi's life may have been full of bitterness, but Ruth showed her the unconditional love of a daughter.

It was Ruth who entered the field of Naomi's distant relative, Boaz, who became enchanted by the young woman; so enchanted that he inquired after her and was told that she had accompanied Naomi back into Bethlehem. Ruth and Naomi hatched a plan for Ruth to seduce Boaz. It worked, and Boaz married Ruth and fathered a child named Obed. In the Bible narrative, women in Bethlehem proclaimed her good fortune.

And the women said unto Naomi, Blessed be the Lord, which hath not left thee this day without a kinsman, that his name may be famous in Israel. And he shall be unto thee a restorer of thy life, and a nourisher of thine old age: for thy daughter in law, which loveth thee, which is better to thee than seven sons, hath born him. (Ruth 4:14–15)

The Bible says that the women named the child and called him a son born to Naomi (Ruth 4:17), instead of a son born unto Boaz or Ruth. Naomi's bitterness began to dissipate, and hope turned into happiness with the marriage of Ruth and Boaz and the birth of their male child. The Bible doesn't say she changed her name back to Naomi, but it also doesn't say that people ever called her Mara.

Rizpah

Perhaps the most dreaded experience a woman has to go through is mourning the death of her child. Rizpah, Saul's concubine, mourned the loss of seven male members of her family after they were murdered by the Gibeonites. Their bodies were left unburied at the beginning of the barley harvests, so that the beasts and vultures could pick the flesh off the bones. This was a terrible violation of the Hebrew ritual treatment of the dead. The ancient Israelites's handling of corpses included a speedy burial—they believed that the soul continued to perceive what was done to the body after death until it was interred. Therefore, it was unthinkable to leave a body unburied as the Gibeonites did to the sons and grandsons of Rizpah. "And Rizpah...took sackcloth, and spread it for her upon the rock from the beginning of harvest until water dropped upon them out of heaven..." (2 Samuel 21:10).

The ancient curse, "May the earth not receive your corpse," finds its parallel in Deuteronomy: "And thy carcass shall be meat unto all fowls of the air, and unto the beasts of the earth, and no man shall fray them away" (28:26). That is why Rizpah, out of love and concern for the souls of the deceased men of her family, undertook her vigil.

To understand why the male members of Rizpah's family were murdered, it is necessary to understand that three years of famine compelled King David to seek answers from God in order to understand why his people were being punished. The Lord told David that Saul and his family were guilty of killing (the ancient word was *smote*) the predecessors of the Gibeonites (the Amorites, some of whom survived to become the Gibeonites) in defiance of a treaty made in the Lord's name between Joshua and the Gibeonites. David went to the Gibeonites and asked them what he could do to make atonement. The Gibeonites didn't want money from the house of Saul, nor did they desire to kill any Israelites. Instead, they asked for seven men from Saul's descendents to be given to them. They told David that they intended to take the men to the mountain (Mount Gilboa, where Saul died) and hang the men before the Lord.

But the King took the two sons of Rizpah the daughter of Aiah, whom she bare unto Saul, Armoni and Mephilbosheth; and the five sons of Michael the daughter of Saul, whom she brought up for Adriel the son of Barzillai the Meholathite: And he delivered them unto the Gibeonites, and they hanged them in the hill before the Lord: and they fell all seven together... (2 Samuel 21:8–9)

Following the revenge killings of two of Rizpah's sons and the five sons of Saul by his wife Merab, Rizpah began a vigil through long days and nights, fending off the wild animals and vultures. The bodies must have bloated, blackened, and withered through the days and weeks, until finally the rains came. The rains were the lifeblood of the earth, ending drought and famine.

Someone told David about Rizpah's loving act, and he took pity upon her. The king arranged for the bodies to be taken down and buried alongside the bones of Jonathan and his father Saul in the family tomb at Zelah, in the territory of Benjamin (2 Samuel 21:14). As so often is the case in acts of war, women like Rizpah bear the burden of sorrow when the babes they carried in their wombs and nursed at the breast die in battle. In Rizpah's case, there wasn't even the honor of battle, just the act of revenge. Yet her love and devotion to her boys saw her through the long days and nights of her mournful vigil.

Thamar

King David's eldest son Amnon, who was heir to the throne, passionately lusted after his stepsister Thamar. A girl of great beauty, Thamar lived with her mother at the royal court of David, although in different quarters than David's other wives, concubines, and serving girls. Following the suggestion of a friend that he should seduce the girl, Amnon pretended he was ill and needed medical attention. When his father visited him, he entreated the king to let Thamar nurse him back to health. So the king sent for Thamar to make Amnon some food and to feed it to him. Once alone with Thamar,

Amnon gave vent to his lustful desire. He said to her, "Come lie with me, my sister." Thamar rebuffed him, saying, "…do not force me; for no such thing ought to be done in Israel: do not thou this folly." She attempted to dissuade him, pointing out that he would be committing an ungodly and foolish act. Then she appealed to his sense of honor over the shame she would have to bear: "And I, whither shall I cause my shame to go?" But Amnon could not control himself; he "…forced her, and lay with her" (2 Samuel 13:11–14).

However, after he had made his conquest, her presence was a constant reminder of his wrongdoing, so he sent her away. Thamar, engulfed in bitter sorrow and probably weeping, encountered her brother Absalom, who coaxed the horrible truth out of her. The king was informed of the unfortunate incident, but levied no chastisement or punishment on his impulsive heir.

QUESTION?

Why didn't David hold his son accountable for the rape of Thamar?
The Bible does not answer that question. The speculative answer might be that perhaps he believed that he and his son were accountable only to God. A powerful and popular king, David was a polygamist with numerous wives and concubines. He committed adultery with Bathsheba, and when she became pregnant, he ordered the murder of her husband.

Absalom took his sister into his home and began to formulate a plan of revenge. He didn't show any outward sign of his anger, but his hatred of Amnon and disrespect for his father festered inside him. For years he waited to avenge his sister, and when the timing was right, he meant to slay Amnon and seize the throne from his father.

Absalom's plan finally began to come together during the annual sheep-shearing festival. There would be the customary first clip of the flocks to be given to the priest, and then a great feast to follow. David sent Amnon to attend the festival in his place. When Amnon had drunk too much wine, Absalom's men overpowered and killed him.

Hearing the dreadful news, David banished Absalom from his court. Absalom used the time away to rally forces in his favor, and to incite discontent with the rule of his father. Then, he found means to return to the good graces of David, all the while secretly plotting to seize the throne. His attempts at a coup failed, however, and Absalom perished.

Absalom was said to be the most beautiful man in David's kingdom. His hair was heavy, luxuriant, and long, but a liability when, during the battle with David's forces in the wood of Ephraim, Absalom's hair became entangled in the branches of an oak tree. As he struggled to extricate himself, his father's general, Joab, thrust three spears through Absalom's chest, instantly killing him.

The Bible says David deeply mourned the loss of his son, and erected a mound of stones at the place where he died. No further mentions are made of Thamar, though it is likely that she, too, mourned the loss of Absalom, the one honorable man who stood up for her.

The Daughters of Amaziah

Amos comes across in the Old Testament as a reluctant prophet. He was a proprietor of flocks and the keeper of sycamore-fig trees who became a prophet during Uzziah's rule as king of Judah, and Jeroboam II's rule of Israel. Amos lived as a simple shepherd in a rural area of the Southern Kingdom. His prophecy was directed at the rulers of Judah and Israel, and the rich and powerful, to keep their religion pure and pursue a course of right action in the name of God, or risk having Israel destroyed (Amos 5:1–15). He was deeply concerned about the plight of the poor and the well-being of the common people.

Amos had a conversation with a priest loyal to Jeroboam II after the latter came to power. The conversation took a prophetic turn when the priest, Amaziah, accused Amos of stirring up dissent against Jeroboam, and told him to stop prophesying. In fact, Amaziah told King Jeroboam that Amos was conspiring against him with the Israelites. Amos told a new prophecy to Amaziah: "Therefore thus saith the Lord; Thy wife shall be an harlot in the city, and thy sons and thy daughters shall fall by the sword, and thy land shall be divided by line; and thou shalt die in a polluted land…" (Amos 7:17).

Amos also said that the Israelites would leave their indigenous land and go into exile. Since Amos made a prophecy about an earthquake that proved true, there was a likelihood that the priest lived to regret his actions. No more mentions are made of the daughters of Amaziah in the Old Testament.

FACT

Jeroboam came to power in 781 B.C. He belonged to the tribe of Ephraim, a powerful tribe among the twelve. He was known to be industrious, bold, and focused. However, his rise to power is not attributed to his own talents and efforts, but the idolatrous practices of Solomon that brought his reign to an end.

The Women of Joppa

The narrative of the women of Joppa is a story of the persecution of the Jews. The ancient Hebrews chafed under the rule of the Seleucid king Antiochus IV Epiphanes, who was Greek. The Hebrews desired to celebrate their cultural and religious ways independent of foreign rule. While they lived in Joppa, they quietly worked in their fields, cared for their flocks, and kept to their own ways; but the Greek king and his generals plotted against the Jews, refusing to let them live in peace. In a terrible act of hatred, the king's soldiers and some of the townspeople of Joppa invited the Jews, their wives, and children to get onto boats for an outing. The unsuspecting Jewish women boarded the boats with their children, who must have been excited to be going out to sea in a boat. The Joppa men steered a course to the open sea and, once there, drowned roughly two hundred Jews. The incident provoked the wrath of the Jewish leader Judas, who organized a night attack upon the town, burning the harbor and boats, and plunging the sword through anyone who had taken refuge near the harbor. The bitterness felt by the women who survived but lost their children must have been terrible. Their story is found in Chapter 12 of 2 Maccabees. The First and Second Book of Maccabees is not included in the Old Testament of the King James Bible, but you can read the narrative of the women of Joppa at: *www .nccbuscc.org/nab/bible/2maccabees/2maccabees12.htm.*

Chapter 10

Beautiful Women of the Bible

Sarah, as seen through Abraham's eyes, was "...a fair woman to look upon" (Genesis 12:11); Rebekah was described as "...very fair to look upon..." (Genesis 24:16); and Bathsheba, desired by King David, was said to be "...very beautiful to look upon" (2 Samuel 11:2). The ancient Hebrews apparently placed higher value on a woman's virtuous character and fertility than on physical beauty, but that's not to say that they didn't "look upon" a woman's beauty with an appreciative eye.

Abigail

Abigail was a woman "...of good understanding, and of a beautiful countenance: but the man [her husband Nabal] was churlish and evil in his doings; and he was of the house of Caleb" (1 Samuel 25:3). So begins the biblical story of Abigail, the attractive wife of Nabal. Her name in Hebrew means "my father is joy." Abigail quietly saved her husband from certain death, then married the king who was about to murder him. Modern writers have portrayed her as beautiful, eloquent, and mismatched in her marriage to the boorish and self-centered Nabal.

Abigail

Abigail and Nabal lived in Maon, which was located in the hills of southern Judea. Nabal owned 3,000 sheep, which he sheared in Carmel. David supported Nabal by supplying security to keep marauding tribes from stealing sheep. As a result, Nabal was prospering. One day, David (who was not yet king) was in the wilderness near Carmel with his men. He heard that Nabal was shearing his sheep nearby. David and his men needed food and water, and he remembered his friendship with Nabal. Nabal, however, either had a lapse of memory or did not wish to honor his friendship with the king, and would not offer him food and water.

When the men returned to David with Nabal's answer, David took 400 soldiers armed with swords and marched straight toward Nabal's house to slice off some heads. A servant who had overheard the plan told Abigail, Nabal's wife. Not only was Abigail beautiful, she was also resourceful, capable, diplomatic, and wise: Abigail quickly considered the options, put together a plan, and implemented a course of action. She pulled together an unbelievable quantity of wine and food for a feast for David and his men, and loaded it on a caravan of donkeys. Then she climbed upon a donkey and headed out through the hills to meet David. She didn't consult Nabal about her plan, nor did she request his permission.

When Abigail saw David, she threw herself at his feet in a sign of deep humility and respect. She offered him food and drink and pleaded with him to forgive Nabal. She asked David to put the blame for the iniquity upon her, arguing that killing her foolish husband wouldn't be prudent. David was won over by her logic, and granted her request. Thus, Abigail saved her husband from the wrath of David and his sword. But the story doesn't end there.

And Nabal answered David's servants, and said, Who is David? and who is the son of Jesse? There be many servants now a days that break away every man from his master. Shall I then take my bread, and my water, and my flesh that I have killed for my shearers, and give it unto men, whom I know not whence they be? (1 Samuel 25:10–11)

Abigail went to Nabal to talk with him, but he was holding a feast in his house and was quite drunk. She waited until morning to speak to him of what she had done. When Abigail told Nabal what had transpired, "…his heart died within him, and he became as a stone. And it came to pass about ten days after, that the Lord smote Nabal, that he died" (1 Samuel 25:37–38).

David must have noticed that Abigail was not only smart, but also quite beautiful. After Nabal died, David sent his servants to Abigail and asked her to become his wife. Abigail accepted his offer, and took five of her attendants to David's house and married him. In time, Abigail gave birth to his son Chileab (2 Samuel 3:3), who was also called Daniel (1 Chronicles 3:1). David, in Hebron, replaced Saul as king. But that did not end Abigail's story.

When the Amalekites (whom King Saul had failed to annihilate when instructed to do so by God) launched raids on the towns of Negev and Ziklag, they took custody of the women there, young and old. They carried off the women, but did not murder them. The Amalekites then burned the city, so that when David and his men arrived, they were devastated. The men with David wept loudly for their wives and daughters. David's two wives, Ahinoam of the Jezreelites and Abigail the wife of Nabal the Carmelite, were among those missing. David and 400 men pursued the Amalekites, coming upon an Egyptian servant of one of the them. The man had fallen ill and had been left for dead. After they fed him and gave him something to drink, the man told them where to find the Amalekites.

And David recovered all that the Amalekites had carried away: and David rescued his two wives. And there was nothing lacking to them, neither small nor great, neither sons nor daughters, neither spoil, nor any thing that they had taken to them: David recovered all. (1 Samuel 30:18–19)

Ahinoam

Two women in the Old Testament were given the name of Ahinoam: the wife of King David who came from Jezreel (who married David before he married Abigail, Nabal's widow); and Ahinoam the daughter of Ahimaaz, who married Saul. Ahinoam may have attracted a man who would be king, but her life was marred by tragedy. Her story is the focus of this section.

Marriage to Israel's First King

Ahinoam's husband Saul was Israel's first king; that made her the Israelite's first queen. Saul ruled from 1020 B.C. to 1000 B.C. The Old Testament book of Samuel states he was the son of Kish, belonged to the Benjamite tribe, and may have been anointed king by the prophet Samuel at Gilgal, although some sources say he may have simply drawn lots or been selected by the majority of a crowd.

Her Husband Falls Out of Favor with God

Saul defeated the Ammonites and started a war with the Philistines. In preparation for his upcoming battle, he made a burnt offering to God, but since such offerings were supposed to be done ritually by a priest, Saul fell out of favor with the Lord (sources note that God's displeasure with Saul was either because of that, or for failing to completely wipe out the Amalikites). This led Samuel to anoint David king in place of Saul.

Ahinoam Produces Heirs

The Bible does not reveal much about Ahinoam's life, apart from her marriage to Saul (Samuel 14:50). The children of Saul included Jonathan, Ishvi, Malchishua, Merab, and Michal. Saul had promised both his daughters to David; however, in the case of Merab, Saul gave her to Adriel the Meholathite. He agreed to let David have Michal as a wife if David first brought him 100 Philistine foreskins (after killing the men first in battle). David met the price for Michal, making Ahinoam his mother-in-law.

QUESTION?

Was Saul Really Samuel?
Some biblical scholars have theorized that a scribe may have tweaked the text of the original book of Samuel. The name of the child born to Hannah and her husband Elkanah may originally have been Saul, and then changed to Samuel. Yet, in a poem in the original book of Samuel (1 Samuel: 2:1–10), Hannah offers God words that, some scholars assert, seem more like praise for a future monarch than the Lord's prophet.

Ahinoam Loses Her Husband and Sons

Saul received a critical wound while waging a battle against the Philistines. As the fighting grew worse, Saul told his armorbearer to run his sword through him so the Philistines couldn't kill him and abuse his body. The soldier could not bring himself to kill Saul, so Saul fell upon his own sword (1 Samuel 31:4). The armorbearer followed his king's example. The next day, the Philistines found not only Saul dead, but also his three sons.

Ahinoam's beauty captivated a king, and she bore him princes, but in the end, she grieved as a mother and widow. As for her son-in-law David, he mourned the passing of Saul in spite of all of the bad feelings between them.

Jemima

Jemima was the first daughter born to Job after God restored him from his tragedies and afflictions. Jemima's father loved and served the Lord for years. Job prospered according to the Old Testament, and maintained a great household. He was well known and respected on both sides of the Euphrates.

The boils afflicting Job may have been leprosy, according to some biblical scholars. The chronic infectious disease, caused by the *Mycobacterium leprae* organism, causes excessive or deficient pigmentation of the skin as well as ulceration, tubercular nodules, loss of fingers and toes, and lack of sensation in certain nerve regions. Leprosy is also known as Hansen's disease, due to the fact that G.A. Hansen discovered it in 1873.

Job and his wife Nahrela produced three daughters and seven sons. Job's prosperity meant that his wife and children had far more free time than others in the Land of Uz, and became indolent and self-indulgent. God allowed Satan to test Job's virtue, piety, and faith, telling Satan that he could take away Job's possessions and cause disease to ravage Job's body, but he could not take away Job's life. The following is a list of Job's tragedies and afflictions:

- The Sabeans took all of Job's donkeys and oxen and murdered the men guarding them.
- Job's sheep were burned along with the shepherds who had watched over them.
- The Chaldeans took Job's camels and killed the servants caring for the animals.
- Job's sons and daughters were in the eldest brother's house eating and drinking when a powerful wind blew down the house, killing all of them.
- Job's body became covered from head to toe with boils.

Job tore his clothes and shaved his head. His wife encouraged him to denounce God and die, but Job continued to have faith in the goodness and omnipotence of God. Three friends visited Job—Elphaz the Temanite, Bildad the Shuhite, and Zophar the Naamathite. They told Job that he must have sinned against God to bring upon himself such calamity. They remained with Job for a period of seven days, perhaps observing a period of mourning for him. To them, Job swore that his intense suffering couldn't be caused by the few little sins that he may have committed; he refused to condemn God for his afflictions.

Finally, a fourth friend, Elihu, arrived and spoke about the moral authority that was God's alone. After the arrival of Elihu, a divine voice from a cloud or whirlwind asked Job if he'd ever had any experience of being responsible for the world in the way that God had. Job said no, but asked for divine forgiveness in the event that he had somehow offended God through a presumption of having such moral authority. Thereafter, God restored Job's good health and blessed him with double the riches and blessings that he previously possessed, including ten new children. His daughters were notable for their exquisite beauty, and were given an inheritance.

He had also seven sons and three daughters. And he called the name of the first, Jemima; and the name of the second, Kezia; and the name of the third, Kerenhappuch. And in all the land were no women found so fair as the daughters of Job: and their father gave them inheritance among their brethren. (Job 42:13–15)

Jezebel

Her name means "unexalted." (See the "Jezebel" entry in Chapter 6.) She was the beautiful daughter of Ethbaal, king of the Phoenicians, and her marriage to Ahab, king of Israel (874 B.C.–853 B.C.), anchored the alliance between the Phoenicians and the Hebrews. In addition to her good looks, Jezebel possessed a strong personality. She zealously introduced the worship of Baal and Astarte to the Hebrews. According to the Bible, at one time she entertained as many as 450 Baal priests at her table.

She is given the blame for undue influence of King Ahab. Perhaps she was too lovely, and he loved her too much, to refuse her anything. Ahab built a pagan temple for the worship of Baal, and permitted idols to be brought into Samaria. His actions prompted the Hebrew prophet Elijah to warn the king that such actions would bring drought upon Israel if the idols and cult of Baal were not destroyed. Of course, that meant that the king would have to defy Jezebel. The outcome of his idolatry and love for Jezebel was a slow death in battle, and evil came upon the houses of his sons after his passing. Ahab's beautiful Jezebel was torn apart by the dogs of Jezreel (1 Kings 21:17–24).

But there was none like unto Ahab, which did sell himself to work wickedness in the sight of the Lord, whom Jezebel his wife stirred up. And he did very abominably in following idols, according to all things as did the Amorites, whom the Lord cast out before the children of Israel. (1 Kings 21:25–26)

A Bible-history Web site details archeological evidence for the existence of Jezebel and Ahab; in particular, an image of the seal of Jezebel and references in other ancient documents. Also, archeologists found plaques of carved ivory where they believe Ahab's palace was located in Samaria, and 1 Kings 22:39 of the Old Testament states he lived in an ivory palace.

Sarah

Sarah, the sensuous, creative, and exquisite daughter of Raguel, was married seven times. Each bridegroom died on his wedding night as he approached Sarah. A demon that loved Sarah, but despised her would-be husbands, had killed each one before the couple could consummate the marriage. The ridicule and scorn of others made Sarah long for her own death.

Tobit, a blind man of great piety and love for God, had a son named Tobiah. The boy's destiny was to marry Sarah, a near relative. One day, Tobiah left his home accompanied by the angel Raphael, who appeared as a man and called himself Azariah. As Tobiah and Raphael approached a river, a large fish jumped up and tried to swallow Tobiah's foot. The angel told him to catch the fish and then remove the gall, heart, and liver and put them aside; Tobiah would need them later. Raphael told him that the heart and liver could be burned to banish a demon, and that the gall, once rubbed onto the eyes of a man with cataracts, would restore eyesight.

FACT

The Book of Tobit, that reveals the story of Sarah and Tobiah, was most likely written in the early second century B.C. It is not included in the Old Testament of the King James Bible, but is found in other versions of the Bible, including the Saint Joseph edition of The New American Bible. The popular story teaches about Jewish piety and morality, and is anchored in oriental folklore.

Raphael reminded Tobiah that they would stop at the house of Raguel, father of Sarah, for the night. There Raphael would ask the girl's father for Tobiah's right to claim her in marriage. Raphael reminded Tobiah that he had promised his father that he would marry a woman from his own family, and he had the right to choose Sarah, his closest relative.

When Tobiah and Raphael arrived at the house of Raguel, they were greeted by Raguel and his wife Edna, along with their daughter Sarah. When Raguel inquired about Tobiah's father, Tobit, and was told that the old man had gone blind, they all wept.

A Marriage Contract Is Made

Raguel agreed to let Sarah marry Tobiah, but fully disclosed what had happened to her other bridegrooms. He had a scroll brought in and wrote a marriage contract for Tobiah and Sarah. He told Tobiah that after they were married, he should take Sarah and return with her to his father's home to live. Raguel must have been a pragmatist, because even as he went forward with the wedding preparations, he ordered his servants to dig a grave so that when Tobiah died, they could bury him without anyone knowing.

Tobiah Burns the Fish Liver and Heart

Tobiah, remembering the counsel of Raphael about purging a demon, burned the fish liver and heart on some incense embers before taking his wife to bed. The smell was awful, and caused the demon to depart to the desert of Upper Egypt (where it was believed demons dwelled).

Tobiah and his new wife prayed, then crawled into bed to consummate their marriage. When the maid found the couple asleep together, she ran and told Raguel that Tobiah had not died. Raguel and Edna fell to their knees and began praising God. Afterward, Raguel told his servants to quickly go and fill in the grave they had dug.

The Wedding Is Celebrated with a Great Feast

Raguel and Edna made a huge feast, and made Tobiah promise that he would remain with them for fourteen days. After that time, the young man could take half of whatever Raguel owned and return to his father with Sarah. Raguel went on to explain that when he and his wife Edna died, Tobiah would receive the remainder of the inheritance.

In the Book of Tobit, Raphael finally revealed his identity as one of the seven angels who eternally serve God. The Bible mentions two others: Michael, whose name appears in the books of Deuteronomy, Jude, and Revelation; and Gabriel, found in Deuteronomy and the Gospel of Luke.

Upon returning home, Tobiah took out the fish gall and rubbed it onto his father's eyes. Using both hands, he then peeled off the cataracts that were the cause of the blindness. The old man looked upon his son, threw his arms around him, and began to praise God. All of the Jews who lived in Nineveh joined Tobit and Anna as they celebrated the marriage of young Tobiah and Sarah for seven days.

Susanna

Susanna was the daughter of Hilkiah. Among the lovely ladies of the Old Testament, this woman was said to have been extremely beautiful and pious. She lived with her husband Joakim, a rich Jew who occupied a place of honor in Babylon. Jews came every day to the house of Joakim, where cases were heard and judged. After the people left each day, Susanna would walk about in the fine garden that adjoined Joakim's house. Two elders, who had been appointed as judges and who held daily court in Joakim's house, began to feel uncontrollable lust for Susanna.

The Judges Confess Their Lust

The two judges told no one (not even each other) of the mounting lust they felt for Susanna as they watched her move about in her garden. One day, they said goodbye to each other at high noon and went their separate ways to have lunch. But suddenly, each man turned back. Meeting up again, both insisted on knowing the reason why the other had returned to Joakim's house. Each finally confessed to the other his desire for Susanna.

A Plan Is Hatched to Seduce Susanna

The two judges waited for an opportunity to seduce the beautiful girl. One hot afternoon, Susanna sent her maids to fetch olive oil and ointments, and told them to shut the garden doors for privacy while she bathed. What she and the maids did not know was that the two judges were hiding in the garden.

Susanna Understands She Is Trapped

When the maids had left and the gates were shut and locked, the men revealed their presence to Susanna. Both confessed their desire to lie with her. She quickly understood her precarious situation: If she agreed to do what the men wanted, she would be put to death; if she did not agree, then she would be at their mercy (since they were judges). Susanna refused their advances and screamed. Her cries for help brought the maids and the villagers to the garden, where the men spoke against her.

The Locals Gather to Hear the Case

The house of Joakim became crowded with people. The two judges were there, along with the villagers. Susanna appeared with her children, parents, and other relatives. The men laid out their case against Susanna. They said they were out of sight in the garden when she came and dismissed her maids. Then she lay with a young man who had been in hiding. Upon seeing her indiscretion, the two judges said that they ran to capture the young man, but he was strong and got away.

Susanna Receives the Death Sentence

Those assembled believed the two judges and condemned Susanna to death. She cried out to God that the men had given false evidence against her. As the people led her away, the Holy Spirit came down upon a young man named Daniel, who shouted that he wanted no part in shedding the innocent blood of Susanna. He told those assembled that they were foolish not to hear all of the facts before rushing to judgment.

Daniel Traps the Two Judges

Daniel separated the two judges (perhaps so they could not support each other's version of the events). He then asked the first judge to tell him under what kind of tree he had seen Susanna and her lover being intimate. The man replied that it was a mastic tree. There must not have been a mastic tree in the garden, for Daniel pronounced that the angel of God would thereupon cut the man's head in two. He put the same question to the second judge, and was told the tree was an evergreen oak—another lie.

Both men were put to death that day. After that day, Daniel became highly respected among the people of Babylon. Beautiful Susanna's ordeal was over, and her spotless reputation remained intact.

Chapter 11

Women Who Were Queens

In ancient Hebrew society, a queen was not so much a ruler as a king's wife. The Aramaic word for queen was *shegal* (meaning "queen-consort" or "queen-wife"). Such a queen had the ear of her husband (sometimes passing along her insights), but she also had responsibilities toward her children. She would instill her religious beliefs and moral values in her sons and daughters. In ancient times, as now, women taught their children largely through example. But some queens were better exemplars than others.

Azubah

Azubah was the daughter of Shilhi and the wife of King Asa of Judah. She bore him a son named Jehoshaphat. When her husband died after forty-one years of rule, Queen Azubah proudly stood by as Jehoshaphat succeeded his father to the throne as the fourth king of Judah. His father Asa had been the third, his grandfather Abijah had been the second ruler of Judah, and his great-grandfather Rehoboam had been the first ruler of the region after the kingdom was divided into Israel and Judah. The Bible reveals much more about Jehoshaphat and Asa than it does about Azubah, but mentions of her are found in 1 Kings 22:42 and 2 Chronicles 20:31. Her name in Hebrew means "forsaken."

She must have instilled her religious values and those of his father in her son, because most biblical and apocryphal sources state that Jehoshaphat was a good and noble king who stayed close to the course his father had set for Judah. He established an accord with the king of Israel that brought peace to both nations.

Jehoshaphat was thirty and five years old when he began to reign: and he reigned twenty and five years in Jerusalem. And his mother's name was Azubah the daughter of Shilhi. And he walked in all the ways of Asa his father…doing that which was right in the eyes of the Lord…And Jehoshaphat made peace with the king of Israel. (1 Kings 22:42–44)

The Bible notes that Jehoshaphat "…walked in all the ways of his father…"; it doesn't say, as it does elsewhere for other princes who became king, that he walked in the sins of his father, and positive contributions of princes' mothers are seldom mentioned. Some kings set bad examples for their sons, taking many wives and having numerous concubines. Solomon, for example, supposedly had 1,000 women in his harem (1 Kings 11:3). But Jehoshaphat's father Asa was a good king, and showed a zealousness in ridding Judah of idols, even kicking out Ma'acah, the queen mother, because of her worship of Baal and Asherah.

From her royal position, Ma'acah encouraged the worship of idols. She had even turned a grove into a place of idol worship, and had erected an outrageous object there to venerate Asherah. King Asa, husband of Azubah, had that idol burned in the Kidron Valley (1 Kings 15:13–14). No other mention is made of Azubah.

QUESTION?

How much power did a queen mother in biblical times possess?
"Malketha" is the biblical word for mother of the king. A queen mother wielded enormous power and influence. Her position in the court was an exalted position, and carried with it social and political importance. Examples of queen mothers and their sons include Bathsheba and Adonijah, Nehushta and Jehoiachin, and Ma'acah and Asa.

Queen Esther

Esther

Esther is one of the most recognized Jewish heroines of the Old Testament, and she is one of only two women in the Old Testament to have a book bearing her name (the other is Ruth). Hadassah, her birth name, means "myrtle," but Esther derives from the Persian word *satarah*, which means "star." Esther, a stunning beauty, was a smart and courageous young woman of the tribe of Benjamin. Following the death of Esther's father, her cousin Mordecai raised her as his own daughter.

Mordecai told her not to remain quiet about being a Jew. There were those in the kingdom who hated Jews, including advisors to the king. One day, Esther was taken into the harem of King Ahasuerus.

The king felt an immediate attraction to her. After he had banished Queen Vashti, the king came to love Esther more than all of the other women available to him. Not knowing Esther was Jewish, King Ahasuerus made her his queen. The book of Esther details her story and makes note of her remarkable courage.

Go, gather together all the Jews that are present in Shushan, and fast ye for me, and neither eat nor drink three days, night or day: I also and my maidens will fast likewise; and so will I go in unto the king, which is not according to the law: and if I perish, I perish. (Esther 4:16)

Haman Planned to Exterminate the Jews

The king's prime minister was named Haman. He was an egotistical and self-aggrandizing man, who hated Esther's uncle Mordecai because the Jew would not bow before him. Haman sought a way to eliminate Mordecai and all of his kind. He went to King Ahasuerus and complained that there were people (the Hebrews) in his realm who did not follow the laws of the king, and that the king should no longer tolerate them. "If it please the king, let it be written that they may be destroyed: and I will pay ten thousand talents of silver to the hands of those that have the charge of the business, to bring it into the king's treasuries. And the king took his ring from his hand, and gave it unto Haman, the son of Hammedatha the Agagite, the Jews' enemy" (Esther 3:9–10).

Haman Refined His Plot

The decree, sealed with the king's ring, went out all over the palace and into every province. Haman's plan was to draw lots in order to determine which day to carry out the massacre of the Jewish people. When word reached Mordecai, he covered himself in ashes and a sackcloth, and sat near the king's gate.

Esther Fasted for Three Days

Esther's heart sank whenever she saw her uncle, but she understood the gravity of the situation: Haman had secured the king's decree to pay 10,000 talents of gold. Mordecai went to Esther and asked her to seek the audience of the king. Once she had his attention, she had to try to thwart Haman's plan to massacre the Jews. What Mordecai had asked Esther to do could have gotten her killed; no one could have an audience with the king unless summoned. Esther, not sure of what to do, undertook a fast for three days.

FACT

The Jewish holiday of Purim is celebrated each year in February or March, in memory of the averted pogrom of the Jews thanks to Esther and her uncle Mordecai. The holy festival is observed with a feast and expressions of joy. Noise is made to drown out the name of Haman as the story is retold. The fasting part of the festival is called the Fast of Esther.

The King Sided with Esther and Her People

Esther must have had a knot in the pit of her stomach as she entered the king's presence. But instead of anger, the king was happy to see her. He promised to give her half his kingdom, whatever she wanted. She invited him and Haman to a banquet that she had prepared.

Esther had captured the king's heart, and when she revealed Haman's plan to exterminate the Jews, including her and her uncle Mordecai (who had previously saved the king's life when two guards had tried to assassinate him), he ordered the death of Haman and his ten sons upon the very gallows that Haman had prepared for Mordecai. The king then made Mordecai prime minister, and granted the Hebrew people the right to mount a defense for themselves when necessary. This enabled a series of attacks by the Jews against their enemies throughout the empire.

Hephzibah

The meaning of Hephzibah is "my delight is in her." She was the wife of King Hezekiah, the thirteenth reigning monarch of Judah, and the mother of Manasseh. Hephzibah's son would assume the throne when he was only twelve, and would reign for fifty-five years (2 Kings 21:1). So Hephzibah was to remain in the royal household for a very long time, guiding her son and, perhaps, her grandchildren.

Archeological evidence supports the historicity of the reign of Hephzibah's husband Hezekiah. The evidence consists of storage-jar handle seals unearthed in modern Israel. Scholars call them LMLK (pronounced *lamelekh*, "belonging to the king") seals. The jar handles with seals were excavated in a layer of earth, or strata, associated with the destruction of Judah by Sennacherib, King of Assyria, during Hezekiah's twenty-nine-year reign (2 Kings 18:13).

Some sources assert that Manasseh, the teenager, may have coreigned with Hezekiah for some years. During his solo rule, however, Manasseh did many things that went against the beliefs and policies of his father. While Hezekiah was considered a good and fair king who instituted many religious reforms, including stamping out idolatry, his son undid much accomplished during his father's reign. Manasseh built altars for the worship of Baal (just as Ahab, king of Israel, had done before him), and Manasseh dealt with familiar spirits (a euphemistic phrase meaning he used necromancers and wizards to call forth the dead). His many evil actions angered the Lord (2 Kings 21:2–9).

Hephzibah's husband is one of the kings mentioned in the New Testament Gospel of Matthew in relation to the genealogy of Jesus. The name in that gospel, however, is spelled "Ezekias" (Matthew 1:10). Hezekah instituted many reforms during his reign: He destroyed the shrines used for idol worship, including the bronze serpent associated with Moses, since the Israelites were worshipping it (2 Kings 18:4); he consolidated the worship and veneration of God (Yahweh) in Jerusalem, while censoring such worship at the many shrines outside of Jerusalem and elsewhere in Judea (2 Kings 18:22); and he invited all of the tribes of Israel, wherever they were scattered, to undertake an annual pilgrimage to Jerusalem to observe the traditional Passover celebration (2 Chronicles 30:5, 13).

Nehushta

Nehushta was the daughter of Elnathan ben Achbor of Jerusalem. She married Jehoiakim, the king of Judah (2 Kings 24:8), and became the mother of Jehoichin. Her son became king when he was eighteen years old, in circa 598 B.C., upon the death of his father, but he only ruled in Jerusalem for three months.

Most sources assert that Nehushta was a minor character in the Old Testament; more attention is given to her husband Jehoiakim, who was the eldest son of Josiah, and her son. She went into Babylonian captivity when Nebuchadnezzar, king of Babylon, lay siege to Jehoiakim's kingdom and exiled and imprisoned the ruling royal family.

Jehoiachin was eighteen years old when he began to reign, and he reigned in Jerusalem three months. And his mother's name was Nehushta, the daughter of Elnathan of Jerusalem. And he did that which was evil in the sight of the Lord…And Nebuchadnezzar king of Babylon came against the city, and his servants did besieged it…And he carried away Jehoiachin to Babylon… (2 Kings 24:8–9, 24:11, 24:15)

When Nebuchadnezzar died, Nehushta and her relatives received their freedom, and treatment befitting a royal family.

Queen of Sheba

An account of the Queen of Sheba's story can be found in the Ethiopian *Kebra Negast* (The Glory of Kings). See *www.sacred-texts.com/chr/kn*. Other references to the Queen of Sheba are found in the Qur'an. Hers is one of the most popular of all of the biblical stories about women, although it is also quite a short account. The Old Testament devotes thirteen verses to her in 1 Kings 10:1–13 (which is repeated in 2 Chronicles 9:1–12). Various names she has been called include Bilqis (Islamic), Nikaule, and Makeda (Ethiopian).

> In the tenth century, the Queen of Sheba ruled over an ancient kingdom along the Red Sea, known as Abyssinia. It is found today in modern Ethiopia or Yemen. Archeologists have been digging in the Nigerian rainforest at Eredo, near what may have been her gravesite.

The Queen of Sheba had heard many tales of the greatness of Solomon, and decided to make a trip from Sheba to Jerusalem to visit the king and test him with "...hard questions" (1 Kings 10:1). The Jewish historian Josephus, who lived during Jesus' lifetime, noted the Queen of Sheba's intense love of knowledge.

The Queen Arrives in Grand Style

The Bible says she arrived in Jerusalem with a "very great train," suggestive of a caravan, loaded with gifts and an entourage to serve her during her stay. She must have been very rich, because she had brought along precious stones and spices (1 Kings 10:1–11), and 120 talents of gold that she intended to give to Solomon (1 Kings 10:10).

The Queen Observes Solomon and His Surroundings

The Queen of Sheba noticed every detail of King Solomon and his house: the feast spread upon his table and the number of servants he kept (and their well-being), as well as the clothing worn by his ministers and cupbearers. In short, nothing about the king and his life escaped her notice. She asked him many riddles, and Solomon must have answered them to her satisfaction, for she told him that all that she had heard about him was true.

Solomon and the Queen of Sheba Commune

She may have been quite beautiful. The biblical account states that the Queen "...communed with him of all that was in her heart" (1 Kings 10:2–3). He also held nothing back. She lavished him with gifts. In turn, he gave her "...all her desire, whatsoever she asked, beside that which Solomon gave her of his royal bounty" (1 Kings 10:13). Some sources assert that this could be a euphemistic phrase for a physical relationship. Haile Selassie, the last emperor of Ethiopia, who lived from 1892 to1975, purportedly claimed to be a descendent of the Queen of Sheba by way of Menelik I, son of King Solomon and the Queen of Sheba. Menelik I began the Ethiopian royal dynasty.

Did Solomon Love the Queen of Sheba?

Solomon, who kept many wives and concubines, may have fallen in love with the Queen of Sheba. She worshipped the Sun, but some modern scholars have suggested that her relationship with Solomon might account for the introduction of Judaism into Ethiopia. Some sources suggest that she may have been the female lover in The Song of Songs (meaning the greatest of songs), attributed to Solomon. In the opening of that lyrical work of poetry, which describes the courtship and marriage traditions of the author's time, the female lover makes a declaration.

The Queen of Sheba

The Song of Songs, according to many scholars, is not about one man's love for a woman, but really about the mutual love of God and his people. The author simply uses the device of human love to describe the relationship between the two entities.

Of all the ancient queens, the Queen of Sheba (or the Queen of the South as she is called in Matthew 12:42) managed to capture popular interest through the ages. Images of her appeared in twelfth- and thirteenth-century cathedral art at Canterbury, Strasbourg, Chartres, Rochester, and Amiens. She was the subject of numerous books, fine art, a ballet, and no less than three operas: *Solomon* (Georg Friederic Händel), *Reine de Saba* (Charles Gounod), and *Die Konigin von Saba* (Karl Goldmark).

Let him kiss me with the kisses of his mouth: for thy love is better than wine… the king hath brought me into his chambers…I am black, but comely, O ye daughters of Jersusalem, as the tents of Kedar, as the curtains of Solomon. (The Song of Solomon 1:2, 4–5)

Vashti

King Ahasueras put aside his wife Vashti, daughter of Belshazzar, to marry Esther after Vashti refused to parade herself naked except for her crown. The king had been drinking and feasting with his subjects for seven days, the Bible says, before he decided to have Queen Vashti demonstrate her beautiful attributes. When Vashti refused to be paraded about as a sex object through the drunken crowd, the king became furious.

Ahasueras Banished Her

The king called together his advisors to ask what he should do. They told him to put her away and to never allow her in his sight again (which possibly meant to banish or behead her). Vashti's banishment was dwarfed by the emergence of Esther in the king's life. Esther became empowered and saved the Jewish people from certain massacre.

The Plot Thickened

The king and Haman behaved badly toward both Vashti and Esther. The king acted foolishly in wanting to parade his wife naked in front of his court. Haman behaved evilly for wanting to kill Mordecai and all of the Jews. In terms of power, Vashti, a nonJewish woman, became powerless when her husband took the counsel of his advisors. He then became enamored of Esther. When the king saw Esther's beauty, and heard her heartfelt plea on behalf of the Hebrew people, he ordered the death of Haman.

How Did the Talmudic Writers Portray Vasthti?

The Talmud states that Queen Vashti made Jewish women remove their clothes and work for her on Shabbat (the Hebrew Sabbath). Further, she refused to comply with the king's summons because she was afflicted with *tzaraat* (a skin disease). She was cruel to Jewish women who served her, and was arrogant, putting down the king with sharp words when he had summoned her. Those two factors sealed her fate.

QUESTION?

Was Vashti cursed?
Midrashic literature (texts written by learned rabbis to explain discrepancies in the Bible) asserts that Vashti was cursed. She acquired the curse through the actions of her Babylonian grandfather, King Nebuchadnezzar, when he destroyed Solomon's Temple and forced the Jews into exile. In many places in the Old Testament, the sins of the parent are borne by later generations.

The Legacy of Vashti for Modern Women

Modern feminists say that Vashti was not a villain, but a valiant heroine and model of virtue. Although Queen Esther is considered the important biblical character to remember during Purim, some Jewish scholars suggest studying both women's roles to understand how both could be celebrated as heroines of the festival.

For Vashti and other queens in biblical times, a glorious and privileged life could shift in a heartbeat: a wife who was a queen might suddenly discover that she had fallen out of favor with the king because of something she had done (or refused to do). She then faced dire consequences, even death.

Chapter 12

Women Healed by Jesus and the Apostles

It is not surprising that many women who felt disenfranchised and cast out by the patriarchal society in which they lived became ardent believers and supporters of Jesus. He treated women in an egalitarian way; He showed them love, kindness, and respect; He healed them of their diseases and afflictions; He invited them to become his followers. His fame soon spread, not just among women, but among all people, of all ages, and all walks of life.

Jairus's Daughter

Jairus was a powerful man, "…and he was a ruler of the synagogue…" (Luke 8:41). Jairus and his wife had only one child, a girl of twelve, who had fallen ill and lay dying. Word had come to him that Jesus had the power to heal, so he sought out Jesus' help. A throng had gathered around Jesus on the way to the house of Jairus. Before Jesus had entered the house with his host, a servant came to tell Jairus that his daughter had died; it seemed that Jesus had arrived too late.

QUOTE

But when Jesus heard it, he answered him, saying, Fear not: believe only, and she shall be made whole. And when he came into the house, he suffered no man to go in, save Peter, and James, and John, and the father and the mother of the maiden. And all wept, and bewailed her: but he said, Weep not; she is not dead, but sleepeth. (Luke 8:50–52)

No one in the room believed Jesus. When they laughed and scorned him, he made them all leave. Alone with the girl, he took her by the hand and said, "*Talitha koum,*" which means, "Little girl, I say to you, get up." The King James Bible gives Jesus' statement and the interpretation of his spoken words: "*Talitha cumi*; which is, being interpreted, Damsel, I say unto thee, arise" (Mark 5:41).

The Gospel of Luke reveals, "And her spirit came again, and she arose straightway…" (Luke 8:55). Jesus told those gathered to give her something to eat. Her parents were astonished. Perhaps, filled with gratitude, they kissed Jesus' feet or thanked him and offered to pay him or do something noble for him; the biblical account in Luke doesn't say. It only says that Jesus told them that they should tell no one about what he'd done. Word about Jesus' miraculous healing of others had spread, and the crowds had begun to follow him wherever he went, and he had begun to seek out isolated places where he could pray and be alone.

Joanna, Wife of Chuza

The canonical gospel accounts are not explicit about the miracle wrought by Jesus upon Joanna, wife of Chuza. She is mentioned as being among some women who had been traveling with Jesus and the twelve disciples. Presumably, some of the women had been healed by Jesus of "evil spirits and infirmities," since the passage in Luke states that among them was, "…Mary called Magdalene, out of whom went seven devils, And Joanna the wife of Chuza Herod's steward, and Susanna, and many others, which ministered unto him of their substance" (8:2–3).

The canonical gospel of Mark, widely considered the earliest of the gospels to have been written, contains the story of Jairus's daughter with traces of Aramaic, the language used by Jesus. That finding supports the story's existence in a very early oral tradition, long before the gospel writers wrote it for a Greek-speaking audience (as they did for most of the narratives of the New Testament).

Joanna's name means "God's gift." Some sources suggest that it's simply a variation of Anna, a name that means "favor or grace." She was married to Chuza, steward in the service of Herod Antipas (he was likely in charge of Herod's treasury or finances). Herod the Great, the father of Herod Antipas, tried to have Jesus killed when he was an infant. Joanna had become a disciple of Jesus. She and some of the other women may have financed his ministry "of their substance." Most scholars agree that the phrase means financial help that might include renting rooms (perhaps the upper room used at the Last Supper) and procuring food and other items that the group might need. As the wife of Chuza, who would have received a substantial salary in his position as Herod's steward, Joanna could have afforded a luxurious lifestyle. Instead, as a believer and follower of Jesus, she chose to throw her money into the group's treasury to be used as needed for the Lord's ministry. She followed him as he traveled throughout the villages, cities, and countryside of Judea and Galilee. Chuza must also have embraced Jesus' teachings, or he would have refused to allow Joanna to use their money and her time for Jesus' work. He also didn't prevent her from traveling with Jesus.

Joanna had walked with other women believers who, according to the Gospel of Luke, discovered the empty tomb on the morning after the resurrection of Jesus. The women had brought spices to anoint the body of Jesus after he had been crucified. When they arrived in the garden where his tomb was located, they discovered the large stone covering the mouth of the tomb had been rolled away. Two men stood by in shining garments, and asked the women why they were searching for the living among the dead. They reminded the women to remember the words Jesus spoke about being delivered into the hands of sinful men to be crucified, and how he would then arise on the third day.

And they remembered his words, And returned from the sepulchre, and told all these things unto the eleven, and to all the rest. It was Mary Magdalene and Joanna, and Mary the mother of James, and other women that were with them, which told these things unto the apostles. (Luke 24:8–10)

Joanna, as a faithful follower of Jesus, was probably among the group of followers who selected Matthias to replace Judas. When everyone gathered on Pentecost, fifty days after the resurrection of Christ, Joanna may also have been with them, and thus would have received the gifts of the Holy Spirit. Some icons in the orthodox tradition show her with a box (for spices and unguents), a traditional image found in the icons of Mary Magdalene, the best-known myrrhbearer.

Peter's Mother-in-Law

One of the earliest miracles recorded in the New Testament involved Simon Peter's mother-in-law, who had taken ill with a fever. She was in bed when Jesus arrived with Simon Peter for a visit to the latter's home in Capernaum. The synoptic gospels of Matthew, Mark, and Luke all record the miracle healing of Peter's mother-in-law. In Matthew 8:14, the text states that when Jesus entered the house, he saw Peter's mother-in-law lying sick with fever. Mark and Luke state that Jesus left the synagogue and entered the house of Simon and Andrew with two other disciples (James and John), and they told Jesus that Simon Peter's mother-in-law was sick with fever. Matthew states that Jesus took her hand, and the fever left her and she rose and served him (Matthew 8:15).

QUESTION?

What are the synoptic Gospels?
The New Testament Gospels of Matthew, Mark, and Luke are similar in content. Scholars say that this suggests that the writers of those accounts relied on the same source material. Side by side, some passages of the synoptic gospels appear to be nearly identical, while the Gospel of John is quite different in structure, content, and style.

The account in Mark 1:31 states that Jesus took her hand and lifted her up, and the fever left her and she served them. Luke 4:39 says, "And he stood over her, and rebuked the fever; and it left her: and immediately she arose and ministered unto them." The point is made (almost verbatim) in all three accounts that the woman was quite ill, consumed with a debilitating fever; in the presence of Jesus, and by his touch, she was healed. In fact, she felt so well that she was then able to serve the men (perhaps cook for them).

Susanna

Susanna was one of many women mentioned in the New Testament gospels. Some of their stories illustrate a teaching or truth, while others' names are simply included in a list of other named women. Susanna falls into the latter category. She is mentioned in the Gospel of Luke 8:2–3 along with Mary Magdalene, Joanna wife of Chuza, and many others. These women appear in Luke during the telling of Jesus moving through every city and village preaching about the kingdom of God. Wherever he traveled, the group of women traveled with him. These women, the gospel notes, "…had been healed of evil spirits and infirmities…" (Luke 8:2).

Susanna may have been sharing her faith with others while she traveled with Jesus. The gospels do not say if she was married or if she was related to Jesus or one of his followers. She was probably respected and wealthy, since she was included in the group of women who had been healed by Jesus and supported his teaching.

Slave Girl Freed from a Divining Spirit

You read about this young woman in Chapter 6. Her powers of foretelling the future brought a nice income for her owners, but when the girl realized that apostles of Jesus were in her community, the girl (in what must have been an act of desperation to be freed of the demon possession) began to follow Paul everywhere he went. Paul became so annoyed that he turned to her, and in the name of Jesus Christ, commanded the spirit possessing the girl to come out, which the demon did (Acts 16:18).

Acts 9:42–43 states, "And it was known throughout all Joppa; and many believed in the Lord. And it came to pass, that he tarried many days in Joppa with one Simon a tanner." That Peter stayed with a tanner is an important point, since Jews considered the work of tanning an unclean occupation.

The owners of the slave girl brought charges against Paul and Silas, and the two were imprisoned. Not long afterward, an earthquake shook open the cell doors, freeing the bonds of Paul and the other prisoners. To see an image of the cave where Paul and Silas were imprisoned for casting the demon from the slave girl, visit *www.biblestudy.org/biblepic/philpris.html*.

Tabitha

Tabitha (also called Dorcas, meaning "gazelle") lived in the city of Joppa, approximately thirty-four miles from Jerusalem, where she was a follower of Jesus. The first mention of her is in Acts, which states that Tabithawas a woman "...full of good works and almsdeeds which she did. And it came to pass in those days, that she was sick, and died..." (9:36–37). Many widows cried over the loss of the woman who, among other things, made cloaks for the poor.

Her body was placed in an upper room, so that it might be washed with water and smeared with aromatic oil in preparation for burial. Some of the disciples of Jesus in Joppa knew that Peter was nearby, in the city of Lydda. They sent two men to entreat him to come to Joppa. It's unclear whether the disciples thought Peter might attend Tabitha's funeral, or if he might perform a miracle upon the lifeless body.

Joppa was located on the coast of the Mediterranean Sea. It served as an ancient Palestinian seaport for the holy city of Jerusalem, which was only thirty-four miles away. Lydda was roughly eleven or twelve miles southeast and inland.

Peter went to Joppa. Perhaps he heard the widows wailing through the windows of the upper room. Perhaps they were wearing some of the clothing Tabitha had sewn. Some sources say she was noted for making not only cloaks, but undergarments and outer garments as well. The widows showed Peter the cloaks. How could he not be moved by the loving work this woman had done for the poor in her community?

Peter, just as Jesus had done when he raised Jairus's daughter from the dead, asked everyone to leave the room. He knelt and prayed. Then, using the words that Jesus had used with the child of Jairus, Peter said, "Tabitha, arise" (Acts 9:40), and she opened her eyes. Finally, as Jesus had also done, Peter gave the woman his hand and lifted her up. He called the people in the house and presented Tabitha to them...alive.

Woman with the Issue of Blood

The story of the woman with an issue of blood is revealed in the Gospel of Mark, Chapter 5. As people gathered around Jesus, pressing in on him, one woman could not touch him. She was considered unclean because she had a bleeding problem. It had persisted for twelve years, and despite spending all of the money she had on doctors, she still suffered.

The ancient Hebrews had many purity laws governing the issue of blood. The Book of Leviticus, Chapter 15, is devoted to explanations of impurities, including the issue of blood, and the rituals and rules of purification.

And if a woman have an issue, and her issue...be blood, she shall be put apart seven days: and whosoever toucheth her shall be unclean until the even. And every thing that she lieth upon in her separation shall be unclean: every thing also that she sitteth upon shall be unclean. And whosoever toucheth her bed shall wash his clothes, and bathe himself in water, and be unclean until the even. (Leviticus 15:19–22)

The New Testament woman with the twelve-year issue of blood had tremendous faith that Jesus could heal her. So great was her faith, that she believed one touch of his clothing would cure her problem (Mark 5:28). That explains why the woman joined the crowd thronging around Jesus and his disciples during their walk toward the house of Jairus, and in a final act of desperation reached out for the man many called the Messiah.

Jairus, a powerful official in the synagogue, had begged Jesus to go to his house and heal his sick daughter. While Jesus walked with Jairus and some of his disciples (Peter, John, and James, among them), the crowd jostled around and pushed in, trying to get near the Lord. From somewhere behind Jesus, the woman with the issue of blood approached, and got close enough to stretch forth her fingers. Now the Hebrews had many rules governing ritual purity, and Jesus knew immediately when she touched him that the virtue (some texts say "power") had gone from him (Mark 5:30) and, in the eyes of the Jewish officials, he had become unclean.

The Disciples Do Not Know Who Touched Jesus

Jesus' disciples told him that it was impossible to know who touched him. They told him that there was a large crowd all around him. They wondered how Jesus could even ask such a question, when anyone there could have done it.

The Woman Confesses

The woman with the issue of blood stepped up, though she was probably afraid. This man of God had divine power to bring about the healing she so desperately sought, and yet to be in the presence of the power of God must have given her some anxiety. Still, she stepped forward and fell at Jesus' feet. There, she trembled and told him she had touched his garment. She explained why, though it must have been exceedingly embarrassing for her to speak of it publicly.

Jesus Lovingly Responds to Her

The Gospel of Mark reveals that Jesus did not berate her or speak to her sternly; he was not angry or offended. He simply said, "Daughter, thy faith hath made thee whole; go in peace, and be whole of thy plague" (Mark 5:34). The Gospel of Luke also presents the story of that woman and states that Jesus said to her upon hearing her confession, "Daughter, be of good comfort: thy faith hath made thee whole; go in peace" (Luke 8:48). Jesus doesn't say he healed her or that his garment healed her, but that her own faith had ended her misery and made her whole.

The gospels are full of stories of miraculous healings by Jesus, effected through touch and words and prayers. Does that mean that everyone who asked for a miraculous healing from the disciples of Christ were made whole, like the women in this chapter? The answer is no. The Gospel of Mark makes the point that it was difficult when the faith of the people was not strong. "And he went out from thence, and came into his own country; and his disciples follow him. And when the sabbath day was come, he began to teach in the synagogue: and many hearing him were astonished, saying, From whence hath this man these things? and what wisdom is this which is given unto him, that even such mighty works are wrought by his hands? Is not this the carpenter, the son of Mary, the brother of James, and Joses, and of Juda, and Simon? and are not his sisters here with us? And they were offended at him" (Mark 6:1–3).

But Jesus, the gospel stated, answered them "A prophet is not without honor, but in his own country, and among his own kin, and in his own house" (Mark 6:4). The next verse reveals that Jesus "…could there do no mighty work, save that he laid his hands upon a few sick folk, and healed them. And he marvelled because of their unbelief" (Mark 6:5–6).

The laying on of hands and praying over the sick is an ages-old practice. The disciples of Jesus, however, were not always able to perform miracles. Jesus explained why his disciples could not heal a boy whose father pleaded with them for help. The father said to Jesus, "And I besought thy disciples to cast him out; and they could not. And Jesus answering said, O faithless and perverse generation, how long shall I be with you, and suffer you?" (Luke 9:40–41).

QUESTION?

What gain is made through suffering? The Book of Psalms offers one answer: "It is good for me that I have been afflicted; that I might learn thy statutes" (Psalm 119:71). The Apostle Paul endured an affliction despite three separate pleas to the Lord from Paul. He was told that the Lord's power was made perfect in weakness, and he would have grace to endure.

Jesus finally reached the house of Jairus. The Bible doesn't say whether he went through any kind of ritual purification after encountering the woman with the blood issue, before entering the room of a dying child. He was a Jew, and in the opinion of the Jewish rabbis, he wouldn't have been exempt from having to undergo the rituals necessary to purify oneself after contact with blood or a dead body. Still, it is one biblical example of how Jesus moved in the world in his own way, and treated others with love and understanding and assistance, instead of shunning them as others might have.

Chapter 13

Women Disciples and Followers of Christ

Jesus found a receptive audience in women. Ancient Hebrews lived by laws and customs that restricted women's lives. The fathers and husbands of women wielded authority over them. They were forbidden to talk with strangers, were married-off early, weren't educated, and couldn't give legal testimony. They couldn't participate equally with men in religious discourse or worship in a synagogue. They had to be doubly veiled before entering public. Jesus, however, showed an egalitarian treatment of women.

Martha

Jesus often visited Martha, Mary, and their brother Lazarus at their house in Bethany, near Jerusalem. The gospels mention members of this family several times, but in one account, Jesus and his disciples visited them in Bethany (Luke 10:38–42). While Martha worked in the kitchen preparing a meal for the guests, Mary, her sister, sat at the feet of Jesus and listened to him discoursing. Martha, annoyed that her sister wasn't helping with the meal preparation, complained to Jesus.

QUOTE

But Martha was cumbered about much serving, and came to him, and said, Lord, dost thou not care that my sister hath left me to serve alone? bid her therefore that she help me. And Jesus answered and said unto her, Martha, Martha, thou art careful and troubled about many things: But one thing is needful: and Mary hath chosen that good part, which shall not be taken away from her. (Luke 10:40–42)

Jesus had made the point succinctly: Martha could spend all of her time worrying about the things of the world (food preparation, entertaining the guests, and being a great hostess), but Mary had chosen to learn about things not of this world. The nourishment Mary sought was not for the body, but for the soul; she had chosen the "good part," and it would never be taken from her.

Jesus taught many women supporters, not just Mary and Martha. The Parable of the Sower follows the text in Luke 8:1–3. Women were with him, and certainly stayed to hear that story. There were so many people gathered there, in fact, that later in the gospel it states that Jesus' mother and brothers came and couldn't get close to him because of the size of the crowd (Luke 8:19–20).

Many people know that women (or a woman—Mary Magdalene—depending on the account) found Jesus' empty tomb, and that women stood vigil at the foot of his cross. But not many may be aware of the nongender-specific language Jesus used, such as calling men and women "children of wisdom," instead of singling out one gender or the other in his stories. The Web site *www.religioustolerance.org/cfe_bibl.htm* makes an interesting case for Jesus telling parallel female/male stories that are found throughout the New Testament gospels and Acts.

When their brother Lazarus died, Martha and Mary sent for Jesus. When she was told he was approaching the town, Martha went to meet the Lord. Mary remained inside the house until her presence was requested. That day, Jesus gave the grieving Martha words of hope after she told him that she believed Lazarus would rise again at the resurrection on the last day. Jesus told Martha that she would see Lazarus before then.

Jesus said unto her, I am the resurrection, and the life: he that believeth in me, though he were dead, yet shall he live: And whosoever liveth and believeth in me shall never die. Believest thou this? She saith unto him, Yea, Lord: I believe that thou art the Christ, the Son of God, which should come into the world. (John 11:25–27)

Mary Magdalene

Mary Magdalene's profile has been raised considerably in the last few years with the release of the bestselling novel and movie *The Da Vinci Code,* which alludes to a possible marital relationship between Mary Magdalene and Jesus, covered up by a church more interested in self-preservation than getting at the truth. The book, it must be remembered, is a work of fiction. The Roman Catholic, Eastern Orthodox, and Anglican churches all recognize Mary Magdalene as a saint. In the Roman Catholic tradition, Mary Magdalene has been called the Apostle to the Apostles. In other traditions, she has been called the Thirteenth Apostle and The Woman Who Knew the All. Her feast day is celebrated on July 22.

Following his death, the risen Jesus appeared to her in the garden (where his tomb was located) and gave her the first apostolic commission to "tell the others." Mary Magdalene's story is recounted on Tuesday after Easter in the Roman Catholic tradition, while Peter's and John's sprint to the garden to see the empty tomb is recounted at Easter Sunday services (John 20:3–10).

The historical Mary of Magdala may have been a leader of the Jesus followers. They were not yet called Christians, and wouldn't be for many years following the death and resurrection of Jesus. The word Christian, meaning "followers of Christ," was first used in Antioch (Acts 11:26). Those individuals making up Jesus' inner circle, including Mary Magdalene, were all Jews.

Mary Magdalene's name appears fourteen times in the New Testament, suggesting her important standing in the community; a woman was never mentioned in texts unless she had social prominence. The Resurrection story has always been at the heart of Christianity, and Mary Magdalene had a central role as eyewitness to the transcendent Jesus.

Where Was Mary Magdalene Born?

Apart from the biblical references to her, little else is known about the historical Mary Magdalene, including whether she had any family or her place of birth. Her name means "Mary of Magdala." Magdala, an Aramaic place name in ancient Palestine, was located on the shore of Lake Gennesaret (the Romans called that body of water the Sea of Tiberias), between the cities of Capernaum and Tiberias, in an area Jesus is known to have traveled during his ministry (Matthew 15:39). The place is mentioned in the works of Josephus, the first-century Jewish historian who was respected by early church leaders for the historical accuracy of his writings.

How Did She Meet Jesus?

Mary of Magdala, also called Miriham, Miriam, Mariamme, and Miryam (meaning "bitter"), most likely met Jesus when he was preaching in or near her town of Magdala. The Gospel of Luke states that Jesus cast out evil spirits and infirmities afflicting some of the women, including Mary Magdalene. Seven devils went out of Mary Magdalene (Luke 8:2, Mark 16:9), suggestive of a protracted or severe illness, since the ancients used the word "devil" as a euphemism for disease. She may have been suffering from a severe mental ailment, or even epilepsy.

Was She Ever a Prostitute?

The short answer is no. There has never been any biblical or historical evidence to support the idea that Mary Magdalene was ever a prostitute. In A.D. 591, a well-meaning Roman Catholic pope—Gregory the Great—drew upon Mary Magdalene, the sinful woman of Luke 8:37, and Mary of Bethany to create a composite image of a repentant fallen woman in order to show the forgiving nature of the church. Unfortunately, that image was associated with Mary Magdalene for centuries. In 1969, the Roman Catholic Church corrected the misconception, its Missal, and the Roman Calendar.

Did She Marry Jesus?

She may have been a wealthy widow, since her name is associated with a place instead of a patriarchal family, as was the custom. She was restored to health by Jesus and followed him. There is no evidence (historical, biblical, or otherwise) to support the theory that Mary Magdalene ever married Jesus, even though the author of the bestselling novel, *The Da Vinci Code*, sets forth a premise that suggests the beautiful ideal of such a union. It is difficult to believe that the biblical writers would have omitted such an important detail if it were fact.

What Was Her True Relationship with Jesus?

The Gnostic Gospels, one of which is named after her, portray Mary Magdalene as an exceptional student, close friend, and confidante of Jesus. Certain scholars of biblical history have suggested that Mary Magdalene was a female leader who held the followers together after the death of Jesus through her faith, leadership, and insightful understandings of Christ's teachings, and who likely had her own following after the Resurrection, just as the other apostles did.

Why Did She Remain at the Cross?

Mary Magdalene maintained a vigil with Jesus' mother, Mary, and other women during his time on the cross. She had to know that the Romans and Jewish priests were watching her and the others—Jesus' male disciples had already retreated into hiding. Why did Mary Magdalene stay? Perhaps she felt an invisible cord connecting her heart with the heart of Jesus. Whenever she had needed him, she knew that she could mentally tug on that cord. Now it was her time to give unconditionally, to show him support, love, gratitude, and appreciation for his gift to her life. And it must have touched the heart of Jesus to see the women who loved him standing vigil during his final hours on earth.

All four canonical gospels include references to the risen Jesus. Mark 16:9 states that "…he appeared first to Mary Magdalene…." The Gospel of Matthew notes that Mary Magdalene was with the *other Mary* (28:1). The Gospel of Luke mentions several women, including Mary Magdalene and Jesus' mother, who saw two men in shining garments who told them Jesus is risen (24:1–10). John 20:14–17 states that Mary Magdalene met the Savior alone in the garden.

Mary Magdalene Found the Tomb Empty

When the body was removed from the cross and taken to the tomb in the garden of Joseph of Arimathea, Mary Magdalene and the other women followers hastened there to prepare the body for burial. However, the arrival of the Jewish Sabbath at sundown on that Friday prevented the work of cleansing and anointing the body. She returned to the tomb on Sunday morning (Matthew 28:1, Mark 16:1), and finding it empty (Matthew 28:5), ran to tell Peter and John (John 20:1–2). Not believing her, they raced to the tomb to see for themselves.

Jesus Appeared to Her

The New Testament portrays Mary Magdalene as the pre-eminent witness to the Resurrection (John 20:15–18). Biblical scholars say the risen Jesus choosing to appear to Mary Magdalene and giving her the first commission suggests the historical truth of the Resurrection event. Why? Jewish law didn't accept testimony of women in first-century Palestine, and even Jesus' male disciples at first didn't believe her.

Some scholars assert that nonbiblical sources show that Mary Magdalene and other women of her time led fellowship and prayer sessions in house churches after the death of Jesus, but as the groups' numbers grew, larger accommodations were needed. Then, as the fledgling communities of Jesus followers moved into larger public buildings, the roles of women as spiritual leaders (and possibly priests and bishops) were diminished or eliminated. Finally, some sources speculate that the Beloved Disciple may have been Mary Magdalene, and that she either provided the eyewitness account or was the writer of the Gospel of John. The Apocryphal Gnostic Gospel of Philip notes that Jesus kissed her often, much to the consternation of the other male disciples; but there is a hole in the text where the word would appear telling the reader *where* Jesus kissed her often, so it remains a mystery.

Mary of Bethany

Mary was a common biblical name. No fewer than six women in the Bible are named Mary: mother of Jesus; Mary Magdalene; Mary of Bethany; Mary, wife of Cleophas; Mary, mother of John Mark; and a Christian woman in Rome. Often, the way the ancients distinguished them was by using place names or patriarchal family names associated with them. Mary of Bethany was the sister of Martha and Lazarus, the followers of Jesus who lived in Bethany. The Gospel of John is the only gospel account that makes an explicit reference to Mary (sister of Lazarus) as the unidentified sinner who anoints Jesus' feet at the house of Simon the Pharisee.

Jesus loved the family of Mary, Martha, and Lazarus who lived in Bethany. One day, Jesus arrived at the home after Lazarus had been dead for four days. After speaking to Martha, Jesus asked for Mary, who had remained in the house weeping. She told Jesus that if he'd been there with Lazarus, her brother wouldn't have died (John 11:21). Jesus was deeply moved by the tears of Mary, and by the weeping of those Jews who were with her, and he asked where Lazarus had been laid.

> *Now a certain man was sick, named Lazarus, of Bethany, the town of Mary and her sister Martha. (It was that Mary which anointed the Lord with ointment, and wiped his feet with her hair, whose brother Lazarus was sick.) Therefore his sisters sent unto him, saying, Lord, behold, he whom thou lovest is sick. (John 11:1–3)*

Jesus wept as he came upon the cave with the stone covering the opening. He ordered the stone to be removed. Martha said to Jesus, "Lord, by this time he stinketh: for he hath been dead four days" (John 11:39). Jesus prayed to God for the sake of those standing nearby, so that they might believe in God's glory, and then commanded in a loud voice, "Lazarus, come forth." Lazarus, still bound in his grave clothes, walked out of the cave (John 11:43–44). This miracle was a pivotal one that caused some of the Jews to run to the Pharisees and report what Jesus had done. The Pharisees plotted how they might put Jesus to death.

In the Roman Catholic tradition, the sinful woman (Luke 7:36–50) who anointed Jesus with costly spikenard from her alabaster box in Luke 7:37 became associated early on with both Mary Magdalene and Mary of Bethany, according to Catholic teachings. However, the Eastern Orthodox churches (in particular, the Greek Orthodox) have always kept the women separate as "the sinner," Mary Magdalene, and Mary of Bethany.

Mary, Wife of Cleophas

This biblical Mary was the mother of James the Less and Joseph (Mark 15:40, Matthew 27:56). She has also been called Mary the mother of James (Mark 16:1, Luke 24:10), but her relationship, if any, to the mother of Jesus is confusing. Some biblical historians have called Cleophas the brother of Joseph

Mary and Martha of Bethany with Jesus

(Jesus' stepfather), meaning that Mary, wife of Cleophas would be the Blessed Virgin Mary's sister-in-law. "Now there stood by the cross of Jesus his mother, and his mother's sister, Mary the wife of Cleophas, and Mary Magdalene" (John 19:25). The Gospel of John certainly states that Mary of Cleophas was among those women who stood by the cross, but the text doesn't make clear if the gospel writer was identifying the Mary, wife of Cleophas, as the sister of the Blessed Virgin. Tradition does not mention the Virgin Mary as having any brothers or sisters. Catholics believe her birth was not associated with original sin and is thus known as the "Immaculate Conception," often confused with the virgin birth incarnation of Jesus.

Sources disagree over whether or not the wife of Cleophas was related to Jesus' family. Consider for a moment that she was mother of James the Less. Who was he? James the Less was one of Jesus' twelve disciples, and served as the head of the Jerusalem congregations with whom Peter, John, and Paul conferred in Acts 15. He has also been called James the Younger and James, the son of Alphaeus. Were Alphaeus and Cleophas the same person? Most likely.

The spelling of Clopas may derive from Klopas (or the King James Version, Cleophas). This individual is also sometimes identified as Alphaeus. Clopas, according to scholars of biblical linguistics, was most likely of Semitic origin. The wife of Cleophas/Alphaeus was the mother of James the Less. She would necessarily also be the mother of Matthew, who was called in the Gospel of Mark 2:14, "Levi the son of Alpheus."

Early church father Eusebius recorded that Alphaeus/Cleophas (Clopas) was the brother of Joseph, husband of the mother of Jesus. That would make Mary, wife of Cleophas a sister-in-law of Jesus' mother Mary, and James the Less a cousin of Jesus.

Salome, Wife of Zebedee

Salome, like Mary, wife of Cleophas, may have been related to Jesus' family. Certainly, she was a faithful follower of the Lord. The Hebrew form of her name may be Shulamit or Shulamith, with the Hellenized form being Salome. She is named in the Gospels of Mark and Matthew among the women present at the crucifixion.

There were also women looking on afar off: among whom was Mary Magdalene, and Mary the mother of James the Less and of Joses, and Salome; (Who also, when he was in Galilee, followed him, and ministered unto him;) and many other women which came up with him unto Jerusalem. (Mark 15:40–41)

Matthew 27:56 offers a parallel passage to the above quote, but says that the mother of Zebedee's children was there as well. The gospel writer of Matthew calls Salome not by her name but as "the mother of Zebedee's children" (Matthew 27:56). Her sons were James the Great and John the Evangelist. Jesus gave called them "Boanerges" or "the Sons of Thunder" (Mark 3:17).

The Gospel of Mark reveals that Salome was with the women who went to the tomb to anoint Jesus' broken and wounded body with unguents and spices. "And when the sabbath was past, Mary Magdalene, and Mary the mother of James, and Salome, had bought sweet spices, that they might come and anoint him. And very early in the morning the first day of the week, they came unto the sepulchre at the rising of the sun" (Mark 16:1–2).

While she's not called a disciple or apostle in the canonical texts, Mary is referred to as a disciple (along with Mary Magdalene) in the Gnostic text, the Gospel of Thomas. She is also mentioned in another Gnostic text, the Gospel of the Egyptians. Modern writers usually refer to her as a devoted follower of Christ.

Chapter 14

Women Workers in Christ

Women, following Jesus' example, exhibited strong spiritual leadership roles in the early Christian church. Historians say that women worked diligently (sometimes with husbands or brothers), using their money, time, and resources to strengthen the faith of followers and to convert nonbelievers. They opened their homes as churches for worship and fellowship sessions, led those sessions, and even administered sacraments. Women like Priscilla, Phoebe, and Junia taught in their roles as evangelist, minister, and apostle.

Apphia

Apphia was the wife of Philemon. Archippus, according to some sources, was their son (although others assert he was a brother in Christ, a "fellow soldier" as some Bibles state. The Apostle Paul may have converted Apphia and her family to Christianity. Apphia's name appears in a letter written by Paul from his prison cell in Rome. The letter entreats Philemon, Paul's wealthy friend and slave owner in Colossae, to consider Onesimus, his runaway slave, as a brother in Christ. The letter included a salutation to "…our beloved Apphia, and Archippus our fellow soldier, and to the church in thy house…" (Philemon 2). Biblical historians believe that Archippus was a minister, possibly in Colossae.

FACT

The village of Colossae, during the time of the early Christians, was located where the roads from Ephesus and Sardis met. The location was considered strategic, because it was on a hill along a major road from Ephesus, and there was plenty of water. Some sources say that Philemon and Onesimus were natives of Colossae.

Paul entreated Philemon to take back Onesimus, not as a slave, but as a Christian and as a helper or partner. It was a common practice in the ancient world among wealthy people to own slaves. However, as Paul wrote: "For as many of you as have been baptized into Christ have put on Christ. There is neither Jew nor Greek, there is neither bond nor free, there is neither male nor female: for ye are all one in Christ Jesus" (Galatians 3:27–28).

Paul's mission was to bring the message of eternal salvation to all, regardless of their bondage on earth. Perhaps Paul believed that appealing to Apphia's husband as one Christian to another on behalf of Onesimus was the approach that would be best for the welfare of Onesimus. Perhaps Paul believed that Philemon's strong Christian moral values would take care of everything else, and produce the best outcome for Onesimus.

With her husband's wealth and her son's passion for the Lord, it is likely that Apphia also played significant roles in the support of the Christian community in Colossae, since Paul's letter mentions the church "in thy house." Paul also points out his love for her in his salutation "our beloved Apphia." She must have provided loving and dedicated service to the Christians who came into her home for fellowship and worship for Paul to have used the term *beloved* toward her.

QUESTION?

Were Apphia and her family able to practice their faith in peace?
It is likely that as anti-Christian tension escalated, Apphia and her husband and son were imprisoned and persecuted for their faith. According to Christian tradition, Paul was beheaded during the reign of Nero, sometime around A.D. 60, and Apphia, Archippus, and Philemon were stoned to death.

Chloe

Reference to Chloe is found in the New Testament in Paul's first letter to the Christians in Corinth. Members of the house of Chloe brought the divisiveness of the teaching and preaching among certain members of the young Corinthian church to Paul's attention. Paul wrote the letter to deplore their dissention, immorality, and wrong thinking, and to answer the Corinthians's questions about marriage and virginity and the sacrificial offerings made to idols. He addressed their moral infractions and helped them better understand the Resurrection of Christ, as well as the Resurrection of the dead.

He had founded the community in or about A.D. 51. The community was established in the ancient city of Corinth, a crossroads of trade in the Mediterranean. It was a virtual melting pot of different people espousing various ideas, including those of pagan cults, and moral depravity was commonplace.

Paul acknowledges that word had reached him from the "house of Chloe," suggestive of a house church that Chloe's family may have owned and occupied. Paul wasted little time with pleasantries in his letter. He tackled the issue of divisiveness head-on.

In the letter, Paul also addresses the problem of moral disorders emerging in the young church. Women who had participated in the church's fellowship and prayer without their veils or head covering were on Paul's agenda. Women may have also wanted to address the gathering, and possibly weren't permitted; they may have been arguing over the right to speak before the gathering.

Now I beseech you, brethren, by the name of our Lord Jesus Christ, that ye all speak the same thing, and that there be no divisions among you; but that ye be perfectly joined together in the same mind and in the same judgment. For it hath been declared unto me of you, my brethren, by them which are of the house of Chloe, that there are contentions among you. (1 Corinthians 1:10–11)

A member had engaged in a sexual relationship with his father's wife. Other church members talked about it openly, as though they were giving praise for the great freedom Christianity ensured. However, Paul insisted that the man had to be removed, and that no Christian should associate with anyone who was immoral (1 Corinthians 5:1–13).

They had legal battles in the pagan courts, and some even may have participated in cult prostitution. Paul did not hesitate to exert his authority when necessary, but he dealt with each the issues using Christian purity and values as his guide.

Chloe, who most likely kept the house church, is not mentioned again in the Scriptures. Whether or not she addressed the assembly in any way remains shrouded in ambiguity. So, too, is the participation of other women of the New Testament, including Lydia (Acts 16:14–15) and Nympha (Colossians 4:15).

Euodia and Syntyche

These two women served as laborers in the Christian community at Philippi, a Roman city in northeastern Greece. The municipality was important because it was situated between the Via Egnatia (a well-traveled road that ran from the Adriatic coast to Byzantium) and the fertile agricultural plain in the shadow of Mt. Pangaeus. In the Apostle Paul's letter to the Philippians (which he wrote from prison), reference is made to Euodia and Syntyche, two women belonging to the congregation in Philippi.

Therefore, my brethren dearly beloved and longed for, my joy and crown, so stand fast in the Lord, my dearly beloved. I beseech Euodias, and beseech Syntyche, that they be of the same mind in the Lord. And I entreat thee also, true yokefellow, help those women which labored with me in the gospel, with Clement also, and with other my fellow laborers, whose names are in the book of life. (Philippians 4:1–3)

This is the only place the women are mentioned in the Bible. Little else is known about them, except that they were working on behalf of the Lord, but were not in accord with each other, possibly over the Scripture or Christian teaching.

Junia

In the case of Junia, Paul writes in the letter to the Romans, "Salute Andronicus and Junia, my kinsmen, and my fellow-prisoners, who are of note among the apostles, who also were in Christ before me" (Romans 16:7). The New American Bible changes the text slightly to say "relatives" in place of "kinsmen," and "prominent" replaces the words, "of note." Paul, in his word choices, seems to be indicating that these two individuals—Junia and Andronicus—are not only his relatives, but have achieved a level of respect and stature in their preaching and commitment to carry forth the work of the fledgling Church. Further, they had been believers and workers in Christ before Paul. Their long service to the Lord's work must have impressed Paul for him to reference it. Although some modern scholars believe Junia(s) was a man, early fathers of the church—Jerome and John Chrysostom, in particular—believed Junia was female; the name was popular for women in biblical times.

Junia may have worked in partnership with her husband (or brother) Andronicus, much like another wife/husband team of Priscilla and Aquila, whose story follows. Of all of the women in the New Testament, Junia is the only woman to be called an apostle.

Feminist theologians and biblical historians place great emphasis on Paul's reference to Junia as "...of note among the apostles..." (Romans 16:7). They assert that his remark proves that women served in all levels of leadership in the infant church, but today, even though they may be spiritually called to serve the Lord, they're forbidden entry into the priesthood.

Some readers might think that to be an apostle, the person would have to have met Jesus and studied with him. It is true that the Twelve knew Jesus, spent time with him, and learned from him while he was still was in his physical body, but Paul never met the earthly Jesus. Paul, formerly Saul, and persecutor of the followers of Jesus, had a powerful conversion experience on the road to Damascus that made him believe in the Lord and repent of his previous actions against the Jesus followers. After that he became known as Paul, and self-proclaimed Apostle to the Gentiles. Read about Paul's conversion in Acts 9:3–9.

Lydia

Lydia was on a riverbank praying quietly among other women when Paul met her. He had recently had a vision of a man pleading with him to go to Macedonia because the people there needed help (Acts 16:9–12). Paul went to the bustling trading town of Philippi to preach to the Gentiles. He found a peaceful retreat along the banks of a river, and away from the noise of the city, he taught those gathered about the gospel. Lydia, a businesswoman, had joined others for worship that day. Acts 16:14 states that she was "...a seller of purple, of the city of Thyatira...."

FACT

In ancient times, Thyatira was located about forty-two miles inland from where the coast of Western Turkey meets the Aegean Sea. The city was famous for its dye trade and textiles. Archeologists have unearthed artifacts with inscriptions from trade guilds that include wool workers, tanners, linen weavers, and dyers. Lydia was believed to have been a dye merchant. Today, the city is called Akhisar.

The Bible reveals that Lydia's heart was opened by the Lord to receive Paul's message, and she and her household were baptized. She then opened her home to the missionaries. Thus, the little Christian community at Philippi was established by Lydia. The Scriptures state that Lydia opened her home another time—when Paul and Silas converted their jailer and were given freedom, they went to Lydia's house. Her home was probably the meeting place of the early Philippian Christians.

Nympha

Paul sent greetings to Nympha at the end of his letter to the Colossians, followers of Jesus making up the community of Christians at Colossae. Paul did not include specific dates or locations, so there's no way to know which prison he was in at the time he wrote the letter. The King James version of the Bible states the verse as follows: "Salute the brethren which are in Laodicea, and Nymphas, and the church which is in his house." However, The New American Bible (St. Joseph edition) refers to Nympha (no final "s"), and asks the Laodiceans to give greetings to Nympha and those of the church who meet in *her* house (Colossians 4:15).

Paul requested that the Laodiceans, meeting in the house church of Nympha (there is no mention of a husband, father, or brother), read the letter openly in church. He also advised the Colossian Christians to read the letter from Laodicea. That letter may have been written by Paul, but is now lost.

Paul had the habit of writing a postscript in his epistles that declared the letter was written in his own hand. In the letter to the Colossians, Paul states, "The salutation by the hand of me Paul" (Colossians 4:18).

Gender changes in biblical texts increase the ambiguity about women in the earliest churches and the kind of leadership roles they had. Many biblical scholars believe that women had active roles in the Apostolic Church, and agree that as Christianity evolved and larger, public buildings replaced the private homes used for worship, the roles of women leaders increasingly diminished.

Phoebe

Phoebe was the name of a deaconess in the Christian church in Cenchreae, which was located along Corinth's eastern harbor. She may have had some wealth, for Paul calls her "…a succourer of many…," including himself. Some sources call her Paul's "patroness." Phoebe's name first appears in the New Testament in a letter to the Romans.

Paul's letters predate all of the written gospels in the New Testament, and it is known that he stayed in touch with the churches he founded in his missionary travels. A Christian community, however, had already been established before Paul wrote the letter to the Romans in which he mentions Phoebe, sometime around A.D. 56 or A.D. 58.

Priscilla, Wife of Aquila

Priscilla and Aquila were Jewish tentmakers (Acts 18:2–3), and their business may have brought them into contact with Paul. While Acts does not reveal much about the life of Priscilla before she met and married Aquila, the text does make several mentions of her, always with her husband. Aquila.

Aquila was born in Pontus, but had recently come from Italy with Priscilla. They met Paul in Corinth after he had departed from Athens and they had fled Rome. The Roman Emperor Claudius had commanded all Jews to leave that city (Acts 18:2). The three shared a common interest in tent making, as well as a love of Christ. They became dear friends, and Paul lived with them for a time.

I commend unto you Phebe our sister, which is a servant of the church which is at Cenchrea: That ye receive her in the Lord, as becometh saints, and that ye assist her in whatsoever business she hath need of you: for she hath been a succourer of many, and of myself also. (Romans 16:1–2)

While in Corinth, Paul spoke in the synagogue, reasoning with those who would listen to his Christian message, and converting many Jews and Gentiles. Priscilla and Aquila, who had been Christians longer than Paul, helped Paul found the Corinthian church and strengthen others there in the faith.

Benefiting from Paul's Passion

When Paul left for Ephesus on the next leg of his journey, Priscilla and Aquila went with him. In Ephesus, Paul left Priscilla and Aquila to go preach in the synagogue. The name of the Lord was greatly magnified as a result of the preaching and healing done (Acts 19:17). Priscilla would have gained the skills to be a missionary from the Paul. She and Aquila are credited with being strong leaders of the Corinthian and Ephesian Christian communities.

Meeting Apollos

Apollos, a man from Alexandria with the gift of eloquent oratory, began evangelizing in Ephesus. Apollos was a Jew who had limited knowledge of the Christian Way; he knew only the baptism of John (Acts 18:24–28). Priscilla and Aquila became friends with Apollos, and gave him a fuller understanding of the Christian Gospel. This enabled him to articulate the ideas of the faith more effectively than ever. Some sources assert that this means that Priscilla, helped by Aquila, was the earliest-known theological teacher after Paul and Jesus.

Sending Greetings to Fellow Christians

Priscilla and Aquila sent their Corinthian Christian friends greetings in a letter that Paul dispatched (1 Corinthians 16:19). The combined greeting suggests that the three friends were still together when the letter was written. Acts 19:21 reveals "After these things were ended, Paul purposed in the spirit, when he had passed through Macedonia and Achaia, to go to Jerusalem, saying…I must also see Rome." In A.D. 54, Emperor Claudius died and Jews returned to Rome.

QUESTION?

Where is Ephesus?
The ruins of the city of Ephesus, with its Temple of Artemis (the Greek goddess of fertility), is located near the coast of the Aegean Sea in modern Turkey, about 50 kilometers south of Izmir (ancient Smyrna). Running through Ephesus was the Sacred Way, a wide paved road used by pedestrians and charioteers during ancient times.

Going Home to Rome

Approximately two years later, Paul salutes Priscilla and Aquila in a letter in Romans 16:3, indicating they had returned to Rome. As was their custom, they opened their home as a house church. Their stay was short-lived, according to some sources, because of Nero's persecution of Christians. They again fled Rome, and this time settled in Ephesus.

Building Upon the House Church of Saint Prisca

There is an old church dedicated to Saint Prisca in Rome, though it is not clear if that saint is the same Priscilla discussed here. Builders constructed the old church on the site of Priscilla's house church. Roman martyrology reveals that Priscilla and Aquila suffered martyrdom in Rome; however, another tradition holds that they were martyred in Asia Minor. The Roman Catholic Church commemorates Priscilla and Aquila on July 8, their feast day.

Chapter 15

Women Who Opposed Certain Men

Women in biblical narrative were seldom pious protagonists, but more often served as antagonists or characters instigating a situation that propelled the narrative forward. In some cases, they simply disobeyed their husbands. In other cases, they exerted pressure on men in their families to do something that was not right in the eyes of God. Certain women were deceivers; others convinced their husbands to deceive. Some women simply withdrew support or ridiculed and openly opposed their mates. These are their stories.

Job's Wife

You may recall Job's story from reading about his daughter Jemima in Chapter 10. Here, you will learn about Nahrela, Job's wife. The Old Testament Book of Job begins by establishing that Job is exceedingly wealthy. Although pious, the same could not be said of his children. Job was so virtuous that each day he burned offerings and prayed to God for his children, in the event that they had "...cursed God in their hearts" (Job 1:5). One day, God spoke to Satan, asking him, "Whence cometh thou?" Satan answered, "From going to and fro in the earth, and from walking up and down in it" (Job 1:7). That exchange set the stage for God's next question.

Satan told God that it was easy for Job to show loyalty and love to God when God gave him such bounty and protection; but what if God were to test Job's loyalty by causing a complete reversal of Job's fortune? Would Job not curse God? Thus, the story of God's testing of Job begins.

All was good in the lives of Nahrela and Job. They lived East of Palestine near the desert border. He garnered the respect of the people in the Land of Uz, his homeland, because he was devout, moral, and ethical in his dealings with others. But suddenly, his fortunes began to erode.

QUESTION?

How did Job's fortunes erode?
His massive herds of oxen and asses were taken away. His sheep were burnt, along with the shepherds guarding them, and the camels were stolen. Finally, Job's ten children were killed when a windstorm caused the house to collapse on them as they were eating and drinking wine.

The Book of Job states, "Then Job arose, and rent his mantle, and shaved his head, and fell down upon the ground, and worshipped, And said, Naked came I out of my mother's womb, and naked shall I return thither: the Lord gave, and the Lord hath taken away; blessed be the name of the Lord. In all this Job sinned not, nor charged God foolishly" (Job 1:20–22). God intensified the testing of Job by inflicting disease upon his body. Job's friends saw that his grief was great, but Nahrela comes across in the biblical narrative as fickle and unsupportive of Job as each new affliction takes its toll on her husband. During Job's trials, his wife distances herself from him, so much so that Job begins to believe that she loathes him. She may blame him for some transgressions against God to which he does not repent. During his darkest moments, when he longs for death and deplores his birth, she seems to take sides with Satan. As Job is covered with boils from the top of his head to the bottom of his feet, she encourages him to speak out against God.

And he took him a potsherd to scrape himself withal; and he sat down among the ashes. Then said his wife unto him, Dost thou still retain thine integrity? curse God, and die. But he said unto her, Thou speakest as one of the foolish women speaketh. What? shall we receive good at the hand of God, and shall we not receive evil? (Job 2:8–10)

Unlike Job, Nahrela sought the easy way out. She did not understand that the suffering her husband was experiencing was God's test of Job's fidelity and love. If Job cursed God and died, it would end the test, but it would not bring back her children. However, if Job remained loyal and accepting of his fate, he would live to be blessed; God would (and did) increase Job's wealth by doubling it.

Job eventually emerged from his trials, and was restored to good health. He must have forgiven his wife her shortcomings, and Nahrela found it in her heart to be a loving wife again, because she became pregnant, eventually giving birth to ten new children. So, once again Job was father to ten children, owner of many herds of animals, and a pious and well-respected man in Uz.

Judith

Judith was a pious Jewish widow whose extraordinary beauty dazzled the Assyrian general, Holofernes. Holofernes had been ordered by the Babylonian king Nebuchadnezzar to wreak vengeance on nations that didn't support his reign. Consequently, Holofernes attacked Bethulia (scholars believe

Judith

the city was the ancient community of Mese-lieh). Judith saved the city as it came close to surrendering to Holofernes.

Judith deceived Holofernes with a story about a nearby town that was besieged. She was invited to join him for a private party. Once there, Judith waited for him to become drunk. When she was certain he was totally drunk, Judith cut off his head. She took his head to Bethulia, and the soldiers then took the head and displayed it before engaging Holofernes's men in battle. Her act permitted the Jews to defeat Holofernes's army.

Some scholars believe that the story of Judith's beheading of Holofernes is pure fiction, but others disagree. The complete story is found in the deuterocanonical Book of Judith.

Bethulia was most likely located in the mountains that towered out of the southern plain of Jezreel. Numerous springs were located in the vicinity. There were two passes (Kefr Adan and Burqin) nearby, each so narrow that only a single horseman at a time could ride through them. This information roughly correlates with the data of the site mentioned in the apocryphal Book of Judith.

FACT

Numerous artists over time have used the decapitation of Holofernes by Judith as a subject for their paintings. Such artists, including Sandro Botticelli, Caravaggio, Andrea Mantegna, Giorgione, Donatello, Hermann-Paul, and others, found the dramatic event worthy of reproducing with vivid imagery in their works.

Lot's Wife

Lot's wife is not named in the Scriptures. She is simply the wife of Lot, who was the nephew of Abraham. But some things can be inferred from reading the Book of Genesis. That text states that Lot moved his family from Ur to Canaan with Abraham (Genesis 11:31, 12:4–5). The herds of Abraham and Lot increased to the point that the animals encroached on the living space of the herdsman, provoking disputes among them. Abraham, in a great gesture of generosity, allowed Lot to select an area of land to occupy. Lot chose the Jordan valley near Sodom, where the land was fertile and well watered. By that time, Lot was already prosperous.

The exact location of Sodom remains unknown, but in ancient times it was the principle town of five nearby communities: Sodom, Gomorrah, Zovoiim, Admah, and Tzoar. The five cities, collectively called a Pentopolis, became known as "The Cities of the Plain." Many scholars place them on the plain of the Jordan River, south of the Dead Sea.

Looking for Ten Righteous Sodomites

Lot moved his family to Sodom because the grazing for his flocks was exceptional there. But God told Abraham that he would no longer tolerate the depravity and sinfulness of the Sodomites, and intended to destroy the city. Abraham pleaded with God not to rain destruction upon Sodom. The Lord agreed not to destroy the city if Abraham could find ten righteous people, but God's angels found only one person—Lot.

Hearing the Outrageous Demand

The two angels of God went to Lot's house to warn him. The Bible says Lot prepared a feast "… and did bake unleavened bread, and they did eat it" (Genesis 19:3), but it seems more likely that Lot's wife prepared and served the food. Since it was evening, Lot pressed them to remain at his house and rest. Even before the angels lay down, the people of Sodom made their way to Lot's house and clamored for the two male visitors so they might have sex with them.

Offering another Option

Lot was outraged, and went out the door, "And said, I pray you, brethren, do not so wickedly. Behold now, I have two daughters which have not known man; let me, I pray you, bring them out unto you, and do ye to them as is good in your eyes: only unto these men do nothing; for therefore came they under the shadow of my roof" (Genesis 19:7–8).

For many readers, this passage is troubling: Why would Lot offer his virgin daughters to be raped by the village men? Some sources say the passage just shows the value of women in that society at the time.

Seeking Understanding

But even Lot's offering of his daughters in place of the angels was not enticing to the village men. What was the reaction of Lot's wife to the sexual depravity of the men whose lust knew no bounds? Was she trying to understand the sudden turn of events? Had her maternal instincts kicked in? Whether it had or not, the Bible doesn't say.

An episode similar to Lot's is described in Judges 19:20–25. An old man in Gilbeah offered lodging and food to Levite. The men of Gilbeah wanted to be intimate with the male guest. Instead the old man offered his daughter and concubine, but the Gilbeahans refused them. The Levite then sent out his concubine, who was raped all night.

As you may recall in reading about Lot's daughters in Chapter 2, the angels again told Lot to leave the city with his family. Lot wanted to warn his sons-in-law first, but they didn't believe him. The angels decided that Lot had been given enough time, so they took hold of his hand and the hand of his wife and two daughters, and escorted them from Sodom, telling them not to look back.

Seeing Sodom for the Last Time

Perhaps Lot's wife felt sad to be leaving. Maybe she had learned to accept and even tolerate the wickedness of the town. Perhaps she and Lot had found suitable men for their daughters to marry. With the arrival of the angels, her life had changed drastically. The male angels told her not to look back, but she couldn't help herself. She stole one last glimpse, and was instantly transformed into a pillar of salt (Genesis 19:26). The Bible says that Abraham got up the next day and, looking toward Sodom and Gomorrah, saw "…the smoke of the country went up as the smoke of a furnace…" (Genesis 19:27–28). Sodom burned as God destroyed the Cities of the Plain.

Michal

Michal, whose name means "brook," was the daughter of King Saul and his wife Ahinoam. Michal fell in love with David, who was destined to become Saul's successor. However, Michal's deep affection for David may not have been returned. He was infatuated with her, but had actually asked for and was promised her older sister, Merab. The king didn't want David as a son-in-law. In fact, he hoped that David would be killed battling the Philistines, attempting to fulfill the conditions set for him to marry Merab. So sure was Saul that David would perish, he gave Merab to another man.

And Saul said to David, Behold my elder daughter Merab, her will I give thee to wife: only be thou valiant for me, and fight the Lord's battles. For Saul said, Let not mine hand be upon him, but let the hand of the Philistines be upon him (1 Samuel 18:17). But it came to pass at the time when Merab Saul's daughter should have been given to David, that she was given unto Adriel the Meholathite to wife. (1 Samuel 18:19)

Saul learned that his daughter Michal loved David. He made a bargain with David: The young man was to offer no dowry, except to bring the king the foreskins of one hundred Philistines. Saul was already beginning to fear

David, and wanted him dead. David slew 200 men and brought their fore-skins to King Saul. The king had no choice but to keep his end of the bargain. The king knew two things for certain: The Lord was with David now, and so was Michal. Saul's hatred of David increased.

FACT

The Philistines were the main adversaries of the ancient Israelites. The Philistines lived along the coast of the Mediterranean in the land of Canaan, at a time when the Israelites desired to settle in that land. Most of the Philistines dwelled in one of five cities known as the Philistine Pentapolis. Those cities included Ashkelon, Gaza, Ekron, Ashdod, and Gath.

Michal Thwarts an Attempted Murder Plot

Saul's messengers went to watch David's house. Michal informed her husband that if he didn't flee that night, the next morning he would be dead. "So Michal let David down through a window...And Michal took an image, and laid it in the bed, and put a pillow of goats' hair for his bolster, and covered it with a cloth" (1 Samuel 19:12–13). She told the messengers (sent to kill him) that he was sick, so they took David's bed to Saul. The king soon discovered the ruse.

Michal and David Endure a Long Separation

Saul confronted Michal and asked her why she had deceived him. Michal explained that David had begged her to let him go and had asked her "...why should I kill thee?" (1 Samuel 19:17). Michal did not see her husband for years after his narrow escape. Most people believed the marriage had ended. David married other women, including Abigail and Ahinoam of Jezreel, and Michal was given to Phalti (1 Samuel 25:40–44).

David Sends for Michal

The house of Saul had suffered and weakened over the years, as David's strength increased. One day David demanded that Michal be returned to him. Michal was brought before her estranged husband, and viewed him with contempt for having taken other wives, and for snatching her away from her current husband, who had wept at her departure. Phalti must have loved her, and perhaps she loved him. In any event, alienated from David, her passion for him was gone.

Michal's Contempt

In a jubilant procession with trumpets and shouting, David and the Israelites took the ark of the Lord into the City of David (Jerusalem). David, caught up in the moment, began leaping and shouting and dancing in celebration with only his linen ephod on. Michal watched from a window, "And as the ark of the Lord came into the city of David, Michal Saul's daughter looked through a window, and saw king David leaping and dancing before the Lord, and she despised him in her heart" (2 Samuel 6:16).

QUESTION?

What is an ephod?
An ephod was part of an ancient priestly garment worn over other clothing, much like an apron. However, scholars suggest that David's linen ephod was possibly more like a loincloth. His dancing while attired in it may have been part of a ritual that was supposed to culminate in intimate relations with Michal.

David's nearly naked dancing irked Michal, who told him, "How glorious was the king of Israel to day, who uncovered himself to day in the eyes of the handmaids of his servants, as one of the vain fellows shamelessly uncovereth himself!" (2 Samuel 6:20). Her outrage brought about the demise of their marriage. David shot back at her that he was dancing before the Lord, not the maidservants, but that they would hold him in honor. Apparently, David never slept with Michal again after she ridiculed him, for the Book of 2 Samuel states, "Therefore Michal the daughter of Saul had no child unto the day of her death" (2 Samuel 6:23).

Sapphira

In the fledgling Christian community at Jerusalem, one couple emerged as deceitful, for lying about the money they were donating to help build the new church. Ananias and Sapphira, his wife, claimed to be giving every cent of the proceeds from the sale of a piece of property to the church to help fund it, but in fact, they weren't; they were withholding a substantial sum. They were faulted for deliberately duping others, and for being hypocrites.

Ananias and Sapphira lived during the time of the Apostles, when the early Christians pooled their money to help establish and support their churches. When the Apostles were alive, the monies were given to them, and they distributed whatever was needed to the poor and others in need.

Ananias sold a piece of his property and, instead of turning over all of the proceeds to the Apostles, he retained some of the money. Sapphira knew what he'd done and how much money he'd kept for them. She knew that he would take the rest and lay it at the feet of the Apostles, but she wouldn't go with him to do it.

But Peter said, Ananias, why hath Satan filled thine heart to lie to the Holy Ghost, and to keep back part of the price of the land? Whiles it remained, was it not thine own? and after it was sold, was it not in thine own power? why hast thou conceived this thing in thine heart? thou hast not lied unto men, but unto God. (Acts 5:3–4)

Ananias dropped dead on the spot. Some nearby young men lifted Ananias from the floor, wrapped his body in a shroud, and buried him. Sapphira, looking for her husband, came to Peter. He asked her directly, "Tell me whether ye sold the land for so much?" And she said, "Yea, for so much." Then Peter said unto her, How is it that ye have agreed together to tempt the Spirit of the Lord? behold, the feet of them which have buried thy husband are at the door, and shall carry thee out" (Acts 5:8–9). And Sapphira, like Ananias before her, fell down dead. They carried her out and buried her beside her husband.

Chapter 16

Women Who Were Concubines

Among the early Hebrews and other groups, men took concubines as well as wives. A concubine was a bondwoman or a legitimate spouse, albeit one with an inferior rank than that of a principle wife. The concubine had certain privileges, but no real authority in her mate's family, and she could quite readily be dismissed. The early Jews had laws that protected concubines. Although the Jewish patriarchs Abraham and Jacob kept concubines, the practice eventually fell out of favor and became viewed as a sin against the sacred institution of marriage.

Abishag

When King David had grown old and his blood circulation wasn't what it used to be, he suffered from being cold. His servants searched about the land for someone to keep him warm. They finally decided upon Abishag, a beautiful young woman from Shunem, in the land of Issachar, north of Jezreel and Mount Gilboa. She was brought to the seventy-year-old monarch as a companion. In 1 Kings 1:4, it states "...the king knew her not," which is biblical language for he didn't have sexual relations with her. However, she was considered his concubine, and slept against his bosom each night. Those close to the king believed that her body lying next to his would serve a two-fold purpose: keep the old man warm, and possibly revive his vitality and restore his powers. Abishag soon saw royal maneuverings that would leave one prince dead, and the other on the throne even while the king lived.

Wherefore his servants said unto him, Let there be sought for my lord the king a young virgin: and let her stand before the king, and let her cherish him, and let her lie in thy bosom, that my lord the king may get heat. (1 Kings 1:2)

Abishag Becomes Attendant, Nurse, and Body Warmer

The young woman learned how to care for David and served as the frail ruler's nurse, becoming his closest attendant. She was considered his property, and by rule of law during that time, would be inherited by David's heir upon his death.

Adonijah Tries to Usurp the Throne

At the time Abishag was brought into King David's home to care for him, David's son Adonijah began to covet the throne for himself. His two older brothers, Amnon and Absalom, were dead. He reasoned that he had a right to be king; moreover, he desired to lay claim to the throne as soon as possible. However, David and the Lord favored Solomon, Adonijah's younger brother, as the next leader of the Hebrew people. Still, Adonijah proclaimed: "I will be king: and he prepared him chariots and horsemen, and fifty men to run before him" (1 Kings 1:5).

The Attempt Is Thwarted

The powerful men that were associates of King David didn't support Adonijah's attempt to usurp the throne. the prophet Nathan was one of them. He went before Bathsheba, mother of Solomon, whom David had promised would succeed him. Nathan told Bathseheba of Adonijah's attempt, and beseeched her to go before the aging king and remind him of his promise that Solomon would ascend to the throne next.

David Proclaims Solomon King

One day, while Abishag was ministering to the king, Bathsheba entered and bowed before David. Bathsheba explained that Adonijah was trying to establish himself as king without David's knowledge. David called for the priest Zadok, the prophet Nathan, and Benaiah, the son of Jehoiada, and told them to get Solomon on the king's mule and take him to Gihon, where Nathan would anoint him king over Israel. After that, Solomon would sit on David's throne as king, even though David was still alive.

Adonijah Tries Again to Take the Throne

Adonijah had been outwitted and humiliated. Solomon could have ordered Adonijah's death, but didn't. Instead, Solomon offered him a conditional pardon. After David died and Solomon began sole rule of Israel, Adonijah went to Bathsheba. He begged Bathsheba to ask Solomon for permission for him to marry Abishag.

Bathsheba Takes Adonijah's Request to Solomon

Bathsheba carried Adonijah's request to Solomon. The king, however, suspected that Adonijah had ulterior motives. It was inappropriate for an ancient Hebrew king's subject (even if the petitioner was one of the king's relatives) to ask the monarch to give him a personal possession such as a royal wife or concubine. Often, it was seen as a maneuver to seize the throne. Thus, Solomon had Adonijah killed to keep him from destabilizing his rule or attempting an overthrow (1 Kings 2:17–25).

And now I ask one petition of thee, deny me not. And she said unto him, Say on. And he said, Speak, I pray thee, unto Solomon the king, (for he will not say thee nay,) that he give me Abishag the Shunammite to wife. And Bathsheba said, Well; I will speak for thee unto the king. (1 Kings 2:16–18)

Remaining Questions about Abishag

Though desired by Adonijah, son of Saul and Haggith, Abishag did not marry the prince. There is little information about what happened to her after Solomon had his brother killed. She most likely remained within the royal household, aligned with Solomon and Bathsheba.

Antiochis

There is little information about Antiochus to be found in the Bible, apart from a mention as the concubine of the Seleucid King Antiochus IV Epiphanes. His wife, Laodice IV, was also his sister. In addition to his wife/sister, he had a stepson named Antiochus V. Eupator and a stepdaughter, Laodice VI. Apart from the children his wife/sister brought to their marriage, the king had a son named Alexander I Balas. It is unclear whether Alexander was born of the king's wife/sister, his concubine Antiochis, or someone else, but he ruled from A.D. 152 to A.D. 145.

King Antiochus IV Epiphanes ruled over the Hellenistic Syrian lands from 175 B.C. to 164 B.C. Known as the Mad King, he may have been mentally ill. Although he established and occupied a special ivory chair or throne from which he delivered judgments over seemingly inconsequential issues, he also constructed great temples to the Greek gods, including one in Athens for Zeus. He adorned and decorated the island of Delos with beautiful statuary and inscribed altars. In Antioch, he had his workers build a temple to Jupiter that included a gold-lined ceiling and gilded-panel walls.

In order to better understand how Antiochus IV Epiphanes could have reached the decision to give two ancient cities to his concubine, causing the people of those cities to revolt, it may be helpful to present a little background information about the ruler and his reign.

FACT

Scholars say that the mother of Alexander I Balas may have been Laodice IV, but the information is spurious. Alexander claimed to be the son of Antiochus IV Epiphanes. He married Cleopatra Thea, daughter of Ptolemy VI Philometor. Like his father, Alexander took to calling himself Epiphanes, "manifestation of the god."

Jason Tries to Hellenize the Jews

In 175 B.C., the high priest Honi passed away. King Antiochus IV Epiphanes then made Jeshu (later known as Jason) the high priest because of bribes that Jason paid to get the appointment. They both desired to Hellenize Judea and make the Hebrews more Greeklike. Jason desired to make Jerusalem a Greek *polis,* or city-state. According to some sources, Jason held the office of high priest for three years.

Jason's Adversary Advances the Process

Menelaus, his adversary, was able to persuade the king to give him the office of high priest after the king became angry with Jason. Menelaus also paid bribes to the king. For the most part, people rejected Menelaus because he had no priestly lineage or Jewish authority for the office. Menelaus and his followers pushed to abandon Jewish law and customs in favor of the people becoming more like the Greeks. Antiochus IV Epiphanes permitted the changes, and a great gymnasium was built in Jerusalem. Many Jews abandoned their way of life.

The King Persecutes the Jews

Believing his kingdom was at last stable and secure, Antiochus IV Epiphanes set his sights on becoming ruler of Egypt. When he had defeated Egypt, he went to Jerusalem and raided the Temple of all of its gold and religious objects, and continued on to Syria. He sent an army to plunder, occupy, and Hellenize Jerusalem. The Jews became savagely persecuted under his reign. Antiochus IV Epiphanes abolished the Sabbath and forbade circumcision, the Hebrew's sign of their covenant with God.

Antiochus IV Epiphanes Outlaws Judaism

He issued a decree in 167 B.C. abolishing the Jewish religion. People living by the Torah were put to death by being burned alive, according to some sources. The persecution of the Jews was just one way Antiochus IV Epiphanes sought to strengthen his Hellenistic empire. But his attempts to Hellenize the Jews caused the Wars of the Maccabees.

The People Revolt

The people of Tarsus and Mallus did not support Antiochus IV Epiphanes. When word that the king had given the cities of Tarsus and Mallus to his concubine Antiochis, the people of those cities revolted. The King had little choice but to hurry off to restore calm. The Book of Daniel provides an apocalyptic narrative about the destruction of the "Ignoble King" that many believe to be King Antiochus IV Epiphanes.

And the king shall do according to his will...shall exalt himself...magnify himself above every god...shall speak marvelous things against the God of gods, and shall prosper till the indignation be accomplished...Neither shall he regard the God of his fathers, nor the desire of women, nor regard any god: for he shall magnify himself above all. (Daniel 11:36–37)

As for Antiochis, it is unlikely she had a very peaceful and fulfilling life as the wife of a man who was so mentally unstable, egocentric, and intolerant of the Jews. His defilement of the Temple in Jerusalem brought about a Jewish revolt, and the Jews (led by the Maccabeans) defeated Antiochus. They then purified their Temple and instituted Jewish rule over Judea.

The Jewish winter festival of Hanukkah, lasting eight days, is celebrated to commemorate the rededication of the Jewish Temple after the victory of Judas Maccabee and his sons against the Syrians, led by Antiochus IV Epiphanes. Traditionally, one candle is lit each night until all are lit. Hanukkah is also known as the Festival of Lights, Feast of Dedication, and Feast of the Maccabees.

Keturah

After Abraham and his wife Sarah married and had lived together for some time childless, Abraham took Hagar, his wife's Egyptian maidservant, as his concubine. He did so at the insistence of Sarah. Hagar subsequently bore Abraham a son named Ishmael (Genesis 16:11). According to Jewish and Muslim tradition, Ishmael is the ancestor of the Arabs. Sarah then became pregnant by Abraham and gave birth to Isaac, who had one wife his entire life and no concubines.

Now the sons of Keturah, Abraham's concubine: she bare Zimran, and Jokshan, and Medan, and Midian, and Ishbak, and Shuah. And the sons of Jokshan; Sheba, and Dedan. And the sons of Midian; Ephah, and Epher, and Henoch, and Abida, and Eldaah. All these are the sons of Keturah. (1 Chronicles 1: 32–33)

After Sarah died, Abraham took Keturah as his wife (Genesis 25:1). But the Bible seemingly contains a contradiction when a few verses later in Genesis 25:5–6, it states: "And Abraham gave all that he had unto Isaac. But unto the sons of the concubines, which Abraham had, Abraham gave gifts, and sent them away from Isaac his son, while he yet lived, eastward, unto the east country." So Keturah, though not mentioned by name, is nevertheless linked with Hagar as Abraham's concubine. In 1 Chronicles, Keturah is again referred to as Abraham's concubine.

Keturah remained with Abraham until he died. Isaac and Ishmael buried Abraham in the cave of Machpelah, in the field that he had purchased when Sarah died. There, the men placed their father next to the great love of his life. Keturah never reached the status of Sarah, even after Sarah was dead. But because of Sarah, Hagar, and Keturah, Abraham became the "father of many nations," as God had promised, by means of his sons and their descendants.

Reumah

Reumah was the concubine of Nahor (elder brother of Abraham). Nahor already had a wife, Milcah, daughter of Haran and sister of Lot and Iscah (Genesis 11:29). Since Nahor and Haran were brothers, Milcah was Nahor's niece. Milcah was born in Ur, the ancient Mesopotamian city. After marriage, Nahor and Milcah made a home on the eastern side of the Euphrates River, in the land of Haran. Milcah bore Nahor eight sons: Huz, Buz, Kemuel, Chesed, Hazo, Pildash, Jidlaph, and Bethuel (Genesis 22:21–22).

Reumah gave birth to four more (Genesis 22:24). The twelve sons of Nahor became the fathers of twelve Aramean tribes. A midrashic account makes Milcah the ancestress of all of the world's prophets.

Meaning of Her Name

Reumah's name has been translated as "lofty," "sublime," "elevated," and "exalted." However, there is little in the biblical references to her to suggest why she was given that name, or if she did something extraordinary to warrant the name. However, scholars say that names were exceedingly important in biblical times, and were not lightly given. Perhaps her parents had an expectation or hope of how her life might unfold, and thus named her Reumah.

Family Ties

Some biblical historians suggest that communication was maintained between Nahor's family (including his wife Milcah, Reumah, and their children) in the land of Haran and Abraham's family in Canaan (after Abraham had moved there). That is, at least until Abraham's grandson, Jacob, deceived his elder brother Essau. After Jacob fled his family home, according to one source, the connection and correspondence between the families ended.

Another Interesting Family Connection

Rebekah, an important female biblical figure, was not related to Reumah through a bloodline, but she was connected to Nahor's family. In fact, she was the granddaughter of Nahor and Milcah, offspring of their son Bethuel and his wife. Rebekah was chosen by the servant of Abraham as a wife for Isaac (Abraham's son). Rebekah's family agreed to let her go with the servant when he returned to Canaan. She married Isaac and bore him Jacob and Essau.

Rizpah

In Chapter 9, you learned that Rizpah was the daughter of Aiah and the concubine of Saul. This section focuses on fleshing out a few more details about her as Saul's concubine, and the heart-wrenching tragedy she endured. Rizpah's boys were named Armoni and Mephibosheth (2 Samuel 21:8). Her name means "coal" or "hot stone." She was caught up in a political turmoil having to do with the legacy of her husband Saul, which resulted in her personal tragedy and grief beyond measure. Her story in the Bible is brief, but shows a woman of tenderness, gentleness, and great resolve.

In the first years of his reign as king, David saw his people suffer through a three-year famine. David asked God the reason for the famine. He was told that it was because of the murder of the Gibeonites by Saul.

Who Were the Gibeonites?

The Gibeonites lived in Gibeon (but also, perhaps, in a trio of several nearby cities). They wanted to establish an alliance with Israel. Meeting the Israelites at Gilgal, they pretended they were foreign ambassadors. The Israelites entered into an alliance with them, but once they discovered the ruse, they relegated the Gibeonites to cutting wood and carrying water. According to the Scriptures, the Gibeonites "...were not of the children of Israel, but of the remnant of the Amorites..." (2 Samuel 21:2). Saul broke the alliance with the Gibeonites by killing some, and trying to kill the rest (2 Samuel 21:1–2, 21:5).

QUESTION?

To which Hebrew tribe did Rizpah belong?
The Bible states that Rizpah was Aiah's daughter, and that Aiah was an Edomite. The Edomites, Moabites, and Ammonites were tribes of ancient peoples, related to the children of Israel but at times antagonistic to them. The nomadic Edomites lived in the Negev Desert in what is today southern Israel, near Jordan. Some biblical sources assert that the nation of Edomites ceased to exist after the Jewish-Roman Wars.

What Did They Demand?

Instead of asking God what should be done and waiting for an answer, David went to the Gibeonites and asked them what he could do to appease them. They demanded revenge upon the men of the house of Saul.

The Bible doesn't say whether or not David had a heavy heart while he considered the Gibeonites demands. The Gibeonites would settle for nothing less, so David was forced to agree, and the deed was accomplished.

How Did Rizpah Deal with the Dead?

The men's bodies had been lying on the ground unburied where the birds and wild animals could freely desecrate them. Rizpah sat down on the sackcloth-covered rock of Gibeah and began a vigil through long days and nights, protecting the bodies. She stayed there watching over her dead for five long months. Eventually, David was informed and took pity on her. He transported the bones of Saul and Saul's son Jonathan, and "the bones of them that were hanged" to the land of Benjamin (Saul was of the tribe of

Benjamin, the smallest of the tribes of Israel). There, he had them buried in the tomb of Kish, Saul's father (2 Samuel 21:12–14).

And Rizpah the daughter of Aiah took sackcloth, and spread it for her upon the rock, from the beginning of harvest until water dropped upon them out of heaven, and suffered neither the birds of the air to rest on them by day, nor the beasts of the field by night. And it was told David what Rizpah the daughter of Aiah, the concubine of Saul, had done (2 Samuel 21:10–11).

After Saul experienced a crushing defeat in the battle of Gilboa, Abner (son of Ner, and a soldier loyal to Saul) made Saul's only surviving son, Ishbaal, king of Israel at the site of Mahanaim. Meanwhile, David was ruling as king of Judah at Hebron. War between the soldiers of the two factions ended in defeat of Abner. When Ishbaal criticized Abner for marrying Rizpah, Abner switched his support to David.

Chapter 17

Women Who Advised, Taunted, or Lied

Pillow talk is a term often used by modern writers to convey the idea of a woman's counsel to her husband in quiet conversation, often at bedtime or in intimate moments. Women have been sharing wisdom and insight since the days of Adam and Eve. In the biblical narratives, there are stories of queens advising their kings, and wives offering suggestions to their husbands or tribal sisters. But there are also stories of women's gossip, lies, and taunts—women's words that hurt instead of helping.

Arsinoe, Sister and Advisor of Ptolemy IV Philopator

Arsinoe was the daughter of the Egyptian King Ptolemy III Euergetes and his queen, Berenice II. According to some sources, the Ptolemy rulers were resented by the Egyptian people because they ran Egypt as their own private reserve, using the land, wealth, and natural resources for their own personal gratification. The dynasty's declining fortunes reflected the abuses, and the lack of leadership brought threats to the throne as well as politico-military intrigues and insurrections. Arsinoe's father was the last of the Ptolemies with any real power at home and in the world. Many Egyptians longed for a return to the traditional rule by Pharoahs.

When Arsinoe's brother, Ptolemy IV Philopator (meaning "father loving"), assumed the throne, he relied on input from his advisors and women, including his sister, to rule. Possibly influenced by the counsel of his closest advisor, Sosibius, Ptolemy IV acquiesced to having his own mother poisoned and his brother murdered by scalding. His knee-jerk response to a rumor (that conceivably started with Sosibius) meant that Arsinoe lost two members of her family in her brother's murderous plot.

In 217 B.C., Arsinoe accompanied Ptolemy IV Philopator into battle against the Syrian king Antiochus III at Raphia, in Palestine. Arsinoe walked along the ranks of soldiers on the battlefield offering each man two *minae* of gold if they prevailed and conquered Antiochus (3 Maccabees 1:4).

QUESTION?

What information is found in The Books of Maccabees?
These books, found in some Bibles, cover the Jewish revolt against the Seleucid kings, persecutors of the Jews, and the recovery of their Temple, among other events in Jewish history. Jews and Protestants consider the books as apocryphal texts, but the Catholic Church regards them as inspired and includes them.

Ptolemy IV and the Egyptian soldiers defeated the army of Antiochus III. When he returned to Egypt, he married his sister Arsinoe, who became queen. Some sources put the date of their marriage at 220 B.C. She may have been called Cleopatra at that point, since taking that name was often the custom among Egyptian queens.

In 204 B.C., Queen Arsinoe was renounced. She died in a fire during a coup at the palace later that year, a short time before the death of her brother-husband. Her death is believed to have been a murder, quite possibly at the behest of Sosibius or Ptolemy IV Philopator.

FACT

Arsinoe III was born in 246 B.C. and died in 204 B.C. She had a son named Ptolemy V from her marriage to her brother, Ptolemy IV. Her brother-husband also took a mistress, a woman named Agathoclea, and their liaison may have produced a child. In addition, Ptolemy IV had another affair with a courtesan named Hippe.

Although Arsinoe exerted some influence over Ptolemy IV Philopator in governmental matters, some scholars assert that the more powerful influence on him was that of his mistress Agathoclea. His reign was marked by feeble rule (causing the loss of a great deal of Ptolemaic Syria, as well as instability in Egypt), sensual indulgences, drunken debauchery, orgiastic religious practices, and a preoccupation with work on various religious temples, including:

- Temple of Isis at Philae
- Temple of Montu at Medamud
- Temple of Horus at Edfu
- Ptolemaic Temple of Hathor at Thebes on the West Bank
- Khonsu Temple at Karnak

Peninnah

The First Book of Samuel reveals the story of a man named Elkanah from Ramathaim who had two wives. He loved Hannah and wed her with the hope of having many children; however, the Lord kept Hannah barren. So,

Elkanah took Peninnah as wife, and she bore him many children. Elkanah made a pilgrimage to Shiloh each year to offer sacrifice to the Lord. According to the Bible, he gave a portion to Peninnah and all of their children, but he offered Hannah a double portion because he loved her so much, and because she remained barren. Year after year, Peninnah used the occasion to taunt Hannah for being childless. Her reproaches caused Hannah to weep and refuse to eat.

On one occasion, after Peninnah had castigated her mercilessly, Hannah wept, prayed, and made a vow that if God gave her a son, she would give the boy to the Lord's work for the rest of his life. Eli, the priest, overheard her praying and told her, "Go in peace: and the God of Israel grant thee thy petition that thou hast asked of him" (1 Samuel 1:17).

The Bible paints the images of Hannah and Peninnah in high contrast. Hannah was sad and disheartened at not having a child, while Peninnah was prideful and provocative in her criticism of Hannah. Their husband endeavored to keep the peace at home between them, while remaining spiritually devoted to God.

Elkanah Reveals His Love for Hannah

Elkanah asked Hannah one day when she was weeping and feeling melancholy about her barrenness, "...am not I better to thee than ten sons?" (1 Samuel 1:8). He showered Hannah with attention and gifts; he showed her love through his faithfulness and tenderness toward her. But the more he focused on Hannah, the more jealous Peninnah became.

Hannah Gives Birth

The Bible states that the Lord heard Hannah's prayer and blessed her with a son. Hannah and Elkanah named their child Samuel. After Hannah had weaned him, she kept her word to God, taking Samuel up to Shiloh and offering him to Eli the priest, so the boy might be brought up to do the work of the Lord for the rest of his life.

Peninnah Blessed Elkanah, Too

The second wife of Elkanah wasn't a mean-spirited woman, and she blessed him with many children. But Elkanah's greater love for Hannah could not be mistaken. The Scriptures do not reveal whether or not the tension between the two women decreased after Hannah bore Samuel. Did Elkanah show more love to Samuel than to Peninnah's children? Peninnah's jealousy may not have subsided, but she could no longer find fault with Hannah or taunt her for being barren. Peninnah fades from the story once Samuel is born.

Hannah Bears Other Children

Hannah didn't forget her son Samuel after giving him to Eli. She went up to Shiloh each year and took him a little coat that she had made. Eli prayed that Hannah and Elkanah might have other children, and Hannah did–three sons and two daughters.

Samarian Women at the Well

In the Old Testament Book of Amos, there is a verse about wealthy Samarian women who spoke about the downtrodden and poor, while at the same time oppressing such people themselves. These women were hypocrites; their mouths spouted platitudes while their actions spoke volumes about the kind of beliefs they really held. The prophet Amos deplored such immoral behavior, and warned of the consequences of engaging in such hypocrisy.

Hear this word, ye kine [women]of Bashan, that are in the mountain of Samaria, which oppress the poor, which crush the needy, which say to their masters, Bring, and let us drink. The Lord God hath sworn by his holiness, that, lo, the days shall come upon you, that he will take you away with hooks, and your posterity with fishhooks. (Amos 4:1–2)

Such abuse of the less fortunate, while at the same time indulging in gluttonous excess, had become visible in the wealthy northern kingdom in the time of Amos. His poetry addressed a litany of such offences against God. In some Bibles the Samarian women are called the "cows of Bashan." In the book of Amos, they aren't mentioned again.

FACT

In ancient times, Bashan was east of the Sea of Galilee, and known for its fertile lands, excellent pastures, and fatted herds—much like the slothful Samarian women to whom Amos refers in his prophecy.

The Book of Amos contains a collection of the oracles of the prophet Amos, a Hebrew shepherd of Tekoa in Judah (in the southern kingdom). After the Lord called Amos, the shepherd became a prophet who spoke out boldly against the excesses of the wealthy in the northern kingdom. He railed against those who became wealthy at the expense of others, who had forsaken their values and devotion to God, and whose lives were in moral decline. At the shrine at Bethel, Amos addressed the offences against the covenant of God by the cities of Damascus, Tyre, Philistia, and Edom. Then he set forth a sweeping indictment of the ancient nation of Israel for her injustices and idolatry.

So outspoken and forceful was Amos in his denunciation of Israel and his criticism of the moral, religious, and social condition of the people, the priest of the temple at Bethel drove him away, but not before Amos pronounced a prophesy for the priest.

Amos prophesied tribulations and dark times when the people would be put into captivity and the royal house would collapse. He believed that the people had not listened to warnings that God had given them through his prophets. The prosperity of the northern and southern kingdoms had reached a peak, and moral decline followed the rise in wealth. According to Amos, the Lord had repeatedly inflicted chastisements upon Israel, but the people had not returned to the Lord, so God's punishment was coming, and was unavoidable. Destruction might open up the possibility of restoration, according to Amos, under the leadership of a future Davidic king.

The Woman at the Well

The Samaritan woman in the New Testament Book of John told other Samaritans of the prophet she met at Jacob's well, and that he had told her about the "living water." She believed he was the Messiah, and Jesus confirmed it. Because of her, many Samaritans came to believe that Jesus was Christ the Savior (John 4:42). But this woman answered one question that Jesus asked in a roundabout way, and he called her on it.

Jesus' travels took him from town to town. He had left Judea and entered Samaria in order to return to Galilee. By the time he reached Sychar, near a plot of land owned by Joseph (Jacob's son), he was tired and thirsty. Jacob had a well, and Jesus went over to it and sat down. His disciples continued on to the town to purchase food. While Jesus rested at the well, a Samaritan woman came to draw water. Jesus asked her to give him a drink.

Then saith the woman of Samaria unto him, How is it that thou, being a Jew, askest drink of me, which am a woman of Samaria? for the Jews have no dealings with the Samaritans. Jesus answered and said unto her, If thou knewest the gift of God, and who it is that saith to thee, Give me to drink; thou wouldest have asked of him, and he would have given thee living water. (John 4:9–10)

The Woman Has Many Questions

The woman observed that Jesus had nothing with which to draw water from the well. She told him the well was deep, and asked him where he got the living water. But she didn't stop there. She might have been a Samaritan woman talking with a Jewish man, but it was the sixth hour, and no one was around. She had more questions for him: Was he greater than Jacob who dug the well, drank from it himself, and provided water from it to his cattle and children? After Jesus told her that his water would give everlasting life, the woman asked him to give her some of the living water.

Jesus told her to go and find her husband and come back. The woman said she had no husband. Jesus replied, "Thou hast well said, I have no husband: For thou hast had five husbands; and he whom thou now hast is not thy husband…" (John 4:17–18).

Jesus Reveals How to Worship God

The Samaritan woman told Jesus that she could see he was a prophet; how else would an ordinary individual know such things about her? Then she pointed out that, "Our fathers worshipped in this mountain; and ye say, that in Jerusalem is the place where men ought to worship" (John 4:20). Jesus replied that the hour was coming in which her people would worship neither on the mountain nor in Jerusalem, for "Ye worship ye know not what: we know what we worship: for salvation is of the Jews" (John 4:21–22). As they talked, Jesus further explained that God is a Spirit, and must be worshipped in Spirit and in truth.

Jesus Reveals He Is the Long-Awaited Messiah

The Samaritan woman became fully engaged in her chat with Jesus. She told him that she believed that the Messiah, who was called Christ, was coming, and when he did, he would explain everything to the people. Jesus made an astonishing and powerful declaration to her: "I that speak unto thee am he" (John 4:26).

When Jesus' disciples returned, they were surprised to discover him talking with the foreign woman, "…yet no man said, What seekest thou? or, Why talkest thou with her?" (John 4:27).

The Woman Shares Her Story

The woman returned to town and told the people that Jesus had been able to tell her everything she had ever done. Then she asked, "…is not this the Christ?" (John 4:29). The townspeople hurried to see the Christ for themselves, and many, after seeing Jesus, believed he was truly the Messiah. They told the woman that they believed, not because of her word, but because they'd heard for themselves, and were convinced that Jesus was the Savior of the world.

Wife of Naaman

Naaman was a man of honor and valor, and well regarded in his position as captain of the host of the king of Syria. However, Naaman, though a mighty army commander, was a leper. In Naaman's household was a young captive from the land of Israel who waited on Naaman's wife. The Bible does not name Naaman's wife, and doesn't reveal any details about her or her relationship with Naaman. One day, the servant girl told her mistress that there was a prophet in Samaria who could cure Naaman of his leprosy.

Naaman's wife must have been excited to learn that there was a possibility her husband could be cured. Apparently she urged him to make the trip to Israel, because the Bible states that Naaman went to the king and told the monarch everything that the servant girl had said to his wife. The king told Naaman that he would send a letter to the king of Israel on Naaman's behalf. Naaman went to Israel and presented his letter to the king of Israel. Instead of providing Naaman an easy introduction to the king, the king misconstrued the letter as an attempt by the king of Syria to provoke a fight.

And it came to pass, when the king...had read the letter...he rent his clothes, and said, Am I God, to kill and to make alive, that this man doth send unto me to recover a man of his leprosy...see how he seeketh a quarrel against me. (2 Kings 5:7)

The Prophet Elisha Asks for Naaman

When the prophet Elisha heard that the king of Israel had rent his clothes, he sent a message to the king. He told the monarch to send Naaman to him so the leper might know "...that there is a prophet in Israel" (2 Kings 5:8). Naaman got into his chariot and rode to the house of Elisha. There he stood at the door, waiting to meet the prophet.

Elisha's Orders

Elisha did not go directly to meet Naaman. Instead, he sent a messenger to the door to tell Naaman to go down to the river Jordan and wash his body seven times. After that, his leprosy would be gone. But Naaman had some preconceived notion of how Elisha might heal him: He believed that the prophet would come out to face him, invoke the Lord his God, strike his hand over the place, and perform the healing. When Elisha did not even greet him, Naaman became upset. If he were just going to wash himself, weren't the rivers in Syria better than the ones in Jordan? Instead of going down to the river, Naaman left, angry.

The Prophet Refuses Naaman's Gifts

The servants in Naaman's retinue called him back and convinced him to go to the Jordan and bathe as the prophet had instructed. To his amazement, as the water covered his body, his flesh became new again, and he was clean. Naaman, feeling grateful and indebted, returned with his entourage to the house of Elisha. He told the prophet, "Behold, now I know that there is no God in all the earth, but in Israel: now therefore, I pray thee, take a blessing of thy servant" (2 Kings 5:15). But the prophet refused to take anything from Naaman.

Elisha's Servant Is Overcome with Greed

Gehazi, Elisha's servant, thought that Elisha should have taken something from Naaman. He decided he would run after Naaman himself and take something from him, on the pretext that Elisha had sent him. He requested a talent of silver, and two changes of garments, but Naaman gave him double what he asked, and continued on his way. Most likely, he returned to his wife to celebrate a complete recovery from the ravages of leprosy.

Gehazi Is Stricken with Leprosy

When Elisha confronted Gehazi about where he went, Gehazi lied and said that he hadn't gone anywhere. Elisha told him that he was present in spirit when Naaman jumped down from his chariot to wait for him, and asked Gehazi, "Is it a time to receive money, and to receive garments, and oliveyards, and vineyards, and sheep, and oxen, and menservants, and maidservants?" (2 Kings 5:26). Elisha told Gehazi that because of his actions, he would now have Naaman's leprosy, and so would the generations of his family, forever.

Elisha must have acquired a great spiritual power from the Divine, and perhaps also from his teacher, the prophet Elijah. After the death of Elijah, Elisha worked many miracles during his lifetime. The Bible contains a story about how a dead man had been cast into the grave of Elisha, but as soon as the body came into contact with the prophet's remains, the dead man returned to life and stood up (2 Kings 13:21).

Wives of Midian's Warriors

Moses went to the Israelites and told them to carry out the Lord's vengeance on the Midianites, starting a war started between the two groups. The Israelites killed all five Midianite kings and all the males, but spared the women, taking them captive along with their children. The Israelites also took possession of the Midianite herds, flocks, and wealth. After they set fire to the Midianite villages and towns, they took the spoils of war to the camp of Moses on the plain of Moab

When Moses saw the women he became infuriated at the officers, soldiers, and commanders. He exclaimed, "Have ye saved all the women alive? Behold, these caused the children of Israel, through the counsel of Balaam, to commit trespass against the Lord in the matter of Peor, and there was a plague among the congregation of the Lord" (Numbers 31:15–16). In other words, these women were believed to have caused the Israelites at Peor to renounce God, and therefore had brought a plague upon the Hebrews.

Moses ordered the soldiers to kill every male child and all of the women who had intercourse with men. He told the men that they could spare and keep for themselves any young virgin. The Bible states that Israelite soldiers took 32,000 virgins, and "…the Lord's tribute was thirty and two persons" (Numbers 31:35, 31:40).

Chapter 18

Women Who Sacrificed and Suffered

The ancient world had experienced a decline in urban communities by circa 2092 B.C. when Abraham entered Canaan. Agrarian-based living had been replaced by a pastoral nomadic life. The tent life of the Canaan culture was difficult for many women, including Abraham's wives Sarah and Hagar, and it remained challenging for future generations. Although ancient women were resourceful and capable, they still suffered and sacrificed as they moved across the ancient landscape. Too often, the worst of what they had to endure came through the dictates of men.

Jochebed, Mother of Moses

Jochebed is regarded as one of the great Hebrew matriarchs of the Old Testament. Her name means "The Lord is glorious." Her parents, Melcha and Levi, had four children: Gershon, Kohath, Merari, and Jochebed. Levi, one of the twelve sons of Jacob, was already sixty-four when Melcha gave birth to Jochebed. The girl grew into womanhood with many excellent qualities, including selflessness, devotion to her family, and a deep and abiding love and commitment to God. Apparently these were exactly the qualities Amram sought in a wife, for he married Jochebed.

Some rabbinical sources assert that Jochebed was none other than Shiprah. You may recall reading about Shiprah, and her counterpart Puah, in Chapter 5. They were the midwives who defied the pharaoh's order to kill all infant boys born to the Hebrew women. God promised them "houses," which many rabbis interpret to mean dynasties of royalty and priesthood. Shiprah's son Aaron became the first high priest.

Others say Jochebed was the matriarch and founder of the nation of Jews. She may have been 130 years old when she gave birth to Moses. Exodus 15:20 states that Miriam, Jochebed's second child, became a prophetess. Her third child, Moses, became known as the patriarch and savior of the Israelites. All three of her children became famous spiritual pillars for the Hebrews.

Moses witnessed the maltreatment of the Jews in Egypt, where they had migrated with Joseph to escape a severe famine. But the numbers of Israelites kept increasing, causing the pharaoh to worry that the Jews were overtaking the Egyptians in a population explosion. He made life even more difficult for the Hebrews.

While Joseph was alive, the pharaoh did little to curtail the increasing numbers of Jews. But a new pharaoh came to power after Joseph died, and that pharaoh didn't favor the Jews. He began a campaign of murder. At the time Moses was born, the pharaoh had just ordered all Hebrew baby boys killed (Exodus 1:22). Before Moses could grow up to become the Savior of the Jews, he had to survive to adulthood. His mother played a paramount role in ensuring that he did.

Jochebed Places Moses in the River

With the help of her husband Amram and her children Miriam and Aaron, Jochebed kept the infant Moses hidden for three months. But as the child grew, she worried that he would be discovered by those loyal to the pharaoh. She hatched a plan to hide her son in a little ark she had fashioned from some bulrushes. She placed the ark in the Nile near some reeds. She knew that the pharaoh's daughter came to that place each day with her attendants in order to bathe, and she hoped that the princess would discover her baby boy.

QUESTION?

What did the Egyptians believe about moral behavior?
The Egyptian word *ma'at* represented truth and order. *Ma'at* was also the goddess who represented this abstraction. The Egyptians believed the universe to be orderly, rational, and in perfect balance. In the moral realm, there was retribution for sin and reward for purity. The Greeks called the universe's underlying rationality and order *logos*, a word adopted by Christians to mean God.

Miriam Keeps a Watchful Eye on Moses

Miriam watched over Moses until the princess came for her bath and discovered the baby crying at the water's edge, floating in his little papyrus ark. Some sources say Miriam was only five years old at that time. The pharaoh's daughter rescued the baby, and fretted about how to calm and feed him. Miriam offered to find a wet nurse from among the Hebrew women. The pharaoh's daughter agreed and sent Miriam away. Miriam went straight to her mother; thus, Jochebed became the Hebrew woman chosen to nurse the infant.

Moses Grows Up in the Pharaoh's Court

The pharaoh's daughter adopted little Moses, but Jochebed most likely cared for him throughout his youth. He undoubtedly received an excellent education, probably at the university level. He also may have served in Egypt's military for a number of years. But Moses always remembered his Hebrew mother and her sacrifice and risk in giving him up in order to save him. His discontent over the treatment of his people at the hands of the Egyptians festered until he was about forty. Then, he saw a Hebrew slave being mistreated by an Egyptian slave master. Moses killed the man and then fled Egypt for Midian. There he remained until the Angel of God told him to bring the Hebrews out of bondage.

QUESTION?

Where was Jochebed buried?
Sources say she was buried in Hebron, along with Leah, Zilpha, Bilhah, Zipporah, Elisheva, and Abigail (wife of King David). Today, the site is considered the second holiest in all of Israel, and is called the Tomb of the Matriarchs.

Jochebed Remains in Bondage

You can't help wondering what happened to the beleaguered mother whose last hope was that her son wouldn't perish by the hands of the Egyptians. She must have heard about the slave master Moses killed. She must have known that Moses had fled. The Bible doesn't say whether she lived to see her son lead the Israelites out of Egypt. But knowing she'd taught him to stay close to God and stand by his principles, she would have known that Moses had the power to triumph in whatever he tried. The Lord had something mighty for Moses to do, but the Bible doesn't say if Jochebed lived to see it.

Mother of Seven Tortured and Murdered Sons

She is referred to in the Second Book of Maccabees, Chapter 7, as "Mother." Her story is linked to the Jewish Festival of Lights, or Hanukkah. Tradition refers to her as Hannah, the mother of seven sons. Her sons were arrested and tortured by King Antiochus (presumably the "Mad King"), who mercilessly beat them with whips to make them eat pork. For the Hebrews, the eating of pork was prohibited.

The Eldest Boy's Tongue is Cut Out

Hannah's eldest child spoke up for the others and told the king that there wasn't any point in questioning them, as they would die rather than violate God's law. His words angered the king, prompting the monarch to have all of the pans and cauldrons brought out and put on fires. While the cookware was heating, the king ordered his men to cut out the tongue of the outspoken lad, and to amputate the boy's hands and feet while his mother and brothers watched in horror.

The Torture Worsens

The king then ordered the boy to be fried alive. Hannah and her sons knew that they wouldn't be spared either if they refused, but were willing to suffer and die. Each, in turn, proclaimed before being murdered that while the king might deprive them of this life, in the afterlife they would be raised up by the King of the world, and that they were willing to die for the laws of that king.

The Mother Says Farewell to Her Last Son

After six of her sons were tortured and murdered, the woman was given the opportunity to persuade her youngest to eat the pork or perish like his brothers. Hannah, according to the legend, told her boy to follow the example of the others, for it was better to die than to break a commandment of the Torah against eating nonkosher meat.

Hannah Gives Him a Message for Abraham

According to legend, Hannah kissed her young son and whispered that when he died and saw the great patriarch Abraham, to tell him something for her—not to feel proud that he had built an altar and prepared for the sacrifice of his only son, because she had sacrificed seven sons. While Abraham's sacrifice was God's test, hers was real; and not only were her seven sons martyred and taken to God, she would be, too. In one day, God would receive the eight martyrs.

In some synagogues, the liturgical poems composed to celebrate Hannah's sacrifice are recited annually on the Sabbath of Hanukkah. Jewish liturgical poems are called *piyyut* (singular) or *piyyutim* (plural), and have been popular for centuries. During religious services, *piyyutim* are either recited or sung.

Prayerful Maccabees Women

These women aren't named in the Second Book of Maccabees, but are referred to as women who tied sackcloth around their breasts, and who raised their hands toward heaven in a kind of collective supplication to God that he might see the anguish of his faithful and help them in their hour of need.

Their story begins during the reign of Antiochus Epiphanes and his son Eupator. A man named Simon, of the tribe of Benjamin, who was superintendent of the Jerusalem Temple, aspired to do something in the city market (perhaps not honorable) that the pious High Priest Onias wouldn't allow. The two had a falling out. and Simon went to Apollonius of Tarsus (then governor of Phoenicia and Coelesyria) to report that untold riches could be found in the Temple. Simon suggested that it all be confiscated and brought under the management of King Seleucus.

Apollonius then went to the ruler to discuss it, and the king decided to seize everything of value from the Temple. He sent his minister, Heliodorus, to oversee the exploitation of the Temple. Heliodorus set off for Phoenicia and Coelesyria, but in reality, he headed straight for Jerusalem, where the high priest cordially received him.

The Priest Reveals the Temple's Wealth

The high priest revealed that, indeed, there were things of value in the Temple (but nothing like what Simon had claimed). The total amounted to roughly a few hundred talents of silver and gold. A portion of the amount was reserved in a fund to care for orphans and widows. The priest also explained that another part belonged to a man of high position and dignity named Hyrcanus, who was a member of the Tobias family. The Bible states that Joseph was the father of Hyrcanus, and Hyrcanus's mother was the sister of Onias II, the high priest.

FACT

The Second Book of Maccabees states that King Seleucus was the elder brother of Antiochus Epiphanes, and that their father was Antiochus the Great. The family of Judas Maccabeus carried out campaigns against Antiochus Epiphanes and his son Eupator after the Temple had been looted and desecrated.

Heliodorus Defiles the Temple

Despite the protests of the high priest, Heliodorus carried out the king's order to seize whatever he could find of value in the Temple. All the priests fell down before the altar and prayed to God. Everyone could see the anguish in the expression of the high priest; nobody knew how to stop the robbing and defiling of the Temple.

The Women Converge onto the Streets

Jews made public supplication. The women wrapped sackcloth or haircloth around their breasts and entered the streets. Even the virgins (who usually stayed inside) came out to witness the calamity. They stretched their arms upright and held their hands open in a gesture of supplication to God; they asked the Divine to preserve their treasure.

Heliodorus Is Struck Down

A richly festooned horse with a rider in a golden suit of armor suddenly appeared and reared up on its hind legs. Its front hooves struck Heliodorus. Two handsome young men, dressed in finery, appeared on either side of the king's minister and began flogging him. Heliodorus soon fell to the ground. The people watching believed that the horse and rider, and the two young men, were the manifestation of the Spirit of God. Heliodorus was carried out on a litter, believed to be dying.

Four rooms in a second-floor apartment of the Pontifical Palace in the Vatican are known as the Stanze of Raphael. One of the rooms is designated the Room of Heliodorus, and features pictorial decoration by Raphael and his students (A.D. 1503 to A.D. 1513).

Friends of Heliodorus Beg for His Life

While Heliodorus remained unconscious, his friends begged the High Priest Onias to pray to God to spare their friend's life. Onias feared that the king would think that Jews had harmed his emissary, so he decided to help the wounded Heliodorus offer a sacrifice for health before God. When Heliodorus returned to the king, and the king asked him who should go to the Temple next, Heliodorus answered: "your enemy." Heliodorus believed the power of God would protect the Temple of the Jews.

Pregnant Women Destined to Be Torn Apart

The Hebrew prophet Isaiah had many visions. He was a great religious man who was both overcome with the beauty of the holiness of God, and disgusted with the depths of sin and degradation of humans who had turned away from the Lord. Isaiah called the children of God to religious reform and spoke of grim consequences for those who refused to hear the message. In Chapter 13 in the Book of Isaiah, the prophet addresses pagan nations, in particular Babylon. His oracle seems to use the point of view of the Divine at times, but he also uses his own point of view to speak out, warning that, "…the Lord of hosts mustereth the host of the battle. They come from a far country, from the end of heaven, even the Lord, and the weapons of his indignation, to destroy the whole land" (Isaiah 13:4–5).

Isaiah favored language that compelled people to action. In the next passage, he speaks of pregnant women (those joined together) who are destined to be run through with swords, and who must watch as their children are murdered.

Every one that is found shall be thrust through; and every one that is joined unto them shall fall by the sword. Their children also shall be dashed to pieces before their eyes; their houses shall be spoiled, and their wives ravished. (Isaiah 13:15–16)

One source asserts that Elisha, a predecessor of Isaiah who prophesied from roughly 892 B.C. to 832 B.C., also foretold a similar event with the same dire fate for expectant mothers. Psalm 137 mentions the dashing "…of thy little ones against the stones…" in an indictment against Babylon. Nahum the Elkoshite, another Old Testament prophet, similarly had a vision of "…young children…dashed in pieces at the top of all the streets" (Nahum 3:10), due to the Lord's wrath and vengeance upon the unfaithful.

The Virgin Daughter of the Elderly Man of Gibeah

The town of Gibeah was at one point a Benjamite enclave. The men there were a wicked lot. One day a stranger passed through their town, a Levite from Ephraim traveling with his concubine and two donkeys on his way back to Ephraim. The two of them passed through the town of Gibeah at dusk. The only person they saw was an old man who was walking in from his field. The man invited the couple to remain in town for the night, offering them his home and a hot meal. After some time, the men of Gibeah knocked at the old man's door and demanded that he send out the Levite—they all wanted to have sex with the visitor. The old man begged them not to rape the Levite.

Then the elderly man offered his virgin daughter, and told the villagers that they could do with her whatever they pleased. However, the men would not listen. This placed the guest and the host in a difficult position. The Levite didn't want to go outside and appease the desire of the Benjamites, and the old man didn't want to send his young daughter out to be attacked. When the Levite realized that the men of Gilbeah were going to continue clamoring for him, he escorted his concubine into the group of men and left her. She was sacrificed to them, and the virgin and the Levite were spared.

Abraham had two concubines, or secondary wives; Gideon had one; David had ten; Nahor had one; Solomon had upwards of three hundred; and Rehoboam had roughly sixty, just to name a few men of the Old Testament who kept multiple women.

The story illustrates the depravity and wickedness common to biblical times. The final verse of the story states, "And it was so, that all that saw it said, There was no such deed done nor seen from the day that the children of Israel came up out of the land of Egypt unto this day: consider of it, take advice, and speak your minds" (Judges 19:30).

Expendable Women

Feminist theologians say that the story of the virgin daughter of the elderly man of Gibeah illustrates that concubines were expendable to the men of ancient times when they were no longer needed, or became a liability or threat. Abraham cast out the bondwoman (Hagar) after Sarah bore him a son. David had ten concubines, and when he fled from Absalom, the concubines stayed in his house. Absalom, his son, came to the house and found the women. He pitched a tent on top of the house and raped the helpless concubines in view of all of Israel (2 Samuel 16:21–22). In the story above, the Levite had only one concubine, but the Old Testament mentions many instances of men taking multiple bondwomen and concubines.

Old Testament women concerned themselves primarily with domestic tasks, caring for the home and bearing heirs and warriors to defend their tribes, city-states, and nations. With the exception of Esther, whose story is detailed in the Book of Esther, and Judith, whose narrative is relegated to the Apocrypha, the women of the Bible, for the most part, did not serve roles generally filled by men.

In some cases, the women were treated as wives, albeit of inferior standing and lacking the authority of the primary wife. In other situations, such as Solomon's harem, it would have been difficult for a woman to believe she had any wifely value other than sexual, due to the fact that her male provider kept several hundred other women for his pleasure. Granted, Solomon was a king, and had the means to support wives and concubines. It is difficult for many modern women not to judge ancient societies using a modern moral compass. Still, as the point is made about women suffering and sacrificing, it is clear that while some ancient women enjoyed a degree of comfort and security within the households of the men who watched over them, others clearly didn't.

Chapter 19

Women Who Showed Courage and Commitment

The Bible reveals the names of women in both the Old and New Testaments who followed their hearts, adhered to their moral values, and showed courage in the face of adversity. Some died when their commitment to their faith meant going against a political ruler's attempt to coerce them into abandoning their ancient way of life. Other women devoted themselves to helping build the first Hebrew Tabernacle after God gave Moses the Ten Commandments. All of them showed devotion to God and an abiding loyalty to their spiritual beliefs.

Mary, Mother of John Mark

Mary was the mother of John Mark, a disciple of the Apostle Peter. She is mentioned briefly in Acts 12:12 following the narrative of Peter's imprisonment and his arrival at her gate. What is known about her comes from mention of her labor and prayers on behalf of the Christians. The Bible doesn't mention a husband, so she might have been a widow. Her son is identified as the Apostle Paul's companion, along with Barnabas, as the three traveled about doing missionary work.

Some traditions assert that the house of Mary, John Mark's mother, was not only used by early Christians as a meeting place, but quite possibly served as the location of the Last Supper, as well as the place where the Holy Spirit descended upon the disciples in the event known as Pentecost.

The text of Acts states that on the night before Peter was to be tried before Herod, he was secured in double chains, and slept with soldiers on either side of him. Beyond the door, other guards stood watch. Suddenly, an angel of the Lord appeared and caused light to illuminate the cell. The angel tapped Peter to wake him up. As he awoke, the chains fell away, and the angel told him to follow him. Peter thought he was having a vision. He and the angel left the dungeon and entered the street, and the angel disappeared. The Bible states that Peter stood there, contemplating what to do. He must have believed that the Christians were still praying for him at Mary's house, for that's where he went.

The Bible states that the Christians prayed for Peter's safe return without ceasing. They were probably used to meeting at Mary's house, and on the night that God had intervened and sent his angel to free Peter, the Christians had once again assembled with Mary to pray. Perhaps they were praying still when Peter arrived at the gate and knocked. Rhoda, the servant girl, became so excited to hear his voice that she ran back to tell the others, leaving Peter standing in the dark. Apparently, she didn't consider that the guards might have woken up and discovered he was gone, or that they could be following him. So overjoyed was Rhoda, that she didn't think to unlock the gate and let Peter in.

Those inside Mary's house didn't believe the servant girl, "But Peter continued knocking: and when they had opened the door, and saw him, they were astonished" (Acts 12:16). They must have also been jubilant, because Peter cautioned them to be quiet. He told them how the Lord had helped him by sending an angel; then he told them to go to James (the Lord's brother) and tell him and the others (Acts 12:17).

Peter then left for another place, the text of Acts reveals. When Herod discovered that Peter was no longer in his custody, he had the soldiers who were guarding Peter killed. Herod then also left Judea and went to live in Caesarea (Acts 12:19).

And when he had considered the thing, he came to the house of Mary the mother of John, whose surname was Mark; where many were gathered together praying. And as Peter knocked at the door of the gate, a damsel came to hearken, named Rhoda. And when she knew Peter's voice, she opened not the gate for gladness, but ran in, and told how Peter stood before the gate. (Acts 12:12–14)

Acts does not offer much more information about Mary. It can be deduced from her brief mention that she had the means to maintain a large home with servants. She risked persecution to allow her home to be used by Christians as a place of worship. Peter and James must have known her and held her in high regard, since Peter knew that she and others were praying for him at her house.

Mothers Put to Death for Having Their Sons Circumcised

The story of these mothers is mentioned briefly in the First Book of Maccabees, written approximately 100 B.C. The author of that text details the attempts by the Seleucid kings to suppress the practices of Judaism in Palestine. The reign of Antiochus IV Epiphanes especially was known for its widespread Hellenization of the Jews. The Maccabees, in particular Judas Maccabaeus (the first to lead a Jewish revolt against the Seleucid rulers), hated his policies, but also despised those Jews who wouldn't uphold the law of God, walk in righteousness, and demonstrate faithfulness and loyalty to God.

FACT

Mary's son, John Mark, is credited with writing the second gospel. It is the first of the canonical gospels written, the shortest, and yet the one providing the most detail about Jesus' work. While tradition says the gospel was written in Rome before A.D. 70, a time of persecutions of both Jewish and Gentile Christians, some modern scholars assert it was composed after that date.

The king sent word throughout his kingdom that the people should abandon whatever customs they were observing, and instead come together as one people and worship in the same way. The king made it clear that whoever didn't obey his orders would be put to death. That decree included women who had circumcised their baby boys. In fact, the text of the First Book of Maccabees, Chapter 1, verses 60–62, reveals that not only were those women murdered, their babies were then suspended from around their necks, and their families were also murdered. Anyone who participated in any way in the circumcision rites was also killed.

It was a dark moment in the history of the Jews, but there was hope in the person of the Hebrew priest Mattathias. When the king ordered the people to engage in pagan worship, Mattathias defiantly refused, and declared that his family would never depart from the beliefs and commandments of their religion. The king ordered a Hellenistic Jew to begin offering a sacrifice upon the altar. Compelled by outrage and filled with zeal for his convictions, Mattathias pounced upon the Jew, killing him. He destroyed the altar and fled into the streets, inciting others of the same conviction to follow him. He went up into the mountains with the king's men in hot pursuit.

Some who had been inspired by the words of the priest fled into the mountainous area of the desert south of Jerusalem. When the king's men found them and were ready to attack, they offered the Jews one last chance to save themselves. The Jews, however, had agreed to die without a fight, so they were all killed. The First Book of Maccabees states that 1,000 Jews—men, women, and children—died that day.

During the rule of Antiochus IV Epiphanes, the Jews were sought out and persecuted. To flaunt the increasing Hellenization of the people, a Greek-style gymnasium was built in Jerusalem, the Temple was desecrated and pagan temples were built, some Jews didn't circumcise their sons, and many Jews, under the threat of death, no longer adhered to God's commandments.

Mattathias grieved over the deaths. He warned his friends that they must resolve to fight, because if they didn't, they would disappear from the earth. Nearing his death, Mattathias again urged his sons and friends to fight on. When Appolonius desecrated and robbed the Temple in Jerusalem, it was Judas Maccabaeus, the third son of Mattathias, who led the revolt that secured the freedom of the Jews from 165 B.C. to 63 B.C. With their victory, the Maccabees established the Hasmonean rule in ancient Palestine and re-established Jewish worship and cultural practices.

Women Who Aided in Sanctuary Construction

After Moses had received the Ten Commandments from God, he gathered the whole Israelite community together and explained the work that the Lord wanted them to do in the construction of a sanctuary. But before he outlined the Lord's plan, he stated that the Hebrew people would work for six days, but would rest on the seventh and hold it as a sacred day; any person found working on the Sabbath would be killed. Moses then sent out a call for a collection of gifts for the construction of the tabernacle (Exodus 35:5–9).

QUESTION?

Who were the Hasmoneans?
The Hasmoneans were Jewish high priests, political leaders, and kings who were brought into power by the Maccabean Revolt. Later, military leaders were included in the Hasmonean dynasty. These Jews regarded themselves as heirs to early biblical kings and judges who ruled over the land of Israel.

Women Inspired to Spin

There were Hebrew women who heard Moses' call and felt inspired to do spinning for the Lord: "And all the women that were wise hearted did spin with their hands, and brought that which they had spun, both of blue, and of purple, and of scarlet, and of fine linen. And all the women whose heart stirred them up in wisdom spun goats' hair" (Exodus 35:25–26). So motivated and exuberant were the Hebrew people, that they supplied more than was needed for the creation of the tabernacle.

The Innermost Tent Curtains Are Completed

Those who were expert at weaving and embroidery made ten sheets of the finest linen and adorned them with delicately detailed cherubim embroidered in various shades of red and purple (Exodus 36:8). Although the King James Version of the Bible says that "wise-hearted men" made the curtains, the New American Bible, Saint Joseph Edition, states that those who sewed the curtains were experts (no gender stated) although previous verses revealed Moses telling the camp, "Let neither man nor woman make any more contributions for the sanctuary" (Exodus 36:6). It is therefore possible that women may have been experts who worked on the curtains. The Scriptures explain the length and breadth of the curtains, and even discuss the blue edging that was applied, along with the fifty gold clasps to join the curtains.

The Dwelling Place of the Lord Further Draped

The tent was then draped in eleven sheets of goat-hair coverings. These were fastened with brass clasps. Following that, a layer of rams' skins dyed red was laid upon the sheets of goat hair. The final covering was made of badgers' skins.

It must have been normal for women to meet and congregate at the door of the tabernacle, because another group of them are mentioned in the First Book of Samuel, albeit with a negative inference. "Now Eli was very old, and heard all that his sons did unto all Israel; and how they lay with the women that assembled at the door of the tabernacle of the congregation. And he said unto them. Why do ye such things? . . ." (1 Samuel 2:22–23).

Wooded Walls Are Erected

The wood was cut in specific lengths and widths to create the walls; the structure had to conform to specific dimensions. The men most likely cut the wood and constructed the walls. There were silver pedestals under the walls. The boards were plated with gold and upon them were fashioned gold rings to hold gold bars (Exodus 36:20–34). The erection of the walls completed the construction of the building.

Experts Craft the Veil and Entrance Curtain

Although the Bible doesn't specify exactly who made the tabernacle veil, it does reveal that the veil was constructed from purple, red, and violet yarn and fine linen that had been embroidered with cherubim. The veil was made to be attached to four wood columns enhanced with gold plating. An entrance curtain was made from variegated linen and yarn.

All Other Tabernacle Items Are Completed

The Hebrews then made the ark and all of the other sanctuary items, including the laver and base. "And he made the laver [wash basin for purification] of brass, and the foot of it of brass, of the lookingglasses of the women assembling, which assembled [women who served and met] at the door of the tabernacle of the congregation" (Exodus 38:8).

Zibiah

Zibiah is briefly mentioned in the Second Book of Kings in a way that indicates she was the mother of Jehoash, who became king, and that she was from Beersheba. The Bible doesn't reveal whether or not she was married, or explain who Jehoash's father was. Jehoash and Joash are different spellings of the same name in the Old Testament, as you will see in the quotes that follow.

In the seventh year of Jehu Jehoash began to reign; and forty years reigned he in Jerusalem. And his mother's name was Zibiah of Beersheba. And Jehoash did that which was right in the sight of the Lord all his days wherein Jehoiada the priest instructed him. (2 Kings 12:1–2)

There is a similar reference a little further on in the Old Testament: "Joash was seven years old when he began to reign, and he reigned forty years in Jerusalem. His mother's name also was Zibiah of Beersheba. And Joash did that which was right in the sight of the Lord all the days of Jehoiada the priest. And Jehoiada took for him two wives; and he begat sons and daughters" (2 Chronicles 24:1–3).

Upon the death of his father, Jeohoash's grandmother, Athaliah, became queen. Athaliah, thirsty for power, went on a murderous rampage, killing all of her son's little boys who might someday lay claim to the throne. She found all of them except Jehoash. The Bible says, "But when Athaliah the mother of Ahaziah saw that her son was dead, she arose and destroyed all the seed royal of the house of Judah" (2 Chronicles 22:10).

A recently discovered sandstone tablet with an inscription that may have been written by King Jeohash has generated heated debate among scholars as to whether it is authentic or a forgery. Some believe it dates from the reign of Jeohash. The stone's crust has been Carbon 14 tested and determined to be 2,300 years old. The inscription references repairs made to the Temple during Jeohash's reign. But experts say the Hebrew in the inscription is a forgery, because it is much too modern.

Jehoash was spared death at the hands of his grandmother thanks to another relative—his aunt Jehosheba, sister of Ahaziah and wife of the high priest Jehoiadia. Jehosheba hid Jehoash and his nurse in a bedchamber. For seven years, Jehoash remained concealed from his grandmother and her minions, but when he turned seven, Athaliah was overthrown and Jehoash became king.

Athaliah was the daughter of King Ahab and his queen, Jezebel. Jezebel was a powerful influence over the compliant Ahab, and during his reign many worshipped Baal. Jezebel banished the Hebrew prophets in an effort to promote pagan worship throughout the land.

Ahab ruled over Israel, the northern kingdom, while Jehoshaphat ruled over the southern kingdom of Judah. The two kings forged an alliance by marrying Ahab's daughter Athaliah to Jehoram, Jehosphaphat's son. Some sources assert that Athaliah was nearly as bad as her mother, who epitomized evil, according to many theologians.

Chapter 20
Remarkable Mothers

The four women featured in this chapter were extraordinary in every way. From Ann, the grandmother of Jesus, to Elisabeth, who bore John the Baptist, to Sampson's mother, and Mary, mother of Jesus, these women collectively stand as a spiritual prism to reflect many of the best and most beautiful qualities and attributes of motherhood. The Roman Catholic Church and orthodox churches proclaimed some of these women saints. Mary, mother of Jesus, and Ann, especially, are revered as saints.

Ann

Ann, the mother of the Blessed Virgin Mary, and her husband Joachim both came from Galilee. Tradition states that Joachim belonged to the house of David and the tribe of Judah, and the couple resided in Nazareth. Ann's name derives from the Hebrew word for "grace." Her family most likely called her Hannah.

Ann and Joachim were ashamed of their inability to conceive a child despite fervent prayers to the Lord for his help. Tradition states that Ann was twenty when she married Joachim, who by then was forty-nine. According to some sources, they had the means to live comfortably in Nazareth.

The Couple Prays for a Child

Ann became pregnant with Mary, their only child, when she was forty and Joachim was sixty-nine. By then, they had been married for twenty years. The ancient Hebrew culture considered barrenness a punishment by God, for only the power of the Lord could open or close a woman's womb. But through prayer, tradition says, the couple was finally blessed with the child they so fervently desired.

FACT

Ann is the patron saint of infertility and family crisis. The Roman Catholic Church celebrates the feast day of Ann and Joachim on July 26. Ann's cult started in the early church, but became popular in the thirteenth century. One of her early shrines was built in Douai, France. Other notable shrines are St. Anne-de-Beaupre in Quebec and St. Anne d'Auray in Brittany.

An Angel of the Lord Appears to Ann

Since Ann isn't mentioned in the New Testament, most of the information that is available about her comes from apocryphal sources, including the Protoevangelium of James. That text reveals that Ann's prayers for a child went unanswered for years, until the day she prayed beneath a laurel tree and an angel appeared and told her that the Lord had heard her prayers. Ann would give birth, and people throughout the world would speak of the one she would bear. After hearing the angel's words, Ann declared that whatever God gave her, whether boy or girl, it would be given to the Lord as a gift to do the Lord's work.

The Protoevangelium of James is a second-century apocryphal gospel. It was known and used by Origen, an early Christian theologian and writer, and was referred to in the writings of Clement of Alexandria, another Christian Church father and writer, and by Justin, the Christian apologist. These men and Eusebius of Caesarea (a third-century theologian) used that gospel to explain that Joseph was Mary's husband in name only.

Ann Gives Birth to Mary

Ann gave birth to Mary, who became the mother of Jesus. Joachim, Mary's father (about whom little is known), has been called the forbearer of God in his role as the father of the Blessed Virgin Mary.

Ann's Placement of Mary

Ann and Joachim must have been jubilant to finally have a child. But in honor of her promise to God, when Mary was three, Ann took the little girl to the Temple of the Lord where she would be consecrated to God. There, Mary would be educated and do the Lord's work. According to the Protevangelium, an angel fed Mary her food, and she was treated like a dove. Ann's placement of her only child in the Temple is similar to the Old Testament story of Hannah's placement of Samuel in the Temple to be educated and raised by the priest Eli (Samuel 1:22–23).

Elisabeth

Elisabeth was married to Zachariahs, a priest who was of the family of Abia. Elisabeth was the daughter of Aaron and his wife Elisheba (Luke 1:5, 1:36). Elisabeth and Zachariahs were a pious couple and kept all of the commandments of the Lord. In addition, they may have been among those Jews who believed in the coming of the Messiah, and who eagerly awaited that event. They were advanced in years and remained childless.

The Angel Appears to Zachariahs

One day while Zachariahs was performing his priestly duties, an angel of the Lord appeared and stood on the right side of the altar of incense. When Zachariahs saw the angel, he was afraid. The angel calmed him, then told him that Elisabeth would bear a son, and that they should name the child John (Luke 1:11–13).

Elisabeth Receives Her Cousin Mary

When Elisabeth's cousin Mary, mother of Jesus, learned of Elisabeth's pregnancy, she went to the hills of Judah where Elisabeth and Zachariahs lived. Mary stayed with the couple for three months (Luke 1:56). When Elisabeth first received Mary into her home, she was filled with the Holy Spirit, and loudly proclaimed Mary to be the Mother of her Lord.

Elisabeth Gives Birth and Names Her Son

Elisabeth gave birth to a boy. Eight days later, according to Jewish tradition, they held the naming ceremony, during which time he was also circumcised. Those gathered wanted to name him Zachariahs, after

Elisabeth receiving Mary into her home

his father. However, Elisabeth said no, and instead named him John. All of their friends and relatives protested, saying no one in the family had that name. So they asked Zachariahs, who couldn't talk because he had been struck speechless, and he wrote "John" on a tablet. After that, the Scriptures say his tongue became loose and he could talk again.

QUESTION?

What is the Jewish naming and circumcision ceremony?
The practice is known as *Brit Milah* (Hebrew for "covenant of circumcision"). In Yiddish, it is simply called a "bris." It dates back roughly 4,050 years, to Abraham and God's covenant with his chosen people.

Elisabeth's Husband Becomes Filled with the Holy Ghost

Following the naming of his son, Zachariahs was filled with the Holy Ghost and prophesied many things, including that his child would be called prophet of the Highest and would, "...go before the face of the Lord to prepare his ways..." (Luke 1:76). And, indeed, his son became known as John the Baptist. The Scriptures state that he was the forerunner of Christ, and also baptized Jesus. The son of Elisabeth and Zachariahs would eventually be beheaded by order of Herod Antipas. He is considered by some to be the last Old Testament prophet, and by others as the first missionary of Christ.

Manoah's Wife, Samson's Mother

This Old Testament mother is not named in the Bible, but she is referred to as Manoah's wife. Like Ann and Elisabeth, Manoah's wife was barren. Judges 13:2 states, "And there was a certain man of Zorah, of the family of the Danites, whose name was Manoah; and his wife was barren, and bare not." Again, like Ann and Elisabeth, the angel of the Lord appeared and told her that she would give birth to a child. In the case of this mother, however, the angel gave some prenatal advice.

Manoah's wife ran and told her husband what the angel had told her, but Manoah wanted to hear it for himself; he prayed that the angel would return. So, the angel came again. This time Manoah's wife was sitting in a field, and again, her husband wasn't with her. So she ran to find her husband and bring him to where the angel remained standing. The angel repeated the message to the husband that he had given the wife. Manoah wasn't sure that the man standing before him was truly a messenger of the Lord, so he offered to prepare food for the angel. The divine being refused, saying it had to be offered to God. Then Manoah asked the angel for his name, and was told it was secret. However, the Lord's messenger finally proved he was an angel when Manoah placed a meat offering upon a rock, and the angel entered the flame and ascended to heaven.

Now therefore beware, I pray thee, and drink not wine nor strong drink, and eat not any unclean thing: For, lo, thou shalt conceive, and bear a son; and no razor shall come on his head: for the child shall be a Nazarite unto God from the womb: and he shall begin to deliver Israel out of the hand of the Philistines. (Judges 13:4–5)

Manoah's Wife Gives Birth to a Son

Manoah's wife fell to the ground at the sight of the angel's ascension to heaven. The angel never returned, but Manoah's wife believed the heavenly messenger. Indeed, she bore Manoah a son, and they called the child Samson. They made him a Nazarite as they had been instructed to do by the angel.

Manoah and His Wife Receive a Request

One day, Samson went to Timnath. There, he noticed a woman that he desired to have as his wife. He went to his father and mother and asked them to get the woman for him. His parents were not opposed to finding a wife for him (marriages were arranged during that time), however, they wanted him to marry a woman from among their tribe, not someone belonging to the "uncircumcised Philistines" (Judges 14:3).

Samson Kills a Lion

Samson took his father and mother to Timnath. In some vineyards, a young lion roared, "And the spirit of the Lord came mightily upon him..." and he killed the lion barehanded (Judges 14:5–6). He didn't tell his father or mother, but continued on until he met with the woman. On the way back, he saw the lion carcass filled with swarming bees and honey. Samson took the honey and gave it to his parents, never telling them that he had killed a lion and taken the honey from its carcass.

FACT

In ancient biblical times, Tinmath was a Philistine city in the land of Canaan. In Samson's story found in the Old Testament Book of Judges, Chapter 14, Samson goes to Timnath, where he sees the Philistine woman he desires for a wife.

Samson's Wife Betrays Him

Samson asked the Philistines a riddle they couldn't answer. They went to Samson's wife and asked for her help. Samson told her that if he hadn't told his own mother and father the answer, he wouldn't tell her. She cried, and because he felt sorry for her, he told her the answer to the riddle, which she then told to the Philistines. When the Philistines gave him the answer to his riddle, Samson knew his wife had betrayed him. In anger, Samson slew thirty Philistines and gave his wife to his friend.

Samson's mother may have been the only woman who didn't betray him, for Samson met another woman, a harlot named Delilah, who also betrayed him.

The Blessed Virgin Mary

Mary's story is found in the New Testament and various Apocryphal accounts, but many details of her life remain vague. A devout Jewish girl who was the daughter of Ann and Joachim, Mary (or the Judeo-Aramaic, *Maryām*) spent her childhood in the Temple (cloistered most likely, since the Temple was a male bastion in those patriarchal times just prior to the beginning of the Christian era).

Matthew's and Luke's gospels assert that Mary was an immaculate virgin who was God's choice to give birth to Jesus. Matthew's account ties the virgin birth into the Hebrew prophet Isaiah's prediction: "Behold, a virgin shall be with child, and shall bring forth a son, and they shall call him Emanuel, which being interpreted is, God with us. Then Joseph being raised from sleep did as the angel of the Lord had bidden him, and took unto him his wife: And knew her not till she had brought forth her firstborn son: and he called his name JESUS." (Matthew 1:24–25).

Immanuel means "God is with us." Early church father Irenaeus, who lived from A.D. 120 to A.D. 202, wrote that the Lord himself gave a sign which humankind had not requested; that is, a virgin would give birth to a son who would be "God with us" and that she would remain a virgin. Some scholars, however, dispute that the Hebrew word *almah* means virgin, and instead assert that the word means a young girl of marriageable age.

Matthew's gospel reveals that after Joseph was espoused to Mary but had not yet known her, he learned that she was with child. "Then Joseph her husband, being a just man, and not willing to make her a public example, was minded to put her away privily" (Matthew 1:19). While Joseph mulled over these thoughts, he was visited by an angel who told him the truth about Mary's pregnancy.

But while he thought on these things, behold, the angel of the Lord appeared unto him in a dream, saying, Joseph, thou son of David, fear not to take unto thee Mary thy wife: for that which is conceived in her is of the Holy Ghost. And she shall bring forth a son, and thou shalt call his name JESUS: for he shall save his people from their sins. (Matthew 1:20–21)

Joseph and Mary weren't married yet, and the marriage went forward as planned. Joseph, however, did not consummate the marriage with Mary, according to the Gospel of Matthew, "…till she had brought forth her first-born son" (Matthew 1:25).

Matthew Provides Linkage to King David

According to 2 Samuel 7: 12–13, Jesus' coming would be through the lineage of King David. Matthew's Gospel 1: 1–17 lists forty-two generations in the lineage of Jesus, extending from Abraham through David to Christ and includes women. Luke's Gospel 3:23–38 offers the genealogy of Jesus in reverse order, extending all the way back to Adam. The prophet Isaiah linked the house of David to the future birth by a virgin of the child who would be called Immanuel. The prophet Isaiah predicted that the future messiah would be linked to the house of David. The Old Testament book of Isaiah states, "Here ye now, O house of David: Is it a small thing for you to weary men, but will ye weary my God also? Therefore the Lord himself shall give you a sign; Behold, a virgin shall conceive, and bear a son, and shall call his name Immanuel" (Isaiah 7:13–14). Immanuel in Hebrew means "God is with us."

QUESTION?

What are some of Mary's titles?
Various names for Mary have evolved from the way she is portrayed, whether as a Blessed Virgin, compassionate intercessor, a grieving mother, the saint of all saints, or the Madonna. Some of her titles include: Mother of Sorrows, Our Lady of the Miraculous Medal, Queen of Heaven, Mother of God, Our Lady of Guadelupe, Our Lady of Mount Carmel, Our Lady of Fatima, and Our Lady of Perpetual Help.

The Angel Gabriel Appears to Mary

The Gospel of Luke states that the angel Gabriel appeared to Mary and told her that she was favored by the Lord. Mary was afraid, and wondered why she had been singled out for such a visitation. The angel told her not to be afraid, but that the Holy Ghost would come upon her, overshadow her, and conceive in her a child that "…shall be called the Son of God" (Luke 1:26–35). Mary replied, "…be it unto me according to thy word" (Luke 1:38).

Mary Visits Elisabeth

The angel Gabriel also informed Mary that her cousin Elisabeth, who had remained barren for so long, had conceived in her old age. Then the angel made a powerful declaration: "For with God nothing shall be impossible" (Luke 1:37). Mary left Nazareth to visit her cousin in the hill country of Judah. The Gospel of Luke states that upon Mary's arrival, when Elisabeth heard Mary's words of salutation, "…the babe leaped in her womb; and Elisabeth was filled with the Holy Ghost: and she spake out with a loud voice, and said, Blessed art thou among women, and blessed is the fruit of thy womb" (Luke 1:40–42).

"Blessed are thou among women, and blessed is the fruit of thy womb"—those exact words have been recited for centuries in the Hail Mary prayer (in Latin called, *Ave Maria*). The prayer is a merging of the angel Gabriel's salutation found in Luke 1:28 and Elisabeth's greeting of Mary in Luke 1:42. The prayer has enjoyed popularity since the eleventh century, and is one of the prayers required in the praying of the rosary.

Mary Accompanies Joseph to Bethlehem

Mary stayed at Elisabeth's house for three months before returning to her own home. Augustus, the Roman Emperor, required that everyone be taxed, and that everyone had to pay the tax in his own city (Luke 2:1–3). Joseph went from the Galilean city of Nazareth up to Bethlehem in Judea (here again, Luke 2:4 repeats that Joseph was of the house and lineage of David) to be taxed with Mary. This is truly remarkable, because Mary was nine months pregnant, the inns were full, and there was no place for her to have privacy and comfort.

Mary Gives Birth

The Gospel of Matthew doesn't mention a tax or census, but states that three wise men were asking how to find the King of the Jews in order to make offerings to him. That brought the birth of Jesus to the attention of King Herod. The wise men followed a star in the East and arrived in Bethlehem to pay homage to the newborn and his mother. Herod asked the wise men to find the baby and advise him of exactly where the baby was located

The Blessed Virgin Mary holding the baby Jesus

so he, too, could go there to worship. Matthew 2:11 reveals that they found Mary and the child, and fell down and worshipped him. After the visit, the wise men had a dream telling them not to return to Herod, so they left town, using a different route back to their country. Joseph was warned to take Mary and the baby to Egypt. Later, when Herod died, the angel told Joseph to return to Israel.

Mary's Baby Is Dedicated

Anna, whom the Gospel of Luke called "…a prophetess, the daughter of Phanuel, of the tribe of Aser," was at the Temple when Mary and Joseph took Jesus up to present him, according to the Hebrew custom. Anna had been a widow for many years (Luke 2:36–37). She didn't live in the Temple, but spent all of her time there serving God through fasting and prayer, and waiting for the arrival of the long-hoped-for Messiah. On the day that Jesus was dedicated, Anna spoke of the Lord to all who hoped for redemption (Luke 2:38).

Mary Expresses Love and Concern for Jesus

When Jesus was twelve, Mary and Joseph took him to Jerusalem. Jesus went missing, and when his parents finally located him in the Temple, Mary was understandably concerned. She confronted Jesus, asking, "Son, why hast thou thus dealt with us? behold, thy father and I have sought thee sorrowing" (Luke 2:48). Jesus answered by asking her how she could not know that he was about his Father's business. When Jesus grew up and embarked upon his ministry, Mary, with other women (some were likely her female relatives), followed her son in his travels around Palestine.

Mary Asks Jesus' Help at Cana

At the wedding at Cana, where Mary and Jesus were guests, the host family ran out of wine during the celebration. The Gospel of John stated what happened next: "And the third day there was a marriage in Cana of Galilee; and the mother of Jesus was there: And both Jesus was called, and his disciples, to the marriage. And when they wanted wine, the mother of Jesus saith unto him, They have no wine" (John 2:1–3). Mary didn't ask for a miracle, but that's what Jesus performed when he turned the water into wine, his first miracle. And the wine was of exceptional quality (John 2:10).

His mother saith unto the servants, Whatsoever he saith unto you, do it. And there were set there six waterpots of stone…Jesus saith unto them, Fill the waterpots with water. And they filled them up to the brim….When the ruler of the feast had tasted the water that was made wine, and knew not whence it was: (but the servants which drew the water knew;) the governor of the feast called the bridegroom… (John 2:5–7, 2:9)

Mary Suffers and Stands Vigil at the Cross

After Jesus' three-year ministry ended with his passion and crucifixion, Mary stood vigil at the foot of his cross near the Beloved Disciple, Mary Magdalene, and others. Jesus addressed Mary from the cross, saying, "Woman, behold thy son!" referring not to himself, but to John the Beloved. He told John, "Behold thy mother" (John 19:26–27).

FACT

The Via Dolorosa (or "Way of Sorrows") is also known as the Stations of the Cross. These fourteen stations each symbolize and commemorate specific events during the suffering of Jesus in the final hours before he was put on the cross. Mary is often depicted in art as the despondent mother, cradling the body of her dead son.

Mary Joins Others in the Upper Room

Mary was mentioned by name in the Book of Acts of the Apostles as being present in the upper room, where roughly 120 of Jesus' followers had gathered to choose the disciple to replace Judas (Acts 1:14). After that, she isn't mentioned again in the Bible. Legend asserts that she spent time in Ephesus with John, and perhaps Mary Magdalene, but some archeologists assert there is no proof. Other traditions say that she remained in Jerusalem.

Chapter 21

Ancient Hebrew Women in Their World

Recently found loom weights and pottery shards of cooking utensils uncovered in Yodefat, Galilee, and elsewhere in the Holy Land have provided archeologists with evidence of women's lives and work during ancient times. The objects show that the center of the ancient Hebrew woman's world was her home, where she fulfilled her duty as wife and mother. Otherwise, her life was severely restricted. She couldn't give legal testimony or talk with strangers. To go outside the home, she had to be veiled. Generally, she was considered inferior by virtue of her gender, and was seen as the property of her father or husband.

Marriage

In the Old Testament world, marriage was referred to as the taking of a wife. Couples weren't joined together because they had fallen in love; marriage cemented alliances between families and had less to do with love than with property and ownership. A girl was the property of her father until she was married, at which time she became the property of her husband. A mother might have some say in her daughter's marriage arrangement, but the father had final say and could decide without input from anyone, as was the case when Judah took a wife for his son Er (Genesis 38:6). Marrying within one's community tended to concentrate property and people within that community, and thus the wealth built up within a village or town remained there. That isn't to say couples never fell in love; they did. But in general, love was something that one hoped would grow out of the marriage alliance.

According to the ancient Hebrew law, marriage between a man and a woman required three things: (1) the man must pay the bride price; (2) the young woman and her father had to consent; and (3) for it to be considered legal, intercourse had to take place.

FACT

Among the ancient Hebrews, it was customary for the father of the groom to pay a *mohar*, or the purchase price or dowry, to the father of the bride. It could be a monetary payment or an exchange of services or property.

Loss of Labor

When a man found a woman from his village or region that he thought would make a good wife, he had to compensate the woman's family for her. After all, the loss of the woman meant the loss of a worker for her family. Some sources assert that the bride price became little more than a symbolic token (certainly not the buying of a woman) in the few centuries just prior to the Common Era. The paying of a bride price may have been the reason that Laban, father of Leah and Rachel, had insisted that Jacob work for seven years to earn the right to marry first Leah, and then Rachel. Of course,

Jacob had only intended to marry Rachel, but Laban and Leah tricked him into marrying Leah first. Jacob's gain was Laban's loss of his daughters and their labor.

Marriageable Age

The most typical marriageable age for a girl was just after puberty. At twelve or thirteen, she would still most likely do exactly what her father told her to do. So, if the marriage was something the father wanted, his daughter generally consented. Once married, the young woman typically moved from her father's house to her husband's. As for the wedding, the ancient Israelites surely had them, but the Bible sheds little light on the ceremony. Most likely, families followed whatever local customs in the couple's village or region dictated.

A Hebrew wedding procession

Expectations

A husband expected his wife to obey him as she had her father. He also expected her to love him and to produce offspring (especially male heirs). The wife was expected to conduct herself in virtuous ways, so that she remained beyond reproach, and was to be faithful to her husband. She was also expected to practice his religion; the ancient Israelites, for the most part, shunned marriages to non-Israelites. The *ketubah*, or marriage contract, was an instrument of understanding that laid out the particulars. The Book of Exodus states, "If he take him another wife; her food, her raiment, and her duty of marriage, shall he not diminish. And if he do not these three unto her, then shall she go out free without money" (Exodus 21:10–11).

The wife expected the husband to provide for her and to love her. Her life was fulfilled if she could bear him children, so there was an expectation that they would try to have a family. The wife might reasonably expect that her new husband would allow her to see her family. Husbands generally married within their communities, villages, or regional areas, so allowing a wife to visit with her family members was usually easy enough to fulfill.

Polygamy

The taking of more than one wife by ancient Hebrew men was permitted, although it didn't happen often. The Old Testament reveals that a few Hebrew patriarchs and kings practiced polygamy. Abraham had three wives—Sarah, Hagar, and Keturah (Genesis 16:1–3, 25:1); Moses had two—Zipporah and the Ethiopian woman (Exodus 2:21, 18:1–6; Numbers 12:1); and Jacob had four—Leah, Rachel, Zilpah, and Bilhah (Genesis 29:23, 29:28, 30:4, 30:9). King David had numerous wives, including Michal, Abigail, Ahinoam, Bathsheba, Abital, Maachah, Haggith, Eglah, and possibly Abishag, who slept with him to keep him warm during the end of his life (1 Samuel 18:27, 25:39–44; 2 Samuel 11:3–4; 1 Chronicles 3), and Solomon had 700 (1 Kings 11:3). Men could take multiple wives, but were required to support them all. Women, however, weren't permitted to take multiple husbands.

QUESTION?

What evidence exists of a marriage contract stipulating a bride price?
The oldest Jewish marriage document (dating to the period after Babylonian exile) was discovered at the beginning of the twentieth century. The contract included a declaration of marriage by As-Hor, the groom, to the bride's father. The bride price was five shekels.

The Levirate Marriage

When a Hebrew man died before his wife could bear him a son (heir), the law allowed for the brother of the deceased man to marry the widow. The law seemed to apply only if the two men lived within the same house. The dead man had no son to carry on his name, so the law justified the marriage of the widow to her brother-in-law so that she might bear a son and heir. In this way, the dead man's name wasn't erased from the history of the Israelites. If the widow conceived and bore a son, he would carry on the genealogical line of the deceased father. The ancient Hebrews considered this a legal arrangement that was respectful of all parties.

If brethren dwell together, and one of them die, and have no child, the wife of the dead shall not marry without unto a stranger: her husband's brother shall go in unto her, and take her to him to wife, and perform the duty of an husband's brother unto her. (Deuteronomy 25:5)

Marriage Between Paternal First Cousins

Another way Hebrew marriages ensured that property stayed in the lineage of a father involved the marrying of daughters to their father's brother's sons. This sounds a little confusing, but basically it was done when a man produced only girls to inherit his property. To keep the property within the father's hereditary lineage, the girls were married to the sons of their uncle (father's brother).

Divorce

A man could easily obtain a divorce. Deuteronomy 24:1 states, "When a man hath taken a wife, and married her, and it come to pass that she find no favor in his eyes, because he hath found some uncleanness in her: then let him write her a bill of divorcement, and give it in her hand, and send her out of his house." Women, however, weren't allowed the same standard. Women couldn't start divorce proceedings against their husbands. Once divorced, it was unlikely that such a woman would marry again; however, if she did, the ancient Hebrews had a rule that applied. If the divorced woman did marry, and upon the death of her new husband found that she again desired her first husband and he desired her, they wouldn't be permitted to marry, because it was considered an abomination. However, if a woman's sister married and then died, the woman could marry her sister's husband if he desired her.

A woman's failure to produce male heirs to carry forward a man's name and genes was problematic. Having no children was often the reason for a man to seek a divorce from the woman he had married. Another reason for getting a divorce was if a man believed he had married a woman who was not a virgin. If he truly thought that he had been deceived, a man could demand proof from his wife's family. Generally, proof was considered blood on the bed sheet that the groom and bride had slept on their wedding night. If the bed linen didn't provide the proof sought by the groom, his bride paid the price with her life—the men of the village stoned her to death (Deuteronomy 22:13–21).

Consequences of Rape

Hebrew law stated that if a man found a woman betrothed to another man in a field and raped her, he would forfeit his life and be put to death for violating another man's property. If he raped a virgin who was not yet betrothed, the rapist would have to pay the girl's father money, marry the girl, and never be able to divorce her (Deuteronomy 22:28–29).

The rape of a woman in ancient Hebrew society was not viewed as an injury or assault against the woman, so much as it was a property offence against the woman's father or husband. This is illustrated in the consequence for the rapist: He atoned by marrying the woman and paying 50 shekels to the man whose woman he violated.

It might have been a little dicey for the woman to remain married to the man who had violated her, but after being raped, she didn't really have any other options. In fact, she was considered unmarriageable. Great emphasis was laid upon women being virgins prior to marriage. Ancient Hebrew men did not marry women who were "damaged goods."

In the event of a man falsely accusing his bride of not being a virgin, and provided her family could prove otherwise, the groom would never be allowed to divorce the woman he had married.

Taboos and Abominations

As previously mentioned, a widow could marry her late husband's brother, but women and men who committed adultery were put to death, since such a commission was a capital offence. The Old Testament records in Leviticus 18 that the Lord gave Moses instructions to pass on to the children of Israel regarding the near relatives of a man with whom sexual relations or marriage was unlawful:

- Biological mother
- Father's wife (assuming she is not his biological mother)
- Sisters and half sisters
- Father's sisters
- Father's brother's wives
- Mother's sisters
- Wife's mother
- Wife's sisters
- Wife's daughters
- Brother's wife
- Daughters-in-law

Women were afforded some protection by the men to whom the belonged. They lived out their lives mostly in the safety of the home. Yet, incidences of incest and abuse must have occurred for Leviticus 18 to provide such detail about what kinds of sexual relationships were forbidden. The chapter also admonished any man who lay with a woman when she was unclean (having her menstrual cycle). In addition, it addressed the wickedness of other types of sexual defilements, such as a man having a carnal relationship with his neighbor's wife. While no Protestant or Catholic religious doctrine adhere strictly to the rules laid out in old Hebrew doctrines, some of the ancient taboos have certainly been incorporated into our modern laws and moral codes of conduct.

The admonishment against a man lying with another man in Leviticus 18:22 has been used as the basis for arguments against homosexuality. Chapter 18 emphasizes the sanctity of sex, and ends by saying that anyone who does not heed the law would be cut off from among his people.

Adultery in ancient times usually began with an accusation against the woman. To prove her innocence, she was forced to drink dirty and cursed water that a priest had mixed from sweepings of the temple floor. If she were guilty, drinking the water would have made her stomach swell and her thighs droop. Perhaps the ritual was so horrific to contemplate that the woman would confess rather than drink the nasty mixture. The commission of adultery among the ancient Hebrews was nothing less than a religious offence. Later, however, the ancients relaxed the double standard, and the rabbinical priesthood took men to task as well. Eventually, adultery came to be viewed as more of a legal and societal issue than a religious crime.

Children and Heirs

Women were expected to produce children. It was important for society to build up its numbers, and for men to have heirs and workers. A woman's value to her husband decreased if she wasn't able to conceive. She could, however, claim to be a mother if her maidservant could produce children by having sexual relations with her husband. Such an arrangement provided an acceptable solution to the problem of childless marriages. However, only women of wealthy families had maidservants. When Sarah believed she would never have Abraham's child, she sent him her handmaid Hagar. The child of Abraham and Hagar was Ishmael. Also, when Rachel couldn't initially bear a child with Jacob, she encouraged him to lie with her handmaid Bilhah. The union produced two boys, Dan and Naphtali, who then became leaders of two of the tribes of Israel. A poor childless woman, who did not have a handmaiden, had no options. Her husband often summarily divorced her.

In the larger Hebrew society, childless couples were often pitied, whereas families with large households of children were favored, especially if those children were male. Leah, wife of Jacob, bore him many children, yet she taunted her sister Rachel for not having any babies.

Widowhood

Life was precarious and often frightening for widows. The lucky ones had families to care for them as they grew old and infirm. But those without families were forced to find ways to take care of themselves. The situation was often dire, and obliged them to depend upon the mercy and generosity of others. By foraging in fields, orchards, and vineyards, they could sometimes find food; for example, fruit left on the vine or trees. The ancient Hebrews harvested their olives, but were admonished to leave what had fallen to the ground for the widows. In the Book of Ruth, Naomi's daughter-in-law picks up the leftover grain in the field of Boaz, since both women have lost their husbands and must somehow survive.

Widowhood

In the patrilineal society of the ancient Hebrews, property wasn't usually left to the wife, but to the male heirs, leaving a widow at the mercy of her sons. Generally, women were not educated, so without a family to provide protection and sustenance, it would have been difficult for a widow to start her own business or find other suitable ways to support herself.

It is recorded in the Old Testament that widows are under God's care. Psalms 146:9 states, " The Lord preserveth the strangers; he relieveth the fatherless and the widow: but the way of the wicked he turneth upside down." The protection of widows is also mentioned in Deuteronomy.

Thou shalt not pervert the judgment of the stranger, nor of the fatherless; nor take a widow's raiment to pledge: But thou shalt remember…the Lord thy God redeemed thee…When thou cuttest down thine harvest in thy field, and hast forgot a sheaf in the field…it shall be for the stranger, for the fatherless, and for the widow… (Deuteronomy 24:17–19)

In the New Testament, the Greeks spoke out against the Hebrews because the Greek widows were being neglected when the allotments of daily food was given: "And in those days, when the number of the disciples was multiplied, there arose a murmuring of the Grecians against the Hebrews, because their widows were neglected in the daily ministration" (Acts 6:1). The Apostles solved the problem by selecting "seven men of honest report" to oversee the whole business (Acts 6:3–6). The Apostle Paul stated in his first letter to Timothy that the widows needed to be shown respect. "Rebuke not an elder, but intreat him as a father; and the younger men as brethren; the elder women as mothers; the younger as sisters, with all purity. Honor widows that are widows indeed" (1 Timothy 5:1–3).

A Woman's Place in Hebrew Society

Society viewed the Hebrew woman almost exclusively as a wife and mother. What else could she do if she wasn't educated, didn't own a business, serve as some kind of leader, or was kept down by lack of resources. Still, there were exceptions in the ancient world of the Hebrews. Deborah, for example, was a wife and a prophetess, but served, in the tradition established by Moses, as a judge of the Israelites. She was intelligent, compassionate, and insightful. She united her people, raised a small army, and (with the help of Barak, a military man) drove out the infidels who had been relentlessly attacking the Hebrews. After all of that, she proved to be a talented singer, composing a victory song over the defeat of Sisera, the enemy of her people, and giving credit to another woman, the tent-dweller Jael.

Judith is an example of another exceptional woman who made a significant contribution to her people. Unlike many widows whose husbands had passed on, Judith was wealthy. She remained pious and virtuous, but wanted to do something to help the Jews. She devised a plan to kill the nemesis of the Hebrews, a general in the Assyrian army whose name was Holofernes. Her plan worked flawlessly, enabling Judith to cut off the head of Holofernes with his own sword as he lay in a drunken stupor.

Religious Responsibilities

The biblical narratives show the importance of women in the history of the Jewish people. Those narratives also underscore women's roles in the practice of faith and the carrying on of tradition. In the home, women shouldered considerable religious responsibility, especially toward their children. In addition, women were expected to obey the Laws given to Moses, and to conduct themselves properly, care for their families in the Jewish tradition, and follow the dietary laws. Although women were restricted from studying the Torah, they were experts in the area of meal preparation and kosher rules.

Although ancient Hebrew society was a male-dominated society, with birthright given to the oldest male heir, a person's Jewishness was (and still is) determined by whether or not that person was born of a Jewish mother.

Women encouraged their men to study and keep Jewish religious law. The Old Testament mentions seven women as seers, or prophetesses, and also mentions that women had a role in the work of building the Tabernacle. Women, such as Huldah in the sixth century B.C., contributed to the understanding of what was authentic Law. After Huldah's lifetime, Judaism continued to evolve, but there was renewed emphasis upon Torah study and daily synagogue worship. Despite the restrictive society they lived in, many women of the Bible left an imprint upon their world and, through the biblical narratives, their lives continue to have relevance.

Chapter 22

Women of the Bible in Popular Culture

Writers, artists, and musicians seeking interesting stories with moments of high drama have only to turn to the Bible. That book remains one of the most widely read books in the world, and contains myriad stories of violence, forbidden sex, exorcisms, prophecy, exploitation, purity laws, rules for moral behavior, and messages of hope and triumphant. The biblical narratives have inspired creativity in popular culture since the first centuries after the Bible was written. The virgin birth of Jesus and the temptation of Eve remain two of the most enduring of the stories featuring women.

Images of Biblical Women in Earliest Christian Culture

As the Apostles of Jesus began their work, they made their way around the lands of the Mediterranean and into Africa and Asia, preaching to both men and women. Jesus had many women followers and some served in leadership positions, but as the age of the Apostles came to an end, the leadership roles of women diminished. Scholars believe that women didn't write the New Testament, although no one knows for sure who wrote those sacred texts. As men served as fathers of the early Church, pondering, thinking, and formulating church doctrine, women kept the biblical stories alive through their storytelling skills, songs, and religious ritual.

In Africa, especially, the seeds of Christianity took hold in the ritual of oral storytelling, and experienced phenomenal growth. Within the first half-dozen centuries after the death of Jesus, Africa produced such notable early Church fathers, thinkers, and writers as Clement, Justin Martyr, Origen, Athanasius, and Augustine (whose mother, Monica, was later canonized as a saint).

The wife hath not power of her own body, but the husband: and likewise also the husband hath not power of his own body, but the wife. Defraud ye not one the other, except it be with consent for a time, that ye may give yourselves to fasting and prayer; and come together again, that Satan tempt you not for your incontinency (1 Corinthians 7:4–5).

Church fathers grappled with many thorny points of theology and conflicting ideas within those first few centuries. Among them was the idea of Eve and original sin, as well as issues around human sexuality. The female characters that were probably the most popular in oral stories of that time were Eve and the Virgin Mary. These two women represented, more or less, polar extremes. Eve was seen as having consorted with the Serpent and bringing sin upon humans through her act of defiance, while a submissive and obedient Mary gave birth to the Savior, sent from the Father, to redeem humankind.

An early Christian father and student of Clement of Alexandria, Origen (A.D. 185 to circa A.D. 254) expressed a belief that sexual intercourse, unthinkable outside of marriage, was impure even within marriage, because of the passion felt and expressed by the couple, although Origen apparently believed that the couple initially had been devoid of any sexual temptation and feelings. The "fall from grace," according to Origen, is what necessitated marriage. The offspring produced within a marriage from a passionate conjugal act made the child impure at birth. Thus, the impurity inherent in sexual relationships continued through generations. According to one source, Origen derived his thinking, in part, from the Apostle Paul's letter to the Corinthians.

Early Christians Grapple with Virginity and Divinity

Origen stressed that love of God must come before all other expressions of love, even that of a man for his wife. He also believed in the human pre-existence as angelic spirits. Once the angel fell from grace, the consequence of his sin was human birth. Stories of angels as messengers of the Lord appear in both the Old and New Testaments. The angels were usually male, as might be expected in a patriarchal culture in which a woman's testimony was not valued or accepted. In the fourth century, Peter of Alexandria disagreed with Origen's thinking and accused his predecessor of borrowing ideas from the Greeks.

Origen believed in the perpetual virginity of the mother of Jesus, and that Mary was first among virgins, meaning her purity exceeded that of all others. Origen and others referred to the young church as being as pure as Mary's virginity; the church was frequently described in the first few centuries of religious writing as the "chaste bride," and "the virgin." Virginity became a sacrifice that one could make for the church. Indeed, many Christian women became virgin martyrs for the faith, offering first their chastity to God, and then their lives for their beliefs.

Like Origen, other men of the early Church wrestled with and wrote about female icons in the Bible, mainly the temptress and the virgin. Athanasius (A.D.296–A.D. 373) and Epiphanius of Salamis (circa A.D. 310–A.D. 420) refer to Mary, Jesus' mother, as the perpetual or "ever" virgin. And while the early church fathers saw a feminine ideal in the Blessed Virgin, they didn't devote major writings to her or her state of virginity; only through her approximation to the Lord does she receive mentions in various writings. As has already been stated, she stood alone as the perfection and strength of womanhood, while Eve represented the weakness.

Augustine (A.D. 354–A.D. 430), who became Bishop of Hippo and named a Doctor of the Church, was born of a Catholic mother and a pagan father at Tagaste, in North Africa. He is widely credited with being one of the most influential contributors to Western Christianity. Augustine addressed the topic of original sin, and underscored his own lustful desires in *The Confessions,* his autobiography. He asked God to grant him chastity and continence…but not right away.

Augustine, like some of the patriarchs of the Old Testament, had a concubine for fifteen years, with whom he had a child. Augustine sent the woman back to Africa from Milan prior to his conversion to Christianity. He confessed that he struggled against the wretched sin of lust, which he saw as an impediment to a life of virtue.

A giant among the great thinkers of his time, Augustine wrote vigorously against literal interpretation of the Bible, even expounding the idea that the universe and everything in it was created simultaneously, rather than in six days. Many writers have asserted that Augustine's understanding of the Genesis creation story translated to a belief in the moral and physical inferiority of women (a belief that Aristotle and Plato also held). However, he did recognize women's value as their mate's helper in the process of procreation. Origen, Augustine, and other early church fathers, both before and after them, didn't alter prevailing societal beliefs about the status of women, but they did define and defend the faith. They were the ones who, early on, grappled with some of the thorniest issues of theology and, through their understanding, clarified many beliefs that Christians held during their lifetimes, and still hold today.

The Esoteric Gnostic Fascination with Eve

In the early centuries of the Christian church in the lands around the Mediterranean, the Gnostics, or "Knowing Ones," developed ideas about the teachings of Christ and his disciples that were at variance with the more traditional forms of Christian thinking. Some Gnostics developed elaborate mythologies based on a fascination with the Old Testament Book of Genesis. An important concept among certain Gnostics was the idea that Eve wasn't simply the second human God created or Adam's mate, but actually the Mother of All of Creation, an illustrious and imminently important role that equaled Adam's position as the Father of Humankind. In the Gnostic culture, women were treated as equals of men. They were seen as spiritual beings as capable as men to receive holy teachings.

According to modern scholars, Gnosticism, which emerged during the period in which traditional Christianity developed, includes numerous religious movements,. At first, what little was known about Gnostic beliefs was gleaned from the writings against heresies by the early Church fathers such as Clement, Origen, and Irenaeus. They saw many ideas originating within the Gnostic sects as heresies infecting Christian teaching. Another early church father, Tertullian (circa A.D. 155–A.D. 230), found it unbelievable that Gnostic sects allowed their women not only to discuss religion, but also to perform such functions as healing, baptizing, and exorcising that were normally performed by men in Christian communities.

In 1945, a priceless collection of Gnostic documents unearthed by a peasant searching for fertilizer near Nag Hammadi, Egypt, enabled religious scholars to better understand some of the Gnostic beliefs and concepts. In the Bible, Eve is an exemplar of sexual temptation by Satan; in the culture of Gnosticism, Eve is portrayed as Barbelo, or emanation of the Godhead in its highest feminine aspect. Other Gnostic texts refer to her as Mother of the Aeons. The Gnostics understood the meaning of *aeon* (Latin for "forever") to be an emanation from the Godhead that had *ennoea,* or thought, as its own inner being.

Included in the body of Gnostic literature that exists today is a controversial text entitled *The Gospel of Mary* [*Magdalene*], the only gospel named after a woman. Only fragments of the gospel survive—two third-century fragments in Greek and a fifth-century version in the Egyptian Coptic script.

References to Barbelo, the Gnostic Eve, can be found in such texts as The Apocryphon of John, The Three Steles of Seth, The Thunder Perfect Mind, The Gospel of Judas, and The Gospel of the Egyptians, among others. In the Apocryphon of John (also called The Secret Book of John and The Secret Revelation of John), Eve, the Mother of All Living, is called Luminous Epinoia. She is the sacred light within and the spiritual capacity of humans to know God. Before the Trinity of the Father, Son, and Holy Spirit became Church doctrine, sects of Gnostic Christians worshipped Luminous Epinoia. The Apocryphon of John proclaims that it is the Savior's teaching given to John, his disciple, and that the teaching reveals the mysteries which are hidden in silence. The Gnostics adhered to the idea that only through inner knowing could humans achieve salvation, and that inner knowing (gnosis) came about in silence.

Medieval Portrayal of the Sacred Feminine and the Witch

From about A.D. 300 to A.D. 600, hostile tribal incursions furthered the breakup that was already taking place within the Roman Empire. The period of Late Antiquity saw the rise and evolution of Christianity displace a thousand years of pagan civilization. A Byzantine Empire that honored The Blessed Virgin Mary and Mary Magdalene (the latter as the Apostle to the Apostles) grew in strength. In the Roman Christian tradition, a male celibate hierarchy of leadership (although some male priests and popes married until 1022, when Pope Benedict VIII prohibited such unions) had become firmly entrenched. During the Middle Ages, women served as wives, mothers, widows, and workers in their roles within Christian society. Some exceptional women embraced the life of monastic retreat. Hildegard of Bingen, Joan of Arc, Julian of Norwich, Mary of Egypt, and others were mystics and visionaries. For many of those women, God was not only male, but also female, and God's Wisdom was a feminine aspect of God.

FACT

The Age of Monasticism began in circa A.D. 500; however, there were ascetics before and during Jesus' lifetime that retired into the desert to do fasting, prayer, and contemplation. Christian religious orders continue to be of three basic kinds: active, semicontemplative, and contemplative. Religious men and women who did good works were in active or semicontemplative orders, whereas the contemplatives emphasized routines of traditional prayer.

Although the medievals did not generally favor educating women, by the ninth century, wealthy women and daughters of nobility did receive some education, meaning that their lives were steeped in the sacred teachings of the Bible and Church. The point was to keep them busy to avoid harmful and impure thoughts. They were expected to live chaste lives in the pursuit of female work—that is, to become wives and mothers. As mothers, their job was to impart religious dogma to their young. The women who desired a monastic life received some educational training, and in some cases had to learn Latin.

Hildegard of Bingen, a Benedictine abbess and mystic who was a prolific writer, musician, herbalist, and healer, personified Wisdom as the Sacred Feminine in her writings and drawings. Hildegard wrote commentaries on the Gospels, among other religious texts, and identified Wisdom as God's bride and Christ as Wisdom Incarnate through the womb of his blessed mother Mary.

But long before Hildegard penned and sketched female images of the Sacred while in an ecstatic trance, the Old Testament books of Ecclesiastes, Psalms, Proverbs, and Solomon's Song represented the Divine in female imagery. God's Wisdom, as a feminine biblical image, dates back to Jerusalem, circa sixth century B.C., when Hebrew holy men believed that the God Yahweh had a counterpart (Asherah).

QUESTION?

Who was Asherah?
In the ancient area of what is modern Israel, thousands of cuneiform tablets were found with depictions of Asherah, a Semetic mother goddess and consort of the Canaanite god El. The Book of Jeremiah opposed the worship of her in Israel and Judah, and refers to her as the Queen of Heaven in Jeremiah (7–18, 44:17).

Sacred Feminine symbols

Catholic clerics dominated the intellectual peak of society, and religion was the focus of medieval literature, art, and music. Village mystery plays constituting the re-enactments of important stories of the Bible were popular among the peasantry, and were performed on particular feast days. A favorite mystery play at Christmas would have been the angel's announcement to Mary that she was pregnant by the Holy Spirit, and the subsequent birth of Jesus.

Ordinary women endured a kind of social subordination in the twelfth century. Perhaps in response to pressures of an increasingly restrictive life, many women turned to the Church. During the twelfth through the fourteenth centuries, there was a surge in women's religious communities.

From some of them emerged women known to be mystics, or who led such saintly lives that they were later canonized.

Women who spoke in tongues or prophesied found themselves at the mercy of others who feared their gifts might be due to the powers of witchcraft rather than the Holy Spirit. In the Old Testament, women endowed with those gifts were called necromancers or prophetesses, and unless it was determined that her gift was the result of possession by an evil spirit (such as the case of the girl possessed by a spirit that the Apostle Paul exorcised), such women were generally well regarded. In some cases, even kings consulted them. But in the twelfth century, such women were constantly on guard, expecting to be accused of being a witch. Such an accusation brought with it torture and death as prescribed by religious and secular courts. Many used the passage in the Old Testament Book of Exodus to justify their actions against women accused of witchcraft: "Thou shalt not suffer a witch to live" (Exodus 22:18).

From the twelfth through the sixteenth centuries, European cultures commonly believed that women possessed an insatiable carnal hunger that would drive some of them to sexual indulgence, even having sex with a demon or the Devil. The medical establishment supported such thinking. After all, Satan could easily deceive a woman; Eve had demonstrated that.

Artistic depictions in which medieval artists condensed the New Testament stories into symbols, signs, and monumental figures were predominant in mainstream culture during the Middle Ages. Particularly popular were church mosaics, illuminated manuscripts, and works of sculpture. Sacred images adorned prayer books, manuscript pages, tapestries, oil paintings, and mosaics. The Blessed Virgin Mary was always a popular image, as was Mary Magdalene, the latter as the repentant sinner. For example, circa 1434, Fra Angelico painted "The Santa Trinita Altarpiece" with Mary Magdalene kneeling at the feet of Christ and kissing his hand. She is dressed in a flowing red gown, and her unbound hair tumbles over her shoulders. The color red and the unbound hair both symbolized the female carnal nature, while kneeling and kissing the hand of the Lord symbolized a repentant attitude. Modern scholarship has since asserted that Mary Magdalene was never a prostitute, repentant or otherwise, despite many painters portraying her as one.

Also in the mid-1400s, Fra Filippo Lippi painted not only altarpieces, but also religious paintings, including "Madonna and Child" and "The Feast of Herod," featuring a white-gowned Salome dancing in preparation for asking for the head of John the Baptist. It seems ironic that Salome would be clothed in white, ancient symbol of purity and innocence. Lippi also painted "The Annunciation," showing a lily-bearing angel leaning toward the Blessed Virgin Mary as hands from an unseen source release the dove that represents the Holy Spirit. Light rays from the dove seem to project toward Mary's womb.

QUESTION?

What is the Marianist Movement?

Mary holds a special place in the hearts of many Christians. She is remembered during the praying of the rosary, and churches throughout the world have special places for Marian veneration. Alfonsus de Liguori (1596–1787) led the cause known as the Marianist Movement to glorify Mary. *The Glories of Mary,* written by de Liguori (canonized as a saint), asserted that Mary rules over half of God's kingdom, in the realm of mercy.

In medieval architecture, the Hagia Sophia, or Church of the Holy Wisdom of God, stands as a striking example of an Eastern Orthodox church that, some would say, represents the personification of Wisdom as the Sacred Feminine. In 1453, the church was converted to a mosque when the Turks overran Constantinople. Today, the church, considered one of the finest of all surviving works of Byzantine architecture, is a museum.

The Renaissance

The influence of the Church on religious art and the most important biblical stories continued to be of paramount importance during the Renaissance. Renaissance art remains some of the finest and most awe-inspiring of all the works that have survived the various art movements over time. Since the Church served as a patron for much of the religious art during the Renaissance, artists aimed to inspire reverence.

QUESTION?

What is *fresco theology*?
It is a term used to describe the popular religious painting on walls of Italian and Greek churches during the Renaissance. Although many artists painted such frescoes, Raphael Sanzo's four frescoes, painted from A.D. 1509 to A.D. 1511 in the papal apartments of Pope Julius II (Disputa, the School of Athens, Parnassus, and the Cardinal Virtues), are probably the most famous.

Ecclesiastical art reached a zenith during the Renaissance, giving the world some of its most notable artists and works of art: Titian, Brunelleschi, Raphael, Donatello, Leonardo da Vinci, Michelangelo, and Rembrandt, to name a few. Masaccio painted his beautiful religious image of the "Virgin with Child," and Sandro Botticelli painted the "Annuciation" and numerous paintings of Mary (often with Jesus as a child and angels). Unlike the flat images of medieval art and iconography, the Renaissance images, because many of the artists studied the anatomy of the human body, portrayed a natural realism with harmonious proportions of all of the elements. Painted portraits and engravings of the Madonna and Child, Eve and Adam, Jezebel, Bathsheba and David, Samson and Delilah, Judith, Susanna, and other biblical subjects became stunningly lifelike in the hands of the Renaissance master artists. Religious art included realistic portrayals of parts of a woman's body that in previous centuries would have been discreetly covered with clothing or a drape. For example, in A.D. 1540, Domenico Beccafumi painted the image of "The Madonna with the Infant Christ and Saint John the Baptist," in which the infant Christ seems totally disinterested in the breast being offered by his mother. Sometime between A.D. 1507 and A.D. 1510, Andrea Solario also painted Jesus nursing at the exposed breast of Mary in "Madonna with the Green Cushion."

Hans Baldung Grien, a contemporary of Matthias Grüenwald (famous for the Isenheim Altarpiece), was a German artist who trained with Albrecht Dürer, and who painted a number of religious pieces. In his work "Eve, Serpent, and Death," a nude Eve stands in high relief against the dark images of the tree, the serpent entwined around it, and Death in the shadows with his hand gripping her wrist.

FACT

In early Renaissance literature, biblical tales were adapted for performance art as plays by French writers. Drawing upon the stories of the Bible for inspiration, the writers reconceived biblical characters to present in their stories.

In 1610, Artemisia Gentileschi, the daughter of painter Orazio Gentileschi, became recognized as an accomplished artist at a time when women had great difficulty in getting accepted into the male-dominated world of art. Known as a Baroque painter, Gentileschi painted religious works that included women figures of biblical narrative, such as "Susanna and the Elders," "Judith Beheading Holofernes," "Conversion of the Magdalene," "Virgin Mary with Baby and Rosary," and "Jael and Sisera."

Images of the Virgin Mary and Eve in the 1700s and 1800s

Popular in Italy in the eighteenth and nineteenth centuries, images of the Blessed Virgin Mary in mosaics, wood or marble carvings, and paintings were framed and placed in niches of exterior walls of homes, churches, and commercial buildings. Often mounted upon shelves with room for a candle or lantern and flowers, the Madonnelles, as they were called, were occasionally covered with small metal canopies to protect them in inclement weather. Some even become associated with healings and other types of miracles.

Catholic piety and its emphasis on Mother Mary continued to be strong during the eighteenth century, and not just in Italy. In Europe and elsewhere during that period, there was increasing interest in Methodism and Protestant beliefs. Incidents of witch hunts in the late Middle Ages, and persecutions of women in the sixteenth and seventeenth centuries, finally began to subside. Some refer to the era as The Great Awakening, and others have called it the Age of Reason. Women could and did join Catholic religious orders, not necessarily to escape the domestic life that obliged them to marry and bear children, but to dedicate their lives to the work of the Church and service to others. A renewed enthusiasm for religion produced a religious revival throughout the United Kingdom and the United States.

In 1785, the English poet, engraver, and artist William Blake created "Job, His Wife, and His Friends: The Complaint of Job" in pen and ink and wash. His image of Job's wife is one of a befuddled woman sitting at her husband's side, hands over her knees with fingers interlocked. She hunches over as though she can't quite understand his quandary and suffering, and has no idea what to do about it. Blake painted other biblical characters as well, in a style that was not appreciated as much in his lifetime as it was after his death. He portrayed other biblical women in his work as well: Bathsheba in "Bathsheba at the Bath," and Eve in "Angel of the Divine Presence Clothing Adam and Eve" and "The Body of Abel Found by Adam and Eve."

PreRaphaelite Portrayals of Mary

In the mid nineteenth century, interest in creating religious art diminished, while secular art grew increasingly more popular. However, some depictions of biblical women found expression in the art of the PreRaphaelite Brotherhood, a band of self-proclaimed revolutionary painters whose works featured romantic images of women. They often painted brightly colored images, inspired by figures from literature including the Bible.

Their founder and leader, Dante Gabriel Rosetti, found the Blessed Virgin Mary a compelling subject. One of his earliest paintings was "The

Girlhood of the Virgin Mary," while another was titled "Ecce Ancilla Domini" ("The Annunciation").

Paintings of Biblical Women in the Modern Era

At the beginning of the twentieth century, religious art wasn't produced in the quantities of previous centuries. Churches, especially in America, proliferated and came in all sizes and shapes. However, many weren't rich and couldn't afford to commission artists to produce panels, frescoes, altarpieces, and elaborate stained-glass windows. However, some artists were still inspired to paint the mother of Jesus and Eve, and stained glass as well as glass-panel painting were still important in creating an atmosphere of holiness.

FACT

The use of stained-glass windows in cathedrals and churches in the high Gothic tradition seems to have reached an apex in the fifteenth century. After this period the artisans became interested in using paler colors (admitting more of the outside light) and larger-than-life figures. Scenes from the life of Christ, Virgin and Child, and images of saints dominated ecclesiastical stained-glass windows and panels.

Austrian artist Gustav Klimt, a leading painter in the Art Nouveau style, portrayed the Hebrew widow Judith explicitly sexualized, with a seminaked torso and confident half-smile suggesting she knew her powers of persuasion over her enemy, Holofernes (whose head she sliced off). One of the most popular French artists of the late 1800s and early 1900s was William Adolphe Bouguereau, a painter in the Academic Style (a painting style that combined the colors of the romantic style with elements of neoclassicism). His "Virgin of the Angels," painted in A.D. 1881, featured the Blessed Virgin without a halo, seated with the Baby Jesus in her arms and surrounded by three angels, two playing musical instruments. Bouguereau created another painting of the Virgin in A.D. 1900 titled, "The Virgin with Angels." That painting of Mary included a halo of nine stars. She appears to have risen from the seat of her throne in heaven, holding the Infant Jesus, while white-clad angels kneel on clouds around her.

In A.D. 1892 John Maler Collier, a British painter in the preRaphaelite style, created "Lilith." The fair-skinned red-headed version of the "first Eve" stands *au naturel,* embracing the serpent that has entwined itself around her body. In complete control, she tilts her head toward her right shoulder as if to affectionately rub her cheek against the serpent's body. In the Old Testament Book of Isaiah, Lilith is a night demon. According to a medieval Jewish tale, she was created as Adam's first wife, but left the Garden of Eden because she did not want to lie beneath him in submission.

FACT

In 1914, John William Waterhouse painted his unforgettable image of the angel Gabriel offering flowers to the Blessed Virgin Mary in "The Annunciation." The angel announced to her that she would conceive a child by the Holy Spirit, and the babe was to be called Jesus (Luke 1:26–38).

In 1900, Henry Ossawa Tanner, an expatriate American who lived in France, painted an image of Mary in the old-fashioned style of Mater Dolorosa (Sorrowful Mother). A somber Mary sits on the floor watching over her sleeping child, who lies hidden beneath a sheet. The strange iconography suggests to some art experts that Mary might perhaps be anticipating the coming Passion and Death of the Savior. Indeed, the sheet appears to be a burial shroud.

Stories of Biblical Women in Movies and Television

By the mid-1900s, movies and television exerted a powerful influence on popular culture and the roles of women in the Bible, as Hollywood began to produce movies that drew upon the biblical narratives. One of the first movies about the life of Jesus, *From the Manger to the Cross,* was made in 1912. Characters included men such as Joseph and Herod, but also women—the Blessed Virgin Mary, Mary Magdalene, and Martha. In 1927, Cecil B. DeMille made the silent movie *The King of Kings,* about the life of Christ. The movie unrealistically portrayed Mary Magdalene in scant attire, wondering where her lover had gone. In the 1930s when a version of the movie with music added was reissued, the film became a hit.

In 1949, DeMille made another biblically themed movie, *Samson and Delilah.* This epic film starred Hedy Lamarr as the lady in the Old Testament who brings down the strongest man in the world (Victor Mature) with a haircut.

In 1951, Susan Hayward starred as a tempestuous Bathsheba in the movie *David and Bathsheba,* the biblical tale of the king who fell in love with a married woman, and then arranged the murder of her soldier husband. Gregory Peck was cast as David, and Jayne Meadows played his wife.

A more recent version of the Samson and Delilah story appeared in 1996, featuring Elizabeth Hurley as Delilah and Eric Thal as Sampson, in a three-hour miniseries titled *When the Son of the Sun Met Desire.* The film combined plenty of Hollywood-style sex and violence for a quick-paced, action-packed portrayal of that well-known biblical tale.

Finally, *The Passion of the Christ,* Mel Gibson's 2004 film on the Passion and Crucifixion of Jesus, has been hailed by some as an accurate portrayal of the gospels, with realistic and sensitive portrayals of Jesus' mother and Mary Magdalene. Pope John Paul II approved of the film and, according to Vatican sources that were widely reported in the media, believed it was powerful and accurate.

Tales of Biblical Heroines and Martyrs in Books

After the worldwide success of the bestselling book by Dan Brown, *The Da Vinci Code,* a plethora of books about the Virgin Mary and Mary Magdalene were published. *The Da Vinci Code* alleges a centuries-old cover-up of the marriage of Jesus and Mary Magdalene and a child of their union who became the ancestress of European royalty. The book was made into a popular film in 2006, starring Tom Hanks and Sophie Marceau, and was directed by Ron Howard.

The discovery in Nag Hammadi of the ancient Gnostic texts and the recent discovery of the Gospel of Judas set the scholarly world abuzz with discussions about the tumultuous beginnings of the Christian religion. One result was a large number of scholarly writings and nonfiction books about early Christianity and the roles of key figures in Jesus' life, especially his mother Mary, Mary Magdalene, and other female followers. A quick search on Amazon.com for books containing the Virgin Mary's name in the title or information about her produced a whopping 33,446 titles, testament to her perpetual popularity as an interesting subject for writers. Books about Mary Magdalene were significantly fewer, but still an astounding 10,881 titles. Other women in the Bible had far fewer numbers of books written about them, but still garnered the attention of writers, publishers, and the public that bought them.

A few recent books that raised awareness of the contribution of women to the biblical narrative include Jonathan Kirsch's nonfiction book *The Harlot by the Side of the Road, Forbidden Tales of the Bible.* The book explores the violent and sexually explicit stories of several of the Bible's females, including Dinah, Tamar, Judith, Zipporah, and Jephthah's daughter, among others.

One Night with the King is a fictionalized version of the story of Esther, Queen of Persia. The film version of the popular book, written by Tommy Tenney and Mark Andrew Olsen, featured Tiffany Dupont in the role of Esther, the kind and courageous Hebrew woman who risked her life to save her people.

Two Women of Galilee is a powerful fictional account of Mary, mother of Jesus and her distant relative, Joanna. The novel was written by Mary Rourke, who holds a Divinity degree from Yale. The book has received critical acclaim.

There have also been several TV movies about notable biblical women:

- *Great Women of the Bible*—focuses on the Bible's best-known women and heroines, including the Virgin Mary, Eve, and Mary Magdalene.
- *Intimate Portrait: Women of the Bible*—a 1995 Lifetime Television documentary series narrated by Sela Ward that reveals the stories of three of the most revered female figures in Christianity: the Virgin Mary, Eve, and Queen Esther.
- *Mary Magdalene: An Intimate Portrait*—narrated by Penelope Miller, examines the life of the most misunderstood woman in the life of Jesus.
- *Mary, Mother of Jesus*—a two-hour film about the life of the Madonna that was produced by Eunice Kennedy Shriver and her son Bobby Shriver, and debuted on NBC TV in 1999.
- *Mary Magdalene: The Hidden Apostle*—a fifty-minute biography of Mary Magdalene's life with research and scholarly interviews, produced by the Arts and Entertainment Channel for airing on television, and also sold as a home video.

Heroines of the Bible in Music

Music has always been a part of the cultural experience of religion. Music plays a role in ritual, devotion, fellowship, and ceremony. Whether for sacrifice or celebration, music was important to the ancient peoples of Israel and Palestine, and was expressed in virtually every aspect of their lives. The women in biblical times played a variety of instruments: "And Miriam the prophetess, the sister of Aaron, took a timbrel in her hand; and all the women went out after her with timbrels and with dances" (Exodus 15:20).

QUESTION?

What are some the instruments ancient women and men played?
Ancient instruments mentioned in the Bible include cymbals, harps, trumpets, pipes, drums, castanets, and rattles.

Singing, clapping, and dancing were as much a part of ancient cultures in biblical times as they are now. Some religious services invoke the name of Mary through music played on guitars, organs, or other instruments. In fact, the Virgin Mary's name has been sung for centuries in religious hymns, devotional chanting, chorale music, ecclesiastical expression, and various Christmas carols throughout many lands. During the Renaissance, when religious songs and madrigal music was popular, the Italian composer Guilio Caccini (circa A.D. 1545–A.D. 1618) wrote "Ave Maria." In 1877, another version was produced by Antonín Dvořák. Other composers also arranged or worked with the composition, including Guiseppe Verdi, César Cui, Franz Schubert, and Charles Gounod. "Ave Maria" has surged in popularity through the performances of modern artists such as Sumi Jo, Charlotte Church, and Andrea Bocelli, among others. Bocelli uses the song in his album of sacred music, titled *Sacred Arias*.

With the popularity of Christian music, modern artists are finding new arrangements for old music inspired by biblical times and figures, including women (Mother Mary especially, ancient biblical females as well).

QUESTION?

What does *Ave Maria* mean?
Ave Maria means "Hail Mary." The prayer is part of the Roman Catholic rosary and derives directly from the words in the Gospel of Luke 1:28 and the greeting of her by her cousin Elizabeth in Luke 1:42.

Certain women of the Old and New Testaments have inspired great cathedrals, works of art, evocative lyrics of poems and songs, and book-length tales of their heroic exploits and accomplishments. Others have served as muses for artists creating or performing operas, chorale music, symphonies, and theatrical works. Still others have had their names become part of popular cultural vernacular: "Jezebel!" "Mother of God!" and "Queen of Sheba." And the women of the perennial bestseller, the holy Bible, will most likely continue to inspire future generations of people, including artists, writers, architects, musicians, clerics, and contemplatives.

Glossary

Ammonites
Lot's descendants through a son born to Lot's daughter after he had incestuous relations with her.

Antiochus IV Epiphanes
He was a Greek ruler of the Seleucid Empire (175 B.C.–163 B.C.). He was born Mithradates, but took the name Antiochus after his elder brother by that name died.

Apocalyptic
Pertaining to the biblical prophecy of the apocalypse or end-time. Revelatory prophesy of the destruction of the universe.

Apocryphal
Various religious literary works of questionable origin. Some regard such works as inspired, but others reject them because of questionable authenticity or authorship.

Apologists
Christian theologians, scholars, and writers who explained and clarified Christian belief for others.

Apostle
One of the twelve disciples the risen Jesus commissioned to teach the gospel. Saul of Tarsus became Paul, the self-proclaimed Apostle to the Gentiles.

Aramaic
The language used by Jesus and many of his disciples.

Benjamite

A member of the Hebrew tribe of Benjamin. Benjamin's mother, Rachel, called him Ben-oni as she died giving birth to him, and his father Jacob changed his name to Benjamin.

Covenant

The promises made by God to man, found in the Scriptures.

Danites

The Hebrew people descended from Dan, who was a son of Jacob and Bilhah.

David

David was Israel's second king and most beloved of the Hebrew leaders after Abraham.

Edomite

The descendants of Esau, who lived along the eastern edge of the Arabah valley, who waged war against the Jews, Syrians, and Assyrians, but finally became merged with the Jews.

Eve

Eve is the first mother of humankind, according to the Book of Genesis.

Gibeon, Gibeonites

The name means "hill" or "hill dwellers" and refers to the city and the people, who, like the Benjamites, lived in the territory of Benjamin. Scholars have associated Gibeon with the town of el-Jib, roughly six miles northwest of Jerusalem.

Hittites

Term for the people who lived in the lands of Asia Minor and Syria from circa 1900 B.C. to 1200 B.C.

Irenaeus

Irenaeus (circa A.D. 130–A.D. 202) was an early Church father who served as Bishop of Lyons, France (during his life, the town was called Lugdunum, Gaul). Recognized as a saint, his feast day is June 28. The Roman Catholic Church regards Irenaeus as a Father of the Church.

Ishmaelites

Descendants of the firstborn son of Abraham and his concubine Hagar. Ishmael means "may God hear," which is suggestive of the plea of Hagar and Ishmael to Abraham after he banished them to the desert.

Israelites

The term used for the Hebrew descendants of Jacob, especially those who lived in the ancient kingdom of Israel.

James the Just

The brother of Jesus and head of the early Christian church in Jerusalem. Assumed to have written the Secret Book of James.

John the Baptist

Jewish teacher and a messianic figure. He is accorded second position in Christianity to Jesus. He baptized Jesus in the Jordan River.

Josephus

Jewish historian (circa A.D. 37–A.D. 107) whose writings about Jews of the first century helped scholars from that time forward to understand and write about that period of antiquity.

Last Supper

The meal Jesus shared with his disciples on the night before he died; also called The Lord's Supper. During that meal, he established the sacrament of the Eucharist.

Levite

A member of the Hebrew tribe of Levi; the priestly clan.

Lilith

She was the first Eve, according to the midrashic texts (see midrash). After Lilith became rebellious and left Adam, God created Eve. A fourteenth-century account, *Sefer ha-Zahor*, or the *Book of Splendor*, says Lilith vanished after saying the unspeakable name of Jehovah. Another midrashic text asserts that she and Adam had a power struggle that resulted in Lilith refusing to lie under Adam during intercourse, whereupon she said the name of God and flew away.

Logos

In Judaism of biblical times, logos meant the "word of God," which had a power through which God could communicate with humankind. In Christianity, logos was equated with the creative word of God, or the "Word," which is an aspect of God, and was also incarnated as the Son of God, Jesus.

Messiah

The promised deliverer of the Jewish people. Christians regard Jesus Christ as having fulfilling the promise of a savior foretold by the Old Testament prophecies.

Midrash

A complex Jewish interpretive system used by learned rabbis to reconcile the contradictions in the Old Testament and to expound upon certain lessons.

Moabites

The ancient people who lived in Moab, a land east of the Dead Sea.

Moses

Old Testament patriarch who served as a leader and lawgiver of the Hebrews, and who occupied an exalted position as the human to whom God spoke.

Nazarite

A Jew who took vows to not imbibe wine or strong drink, to refrain from cutting his hair, to lead a pure life, and to be devoted to God.

Passion

The suffering of Jesus as the Romans tortured and crucified him upon the cross.

Patriarch

Abraham, Isaac, or Jacob, or any of Jacob's twelve sons, who became founders of the twelve tribes of Israel according to the Old Testament. Otherwise, it means the leader, father, or founder of a family, tribe, or clan.

Pentateuch

The first five books of the Hebrew Scriptures, also known as the Torah.

Pentecost

Refers to the feast that takes place fifty days after Easter. In the time of the Apostles, Pentecost took place fifty days after the Resurrection of Christ, and on that day, the Holy Ghost descended upon them and empowered them with divine gifts, such as the ability to speak in tongues.

Philistine

People of Aegean lineage who lived along the southern coast of ancient Palestine in the twelfth century B.C.

Synoptic Gospels

The Gospels of Matthew, Mark, and Luke are so similar in content that scholars assert the gospel writers may have all relied on the same source material.

Tanak

A term that specifically means the "Hebrew Scriptures."

Torah

The first five books of the Hebrew Scriptures: Genesis, Exodus, Leviticus, Numbers, and Deuteronomy.

Additional Resources

Scriptural Texts

American Bible Society. *The New Testament of our Lord and Saviour Jesus Christ.* **New York: American Bible Society, 1869.**
Translated from the original Greek, Dutch-English edition.

Catholic Book Publishing Co. *Saint Joseph Edition of the New American Bible.* **New York: Catholic Book Publishing Co., 1991.**
Translated from the original languages with critical use of all the ancient sources, including the revised New Testament and the revised Psalms.

Catholic Church. *Catechism of the Catholic Church.* **New York: Doubleday, Division of Random House, 1995.**
Revised in accordance with the official Latin text promulgated by Pope John Paul II, second edition.

The World Publishing Company. *The Holy Bible: Old and New Testaments.* **Cleveland and New York: The World Publishing Company. (No copyright or publication date available.)**
Self-pronouncing edition, conforming to the 1611 edition, commonly known as the Authorized or King James Version.

Other Texts

Collins, Michael and Matthew A. Price. *The Story of Christianity: 2000 Years of Faith.* New York: DK Publishing, 2003.

del Mastro, M. L. *All the Women of the Bible.* Edison: Castle Books (Division of Book Sales, Inc.), 2004.

Haskins, Susan. *Mary Magdalen, Myth and Metaphor.* New York: Berkeley Publishing Group, Riverhead Books, 1993.

Jordan, Michael. *Mary, The UnAuthorized Biography.* London: Weidenfeld & Nicolson, 2001.

Klein, Peter. *Catholic Source Book, a Comprehensive Collection of Information about the Catholic Church.* Dubuque: Harcourt Religion Publishers, 2000.

Lester, Meera. *The Everything® Mary Magdalene Book: The Life and Legacy of Jesus' Most Misunderstood Disciple.* Avon, MA: Adams Media, 2006.

Lockyer, Herbert. *All the Women of the Bible.* Grand Rapids: Zondervan, 1967.

Meeks, Wayne A. *The First Urban Christians: The Social World of the Apostle Paul.* Second Edition. New Haven and London: Yale University Press, 2003.

Pfeiffer, Charles F., Howard F. Vos, and John Rea, Eds. *Wycliffe Bible Dictionary.* Peabody, MA: Hendrickson Publishers, Inc., 1988.

Walsh, Michael. *Butler's Lives of the Saints.* New York: Harper Collins, 1991.

Web Sites

Aish.com
Aish.com is a large Jewish content Web site with over 6,000 articles on careers, dating, parenting, spirituality, and more.
✐ *www.aish.com*

Answers.com
This is a free online encyclopedia, dictionary, and almanac in one. Information on a wide variety of subjects consists of licensed content from brandname publishers.
✐ *www.answers.com*

Bibletexts.com
This site explores the original biblical texts, early Christian writings, and Christian values, practices, teachings, and history prior to A.D. 313.
✐ *www.bibletexts.com*

Internet Sacred Text Archive
This is a large archive of full-text books about religion, mythology, folklore, and the esoteric.
✐ *www.sacred-texts.com*

JewishEncyclopedia.com

This Web site contains the contents of the twelve-volume Jewish Encyclopedia, which was originally published between 1901 and 1906. The Jewish Encyclopedia, which recently became part of the public domain, contains over 15,000 articles and illustrations.

✎ *www.jewishencyclopedia.com*

Jewish Virtual Library

This online library is separated into a number of different categories, including history, women, travel, religion, politics, and more.

✎ *www.jewishvirtuallibrary.org*

Judaism 101

This online encyclopedia covers Jewish beliefs, people, places, things, language, scripture, holidays, practices and customs.

✎ *www.jewfaq.org*

Mysteries of the Bible

This Web site is run by Michael S. Sanders, a biblical scholar of Anthropology, Egyptology, and Assyriology. The site has a search feature that allows you to look up any topic you wish.

✎ *www.biblemysteries.com*

Sacred Destinations Travel Guide

This site has information about different places in the world with spiritual heritage. There is information about destinations and trip planning, as well as maps and photo galleries.

✎ *www.sacred-destinations.com*

Vincent Art Gallery

An art gallery with over 5,000 oil reproductions in its collection. Use this site to find famous art works of various biblical figures.

✎ *www.vincent.nl*

Wikipedia

Wikipedia is a free online encyclopedia that anyone can edit. It has a wealth of great information, but always be sure to check with another source or two to be sure the information you're getting is correct.

✎ *http://en.wikipedia.org*

Women in the Bible

This site contains a different section for each of the most prominent women in the Bible. The site offers information and images (paintings, photos from films, etc.) for each woman.

✎ *www.womeninthebible.net*

Index

Abigail, 56, 108–10, 168, 234

Abishag, 172–74, 234

Abominations and taboos, 237–38

Abraham
  Hagar and, 48–50, 76, 204, 238
  Keturah and, 177–78
  Reumah and, 178–79
  Sarah and, 73, 74–77, 204, 238
  Sodom/Gomorrah and, 166, 167
  wives of, 234

Absalom, 104–5, 172, 204

Adam and Eve, 2–6

Adulterous women, brought before Jesus, 14–15

Ahab, 89
  Athaliah (daughter) and, 28–29, 64, 215
  Jezebel (wife) and, 63–65, 113–14
  prostitutes washing in blood of, 89

Ahinoam, 110–11, 167, 168, 234

Amaziah, daughters of, 105–6

Amnon, 103–4, 172

Ann, mother of Mary, 218–19

Anna, 36–37, 227

Antiochis, 174, 176–77

Antiochus III, 184

Antiochus II Theos, 32

Antiochus IV Epiphanes, 174–77, 200, 201, 210, 211

Apphia, 152–53

Aquila, 156, 158–60

Arsinoe, 184–85

Art, women in. *See* Popular culture, women in

Asenath, 96–97

Athaliah, 28–29, 64, 215

Azubah, 120–21

Babylonian sacred sex workers, 82–83

Bathsheba, 15–18, 104, 121, 173–74, 234, 253, 255, 258

Berenice, 97–98

Bilhah, 10, 47, 53, 198, 234, 239

Blood, issue of, 138–40

Books, 258–60, 268

Children and heirs, traditions, 238–39

Chloe, 153–54

Chuza, wife of, 133–34, 135

Circumcision, 11, 12, 97, 99–100, 176, 221

Circumcision, women killed in name of, 210–11

Cozbi, 83–84

David
  Abigail and, 108–10
  Abishag and, 172
  Adonijah and, 172–73

Bathsheba and, 15–18, 253, 258
  concubines of, 204
  Gibeonites and, 179, 181
  Jesus connected to, 225
  making Solomon king, 173
  Michal and, 73, 111, 167–69
  Rizpah and, 102, 103, 179, 180–81
  Thamar and, 103, 104–5
  wives of, 234

Deborah (prophetess), 31–32, 56–59, 240

Deborah (Rebekah's nurse), 46

Delilah, 18–21, 223, 253, 258

Dinah, 98–100

Divorce, 235–36

Drusilla, 21–22

Elisabeth, 220–21

Elisha, 77–79, 191–93, 203

Elisheba (Elisheva), 70–71, 220

Elkanah, 72, 73, 111, 185–87

Esther, 56, 121–23, 128–29, 205, 259, 260

Euodia and Syntyche, 154–55

Eve
  bringing sin upon humans, 4–5, 244–45

eating from tree of knowledge, 2, 4–6

as equal to Adam, 3

as first woman, wife, mother, 2–4

Gnostic fascination with, 247–48

historical works about, 254–55, 257

Lilith as, 2, 257

longing for knowledge, 3–4

losing innocence, 4–5

punishment by God, 5–6

representing weakness, 244–45, 246

sexuality and, 5, 244–45

Expendable women, 204–5

Gibeah, virgin daughter from, 203–4

Glossary, 263–67

Gnostic fascination with Eve, 247–48

Gomer, 85–87

Hagar, 48–50, 74–75, 76–77, 177, 178, 204, 234, 238

Haman, 122–23, 128–29

Hannah, 56, 72–73, 185–87, 199–200

Harlots. *See* Prostitute(s)

Hasmoneans, 211, 212

Hassophereth, 6–7

Hebrew society, women in, 240–41

Heliodorus, 200, 201, 202

Hephzibah, 124–25

Herodius, 29–30, 33

Hosea, 85–87

Huldah, 56, 59–60, 241–42

Isaiah, wife of, 60–61

Jael, 31–32, 57, 241, 254

Jairus, daughter of, 132, 138

Jemima, 112–13

Jephthah's mother, 87–88

Jesus

adulterous women brought before, 14–15

King David and, 225

Mary Magdalene and. *See* Mary Magdalene

Samaritan woman at well, 189–91

Sinful Woman who washed feet of, 92–93

water into wine miracle, 228

woman with issue of blood and, 138–40

women healed by, 132–35

Jezebel, 63–65, 113–14, 215, 253, 261

Joanna, wife of Chuza, 133–34, 135

Job, 112–13, 162–63, 255

Job, wife of, 112, 162–63

Jochebed, 37–38, 196–98

John the Baptist, 29, 30, 33–34, 221, 252

Joppa, women of, 106

Joshua, 90–91, 102

Judith, 163–64, 241, 253, 254, 256, 259

Junia, 155–56

Keturah, 83, 177–78, 234

Laodice, 32, 174, 175

Lilith, 2, 257

Lot, daughters of, 22–23

Lot, wife of, 165–67

Lydia, 65, 67, 154, 156–57

Maccabees women, 200–202

Manoah, wife of, 221–23

Marriage traditions, 232–35, 237–38

Martha, 142–43, 147, 148, 258

Mary, mother of Jesus, 224–29

angel Gabriel appearing to, 225–26

Anna and, 36, 227

birth of Jesus, 224–25, 226–27, 244–45, 250

in books, 258–60

at cross, 228–29

Elisabeth and, 220, 226

images/portrayals throughout history, 248, 249, 251, 252, 253–57

Mary, mother of Jesus
  (continued)
  love/concern for Jesus,
    227–28
  Marianist movement
    and, 252
  mother of, 218–19
  titles of, 225
  in Upper Room, 229
  virginity and, 245–47
  water into wine miracle
    and, 228
Mary, mother of John Mark,
  208–9
Mary, wife of Cleophas, 148–
  49
Mary Magdalene, 134, 135,
  143–47, 251–52, 258–59, 260
  as apostle, 143–44, 145,
    150
  birth of, 144
  at cross, 146, 149, 228
  Jesus appearing to, 147
  at Jesus' tomb, 142, 146
  meeting Jesus, 144–45
  overview, 143–44
  prostitution question,
    93, 145, 252
  relationship with Jesus,
    145
  Sinful Woman and, 92–
    93, 148
Mary of Bethany, 93, 145,
  147–48
Michal, 73, 111, 167–69, 234
Midianites, 24, 83–84, 193

Midian warriors, wives of, 193
Midwives, 50–52, 196
Miriam, 37–40, 56, 70, 71, 196,
  197
Moabites, 22, 40–41, 83–84,
  101, 180
Moses
  Elisheba and, 70–71
  Ethiopian wife of, 39,
    234
  Jochebed (mother) and,
    37–38, 196–98
  Miriam (sister) and, 37–
    40, 70, 71, 196, 197
  smiting Midianites, 83–
    84, 193
  women helping
    construct sanctuary,
    212–14
  Zipporah (wife) and,
    11–12, 39, 83, 198, 234,
    259
Mother, killed for not
  circumcising sons, 210–11
Movie/television stories, 257–
  58

Naaman, wife of, 191–93
Nabal, 108–9
Nahrela, 112, 162–63
Naomi, 40–44, 100–101
Necromancer of Endor, 61–63
Nehushta, 125
Nympha, 154, 157

Peninnah, 72, 185–87

Peter, mother-in-law of, 134–35
Phoebe, 158
Polygamy, 234
Popular culture, women in,
  243–61
  books, 258–60, 268
  earliest Christian culture,
    244–45
  eighteenth/nineteenth
    centuries, 254–55
  esoteric Gnostic fascination
    with Eve, 247–48
  medieval portrayal of
    sacred feminine/witch,
    248–52
  modern paintings, 256–57
  movie/television stories,
    257–58
  music, 260–61
  portrayals of Virgin Mary,
    248, 249, 251, 252, 253–57
  Renaissance, 253–54
  virginity/divinity and, 245–
    47
Potiphar, wife of, 24–25
Pregnant women, torn apart,
  202–3
Priscilla, wife of Aquila, 156,
  158–60
Prostitute(s)
  forcing Solomon to split
    baby, 26
  Gomer as, 85, 86–87
  Jephthah's mother,
    87–88

Mary Magdalene
    question, 93, 145, 252
Rahab, 90–91
sacred sex workers,
    82–83
washing in Ahab's
    blood, 89
Puah and Shiphrah, 50–51

Queen of Sheba, 125–29, 261

Rachel, 9–11, 47, 52, 73, 232–
    33, 238–39
Rachel's midwife, 52
Rahab, 90–91
Rape, consequences of, 236–
    37
Rebekah, 7–9, 46, 73, 107, 179
Religious responsibilities, of
    women, 241–42
Renaissance, 253–54
Resources, 268–69
Reumah, 173–79
Rhoda, 52–53, 208–9
Rizpah, 101–3, 179–81
Ruth, book of, 44
Ruth and Naomi, 40–44, 101

Sacred sex workers, 82–83
Salome, daughter of Herodius,
    29, 30, 32–34, 252
Salome, wife of Zebedee, 150
Samarian women at well,
    187–88
Samaritan woman at well,
    189–91

Samson, 18–21, 222–23, 253,
    258
Samson, mother of, 221–23
Sanctuary construction,
    women aiding in, 212–14
Sapphira, 170
Sarah, 56, 74–77, 204
    Abraham's test and,
        76–77
    Hagar and, 48–49, 50,
        74–75, 76, 234, 238
    Keturah and, 177–78,
        234
    pregnant at ninety, 76
Sarah, daughter of Raguel,
    114–16
Saul
    Ahinoam and, 110–11
    death of, 111
    Michal and, 167–69
    Necromancer of Endor
        and, 61–63
    Rizpah and, 101–3,
        179–81
Sechem, 96, 97
Seven sneezes, 78, 79
Sheba, Queen of, 125–29, 261
Shechem, 99–100
Shiphrah and Puah, 50–51
Shunammite mother, 77–79
Sisera, 31–32, 56–57, 58, 241,
    254
Slave girl, freed from divining
    spirit, 136
Slave-girl soothsayer, 65–67
Solomon

Adonijah and, 172–74
harem of, 120, 205, 234
mother of, 18
proclaimed king, 172
prostitutes influencing, 26
Queen of Sheba and, 126–
    28
Sophereth, 6–7
Starving mothers, 34
Susanna, 117–18, 135–36, 253
Synoptic gospels, 134–35
Syntyche and Euodia, 154–55

Tabitha, 137
Taboos and abominations,
    237–38
Television/movie stories,
    257–58
Thamar, 103–5
Tobiah, 114–16
Tobit, 114–15

Vashti, 122, 128–29
Virgin daughter, from Gibeah,
    203–4
Virginity and divinity, 245–47
Virgin Mary. See Mary, mother
    of Jesus

Whore of Babylon, 82–83
Widowhood, 239–40

Zibiah, 214–15
Zilpah, 53, 234
Zipporah, 11–12, 39, 83, 198,
    234, 259

THE EVERYTHING SERIES!

BUSINESS & PERSONAL FINANCE

Everything® Budgeting Book
Everything® Business Planning Book
Everything® Coaching and Mentoring Book
Everything® Fundraising Book
Everything® Get Out of Debt Book
Everything® Grant Writing Book
Everything® Home-Based Business Book, 2nd Ed.
Everything® Homebuying Book, 2nd Ed.
Everything® Homeselling Book, 2nd Ed.
Everything® Investing Book, 2nd Ed.
Everything® Landlording Book
Everything® Leadership Book
Everything® Managing People Book
Everything® Negotiating Book
Everything® Online Business Book
Everything® Personal Finance Book
Everything® Personal Finance in Your 20s and 30s Book
Everything® Project Management Book
Everything® Real Estate Investing Book
Everything® Robert's Rules Book, $7.95
Everything® Selling Book
Everything® Start Your Own Business Book
Everything® Wills & Estate Planning Book

COMPUTERS

Everything® Online Auctions Book
Everything® Blogging Book

COOKING

Everything® Barbecue Cookbook
Everything® Bartender's Book, $9.95
Everything® Chinese Cookbook
Everything® Cocktail Parties and Drinks Book
Everything® College Cookbook
Everything® Cookbook
Everything® Cooking for Two Cookbook
Everything® Diabetes Cookbook
Everything® Easy Gourmet Cookbook
Everything® Fondue Cookbook
Everything® Gluten-Free Cookbook
Everything® Glycemic Index Cookbook
Everything® Grilling Cookbook

Everything® Healthy Meals in Minutes Cookbook
Everything® Holiday Cookbook
Everything® Indian Cookbook
Everything® Italian Cookbook
Everything® Low-Carb Cookbook
Everything® Low-Fat High-Flavor Cookbook
Everything® Low-Salt Cookbook
Everything® Meals for a Month Cookbook
Everything® Mediterranean Cookbook
Everything® Mexican Cookbook
Everything® One-Pot Cookbook
Everything® Pasta Cookbook
Everything® Quick Meals Cookbook
Everything® Slow Cooker Cookbook
Everything® Slow Cooking for a Crowd Cookbook
Everything® Soup Cookbook
Everything® Tex-Mex Cookbook
Everything® Thai Cookbook
Everything® Vegetarian Cookbook
Everything® Wild Game Cookbook
Everything® Wine Book, 2nd Ed.

CRAFT SERIES

Everything® Crafts—Baby Scrapbooking
Everything® Crafts—Bead Your Own Jewelry
Everything® Crafts—Create Your Own Greeting Cards
Everything® Crafts—Easy Projects
Everything® Crafts—Polymer Clay for Beginners
Everything® Crafts—Rubber Stamping Made Easy
Everything® Crafts—Wedding Decorations and Keepsakes

HEALTH

Everything® Alzheimer's Book
Everything® Diabetes Book
Everything® Health Guide to Adult Bipolar Disorder
Everything® Health Guide to Controlling Anxiety
Everything® Health Guide to Fibromyalgia
Everything® Hypnosis Book
Everything® Low Cholesterol Book

Everything® Massage Book
Everything® Menopause Book
Everything® Nutrition Book
Everything® Reflexology Book
Everything® Stress Management Book

HISTORY

Everything® American Government Book
Everything® American History Book
Everything® Civil War Book
Everything® Irish History & Heritage Book
Everything® Middle East Book

GAMES

Everything® 15-Minute Sudoku Book, $9.95
Everything® 30-Minute Sudoku Book, $9.95
Everything® Blackjack Strategy Book
Everything® Brain Strain Book, $9.95
Everything® Bridge Book
Everything® Card Games Book
Everything® Card Tricks Book, $9.95
Everything® Casino Gambling Book, 2nd Ed.
Everything® Chess Basics Book
Everything® Craps Strategy Book
Everything® Crossword and Puzzle Book
Everything® Crossword Challenge Book
Everything® Cryptograms Book, $9.95
Everything® Easy Crosswords Book
Everything® Easy Kakuro Book, $9.95
Everything® Games Book, 2nd Ed.
Everything® Giant Sudoku Book, $9.95
Everything® Kakuro Challenge Book, $9.95
Everything® Large-Print Crosswords Book
Everything® Lateral Thinking Puzzles Book, $9.95
Everything® Pencil Puzzles Book, $9.95
Everything® Poker Strategy Book
Everything® Pool & Billiards Book
Everything® Test Your IQ Book, $9.95
Everything® Texas Hold 'Em Book, $9.95
Everything® Travel Crosswords Book, $9.95
Everything® Word Games Challenge Book
Everything® Word Search Book

HOBBIES

Everything® Candlemaking Book

Bolded titles are new additions to the series.
All Everything® books are priced at $12.95 or $14.95, unless otherwise stated. Prices subject to change without notice.

Everything® Cartooning Book
Everything® Drawing Book
Everything® Family Tree Book, 2nd Ed.
Everything® Knitting Book
Everything® Knots Book
Everything® Photography Book
Everything® Quilting Book
Everything® Scrapbooking Book
Everything® Sewing Book
Everything® Woodworking Book

HOME IMPROVEMENT

Everything® Feng Shui Book
Everything® Feng Shui Decluttering Book, $9.95
Everything® Fix-It Book
Everything® Home Decorating Book
Everything® Homebuilding Book
Everything® Lawn Care Book
Everything® Organize Your Home Book

KIDS' BOOKS

All titles are $7.95
Everything® Kids' Animal Puzzle &
    Activity Book
Everything® Kids' Baseball Book, 4th Ed.
Everything® Kids' Bible Trivia Book
Everything® Kids' Bugs Book
Everything® Kids' Christmas Puzzle
    & Activity Book
Everything® Kids' Cookbook
Everything® Kids' Crazy Puzzles Book
Everything® Kids' Dinosaurs Book
**Everything® Kids' Gross Hidden Pictures
    Book**
Everything® Kids' Gross Jokes Book
Everything® Kids' Gross Mazes Book
Everything® Kids' Gross Puzzle and
    Activity Book
Everything® Kids' Halloween Puzzle
    & Activity Book
Everything® Kids' Hidden Pictures Book
Everything® Kids' Horses Book
Everything® Kids' Joke Book
Everything® Kids' Knock Knock Book
Everything® Kids' Math Puzzles Book
Everything® Kids' Mazes Book
Everything® Kids' Money Book
Everything® Kids' Nature Book
**Everything® Kids' Pirates Puzzle and Activity
    Book**
Everything® Kids' Puzzle Book

Everything® Kids' Riddles & Brain Teasers Book
Everything® Kids' Science Experiments Book
Everything® Kids' Sharks Book
Everything® Kids' Soccer Book
Everything® Kids' Travel Activity Book

KIDS' STORY BOOKS

Everything® Fairy Tales Book

LANGUAGE

Everything® Conversational Japanese Book
    (with CD), $19.95
Everything® French Grammar Book
Everything® French Phrase Book, $9.95
Everything® French Verb Book, $9.95
**Everything® German Practice Book with CD,
    $19.95**
Everything® Inglés Book
Everything® Learning French Book
Everything® Learning German Book
Everything® Learning Italian Book
Everything® Learning Latin Book
Everything® Learning Spanish Book
Everything® Sign Language Book
Everything® Spanish Grammar Book
Everything® Spanish Phrase Book, $9.95
Everything® Spanish Practice Book
    (with CD), $19.95
Everything® Spanish Verb Book, $9.95

MUSIC

Everything® Drums Book (with CD), $19.95
Everything® Guitar Book
**Everything® Guitar Chords Book with CD,
    $19.95**
Everything® Home Recording Book
Everything® Playing Piano and Keyboards
    Book
Everything® Reading Music Book (with CD),
    $19.95
Everything® Rock & Blues Guitar Book
    (with CD), $19.95
Everything® Songwriting Book

NEW AGE

Everything® Astrology Book, 2nd Ed.
Everything® Dreams Book, 2nd Ed.
Everything® Love Signs Book, $9.95
Everything® Numerology Book
Everything® Paganism Book
Everything® Palmistry Book

Everything® Psychic Book
Everything® Reiki Book
Everything® Tarot Book
Everything® Wicca and Witchcraft Book

PARENTING

Everything® Baby Names Book, 2nd Ed.
Everything® Baby Shower Book
Everything® Baby's First Food Book
Everything® Baby's First Year Book
Everything® Birthing Book
Everything® Breastfeeding Book
Everything® Father-to-Be Book
Everything® Father's First Year Book
Everything® Get Ready for Baby Book
Everything® Get Your Baby to Sleep Book,
    $9.95
Everything® Getting Pregnant Book
Everything® Homeschooling Book
Everything® Mother's First Year Book
Everything® Parent's Guide to Children
    and Divorce
Everything® Parent's Guide to Children
    with ADD/ADHD
Everything® Parent's Guide to Children
    with Asperger's Syndrome
Everything® Parent's Guide to Children
    with Autism
Everything® Parent's Guide to Children with
    Bipolar Disorder
Everything® Parent's Guide to Children
    with Dyslexia
Everything® Parent's Guide to Positive
    Discipline
Everything® Parent's Guide to Raising a
    Successful Child
Everything® Parent's Guide to Raising Boys
**Everything® Parent's Guide to Raising
    Siblings**
Everything® Parent's Guide to Tantrums
Everything® Parent's Guide to the Overweight
    Child
Everything® Parent's Guide to the Strong-
    Willed Child
Everything® Parenting a Teenager Book
Everything® Potty Training Book, $9.95
Everything® Pregnancy Book, 2nd Ed.
Everything® Pregnancy Fitness Book
Everything® Pregnancy Nutrition Book
Everything® Pregnancy Organizer, $15.00
Everything® Toddler Book

Everything® Toddler Activities Book
Everything® Tween Book
Everything® Twins, Triplets, and More Book

PETS

Everything® Boxer Book
Everything® Cat Book, 2nd Ed.
Everything® Chihuahua Book
Everything® Dachshund Book
Everything® Dog Book
Everything® Dog Health Book
Everything® Dog Training and Tricks Book
Everything® German Shepherd Book
Everything® Golden Retriever Book
Everything® Horse Book
Everything® Horse Care Book
Everything® Horseback Riding Book
Everything® Labrador Retriever Book
Everything® Poodle Book
Everything® Pug Book
Everything® Puppy Book
Everything® Rottweiler Book
Everything® Small Dogs Book
Everything® Tropical Fish Book
Everything® Yorkshire Terrier Book

REFERENCE

Everything® Car Care Book
Everything® Classical Mythology Book
Everything® Computer Book
Everything® Divorce Book
Everything® Einstein Book
Everything® Etiquette Book, 2nd Ed.
Everything® Inventions and Patents Book
Everything® Mafia Book
Everything® Mary Magdalene Book
Everything® Philosophy Book
Everything® Psychology Book
Everything® Shakespeare Book

RELIGION

Everything® Angels Book
Everything® Bible Book
Everything® Buddhism Book
Everything® Catholicism Book
Everything® Christianity Book
Everything® Freemasons Book
Everything® History of the Bible Book
Everything® Jewish History & Heritage Book

Everything® Judaism Book
Everything® Kabbalah Book
Everything® Koran Book
Everything® Prayer Book
Everything® Saints Book
Everything® Torah Book
Everything® Understanding Islam Book
Everything® World's Religions Book
Everything® Zen Book

SCHOOL & CAREERS

Everything® Alternative Careers Book
Everything® College Major Test Book
Everything® College Survival Book, 2nd Ed.
Everything® Cover Letter Book, 2nd Ed.
Everything® Get-a-Job Book
Everything® Guide to Being a Paralegal
Everything® Guide to Being a Real Estate
       Agent
Everything® Guide to Starting and Running
       a Restaurant
Everything® Job Interview Book
Everything® New Nurse Book
Everything® New Teacher Book
Everything® Paying for College Book
Everything® Practice Interview Book
Everything® Resume Book, 2nd Ed.
Everything® Study Book
Everything® Teacher's Organizer, $16.95

SELF-HELP

Everything® Dating Book, 2nd Ed.
Everything® Great Sex Book
Everything® Kama Sutra Book
Everything® Self-Esteem Book

SPORTS & FITNESS

Everything® Fishing Book
Everything® Golf Instruction Book
Everything® Pilates Book
Everything® Running Book
Everything® Total Fitness Book
Everything® Weight Training Book
Everything® Yoga Book

TRAVEL

Everything® Family Guide to Hawaii
Everything® Family Guide to Las Vegas,
       2nd Ed.
Everything® Family Guide to New York City,
       2nd Ed.
Everything® Family Guide to RV Travel &
       Campgrounds
Everything® Family Guide to the Walt Disney
       World Resort®, Universal Studios®,
       and Greater Orlando, 4th Ed.
Everything® Family Guide to Cruise Vacations
Everything® Family Guide to the Caribbean
Everything® Family Guide to Washington
       D.C., 2nd Ed.
Everything® Guide to New England
Everything® Travel Guide to the Disneyland
       Resort®, California Adventure®,
       Universal Studios®, and the
       Anaheim Area

WEDDINGS

Everything® Bachelorette Party Book, $9.95
Everything® Bridesmaid Book, $9.95
Everything® Elopement Book, $9.95
Everything® Father of the Bride Book, $9.95
Everything® Groom Book, $9.95
Everything® Mother of the Bride Book, $9.95
Everything® Outdoor Wedding Book
Everything® Wedding Book, 3rd Ed.
Everything® Wedding Checklist, $9.95
Everything® Wedding Etiquette Book, $9.95
Everything® Wedding Organizer, $15.00
Everything® Wedding Shower Book, $9.95
Everything® Wedding Vows Book, $9.95
Everything® Weddings on a Budget Book,
       $9.95

WRITING

Everything® Creative Writing Book
Everything® Get Published Book, 2nd Ed.
Everything® Grammar and Style Book
Everything® Guide to Writing a Book Proposal
Everything® Guide to Writing a Novel
Everything® Guide to Writing Children's Books
Everything® Guide to Writing Research Papers
Everything® Screenwriting Book
Everything® Writing Poetry Book
Everything® Writing Well Book

Available wherever books are sold!
To order, call 800-289-0963, or visit us at *www.everything.com*
Everything® and everything.com® are registered trademarks of F+W Publications, Inc.